Disconnected

An Odyssey Through Covid America

Christopher Gajewski

Disconnected
An Odyssey Through Covid America

Christopher Gajewski

This book is a compilation from the website,
www.thechrischronicles.com. Photos, supporting material and
more columns can be found there.

Table of Contents

Introduction

The 2020 Covid-19 pandemic caught me at a much different place than others. I was already adrift when the Covid tsunami swept across the globe, uprooting the anchors that we all cling to in our daily lives. Before the world began its midlife crisis, I was already in the middle of mine.

At the beginning of 2019, with the pandemic a little more than a year away, I put things in motion to sell my business and my home, to disconnect with everything that I knew and go in search of the unknown. I asked both my wife and my business partner for a divorce. My wife took it better.

Throughout 2019, after allowing work to consume me for decades, I began to take dips into the ocean that was America. Extended weekends away from my home in Chadds Ford, PA became more of a norm, relearning how to do things like pack a suitcase and wander distant places alone.

Family and friends thought I was going crazy—or having a midlife crisis. They may have been right. 50 was creeping up on me and if it waddles like a duck and quacks like a duck?

But what if it wasn't a duck?

What the hell was I doing?

I was running away from home. There was the business I had built up over the past 15 years and the career for the last 30, the dream house I had bought seven years ago, a troubled marriage to a beautiful woman and the easy comfort of friends and family that surrounded me.

I was tired, a soul wearied exhaustion that seeped into everything that I did and was. Burned out, I started exploring, searching for something.

Plan A was a very long sabbatical. There was no Plan B; Plan A was so broad there was no need for a Plan B. With the profits I would make from selling my business, I'd start off with a family trip to Poland for two weeks at the end of April in 2020. Then, I had an apartment rented in Pescara, Italy for May. Next was an apartment on Milos, an island off the coast of Greece for July. After that, I'd shrug into a backpack and start wandering the world. Walkabout. --Until my money or my back gave out.

My business finally sold at the end of December 2019. A large portion of my money went to helping my wife buy a new house. We exchanged the down payment for her new house for the expected proceeds of our current house. With the house up for sale and planning on being somewhere in Europe when it sold, I got rid of everything. I was not even sure if I was coming back, so I gave my wife everything that she wanted.

What was left of my possessions, I sold what I could. What I could not sell, I gave away. What I couldn't give away, I donated to charity. What I could not donate to charity found its way into a dumpster. At the beginning of February 2020, all that remained was a bed, a television, a sofa, a coffee table, a chair in front of my fireplace, and my coffee maker.

There was nothing on the walls. My stepdaughter had been the artist and the art gallery that the house had been to her paintings and photography all went to the new house. The small pictures and art that I had collected during my bachelor years and had been relegated to my office were now in the small 5x5 storage area I had rented for the few personal effects I was keeping.

I closed off unused parts of the 4,000 sqft, three floor, five-bedroom house so the echoes wouldn't talk to me so loudly.

The chair in front of the fireplace became the most used piece of furniture during a winter that seemed to cling to the northeast longer than usual.

On a plane in early March 2020, I coughed on board a flight that would be my last before the pandemic. I continued to cough on the plane returning from Ft. Myers, FL. Everybody would turn around and stare with each cough. I finally remembered the reports coming out of China and held up my pack of cigarettes to show people I was only killing myself and not them.

As I sat in my empty house through March, eagerly awaiting the mid-April departure to Poland, more information started coming out of China. And Italy. And Greece. And Poland. I watched red dots overlaying a map on my computer, virus hot spots. The dots started to blossom and spread. The area around Pescara, Italy was first. The dots bloomed until Europe was engulfed and all international tourist travel was banned.

So much for Plan A.

Yes: I took the damn pandemic personally. Aye, I've lived an absurd kind of life and can be an absurd kind of person. The final indignity came at the beginning of April: Governor Tom Wolf of Pennsylvania, in all his glory and wisdom, made PA the only state where homes could not be bought or sold.

The "For Sale" sign sitting on my front lawn got taken down, stored away in the empty four car garage.

I was screwed.

Instead of packing a couple suitcases to join my family on a four-city bus tour of Poland, I was sitting in front of my fireplace contemplating Murphy's Law: "Anything that can go wrong will go wrong at the worst possible time." Instead of finding out first-hand what the Italian decency laws were as I stripped out of my clothes and went diving into the ocean, I was thinking that I just wanted the universe to leave me the hell alone.

Whether or not it was a midlife crisis, I had earned it. I had worked hard for it. I had dedicated my entire life to it. I had survived train wrecks, hurricanes, and a multitude of other absurdities to arrive at this final absurdity.

Now, I found the world at large was joining me in this absurdity. As I was deconstructing my life, disrobing from my many titles of husband, business owner, son and brother, the American government was deconstructing facts, truth, and science and disrobing from reality.

A novel virus, Covid-19, was sweeping the globe. Death tolls were mounting with stories of overrun hospitals and doctors having to decide who lived and who died because they didn't have enough equipment to treat everybody. Respirators were being saved for the most likely to survive.

Or was it?

In 2016, with the election of Donald Trump as the 45th president of the United States, America had become more fractured than I had ever seen it in my life. Moderates like myself were drowned out in the cacophony from the extreme left and right. Before "Covid-19" and "nasal swabs" entered our vernacular, other words and phrases had entered it like "alternate facts" and "fake news."

"My hospital isn't overrun," I heard a lot and saw on Facebook. "Those overrun hospitals and bodies are all staged by the radical left-wing press so the government can take away our freedoms," was something else I was reading and hearing. "Everybody who dies anymore is being called a victim of Covid." Marginalized conspiracy theories were taking center stage and being amplified by social media.

Respected news organizations and journalists had been under attack since Trump began his bid for the White House in 2015. In one primary debate, he used the National Enquirer to attack one of his Republican opponents. In between stories of UFO sightings and naked celebrities, there had been a story about Senator Ted Cruz's family connection with the JFK assassination.

"You can't believe anything you see on those channels," I was told. "You have to watch such and such for the real facts." –the "such and such" being radical right-wing tabloids with no relationship to the truth or journalism but neck deep in national and worldwide conspiracies.

I wasn't watching television.

Centrist and respected newspapers such as The New York Times and The Wall Street Journal were being dismissed because they were not following the left or right radical party lines.

"So, what you are saying," I asked a friend of mine, "is that the pandemic is actually a conspiracy orchestrated by George Soros, the Democratic Party, and 187 countries around the world to make President Trump look bad for his reelection bid?"

"Well, yes," he replied.

Personally, I felt everybody was to blame. Yes, I am a moderate and damn proud of it. As with all good conspiracy theories, there are kernels of truth. Was the press a mouthpiece for the far left? Was the rise of the far right and nationalism just a reaction to the radical agenda of the left? I could even go further back and discuss the erosion of critical thinking skills due to a test-based culture while art and music were being expunged from our elementary schools.

It was the perfect storm that descended upon America and I was adrift in my little dingy.

I couldn't care less anymore.

All I knew is that I needed toilet paper.

Part One: Struggling in Lockdown

On Pause; April 3, 2020

The world was hushed, on pause, with no idea how long the pause would last.

We entered a new age, a new reality. We entered the age of masks, of social distancing, of lockdowns and isolation. International travel was banned, and even domestic travel was restricted to essential travelers. The world's economy ground to a halt.

On March 19th, California became the first state to issue a stay-at-home order. The rest of the states would soon follow. Delaware on March 24th. Pennsylvania's took effect on April 1st.

Nursing and retirement homes became prisons, with each resident in solitary confinement. Visitors were not allowed in them or hospitals to help prevent the spread of the virus.

I remember one story a woman related on Facebook when she went to visit her father with dementia. She would always take him home for the weekend. Now, she could only she him through thick glass. He had no idea what was going. He was in tears.

"What did I do wrong," he cried. "I promise not to do it again."

Countries like Spain instituted national lockdowns where people were not allowed to leave their homes and could be arrested if they did not have a doctor's note.

I was bored and wondering what to do with myself.

At the end of February, I had helped my wife move into her new home. I was left sitting in a beautiful home that was mostly empty. I had asked my wife for some things back but that didn't go so well. Everything was still packed up apparently. I did get a comforter back, the one the dogs had shredded.

Lamps are important when you don't have any. Knives are nice. Pots and pans help. I had held out hope for a quick end to the pandemic, but I finally had to start spending money. I had no idea how long I would be stuck and, besides, spending money was something to do. The big box stores were considered "essential" so you could enter them, with masks, where there were large, red "x's" taped off on where to stand while in line at checkout. Target, Walmart, Home Depot, and the grocery stores became part of my new morning routine.

My friends thought it was hilarious. I had never done mornings. Aside from bootcamp when I was 18, I had always set my own hours. I had been starting my day when my friends were on their lunch break for decades. Now that we could sleep in, I couldn't. I was waking up each morning at about 5am and waiting for the stores to open.

I became a scavenger.

I still have no idea why toilet paper became scarce. I could understand the cleaning supplies, hand sanitizers and over the counter medications, but toilet paper? For a virus that had nothing to do with bowel movements? Friends and family were either afraid to go to stores or their essential jobs limited them to when they could go. The best time to find the necessary things was as soon as the stores opened. I even got the low down on what days they received their shipments.

Each store quickly instituted policies. Two per customer of the items in short supply. By mid-morning, my SUV, a Subaru Outback, was loaded with toilet paper, paper towels, napkins and anything else I could find at various stores. By the afternoon, the Outback was empty with various packages of supplies placed on people's doorsteps.

I'd knock on the door and then step back a few feet. They would come out with a mask on, thank me while keeping their distance, and bring everything inside to be wiped down with bleach.

One package of toilet paper I kept in a closet, waiting for the call.

I had called my dad one day from Target. "Do you need toilet paper?"

"I'm getting low," he said.

"I'm at Target now. I can grab you a 12-pack."

"What kind," he asked.

"Dad, there is a pandemic. Nobody can find toilet paper. I can. Do you want some or not?"

"Is it Charmin?"

"Yes, it's Charmin."

"Is it the extra soft?"

I scanned the few packages in the almost empty aisle.

"No, just the soft."

"I'll be okay," he said.

I picked it up anyway. He eventually called for it and I dropped it off on his porch in South Philly.

In the afternoons, I became an electrician. When we had moved into the new house seven years prior, my wife had had everything repainted, from earth tones and reds to teals, azures, and whites. The ivory-colored receptacles and plates had bothered me ever since. I started stocking up on white ones at Home Depot. Do you have any idea how many receptacles, plates and outlets there are in a 4,000 sqft house? Over 100. Aye, it kept me busy for a few weeks.

I also added "bootlegger" to my resume. Chadds Ford, PA is about 10 minutes from Delaware and 20 minutes from Maryland. Yet another thing I never understood about PA was beer stores stayed open, but the liquor and wine stores, State Stores, closed. What could be more essential than wine and liquor when you are stuck at home 24/7 with people that you might love but are only used to seeing a few hours a day?

My people needed their booze—it was a mission of mercy. I had an "in" in Delaware, where people from out of state were now being stopped by the state troopers after decades of unlimited access. (Though it is ignored, it is technically illegal to transport booze across state lines. Pennsylvanians has been buying their booze in Delaware for their no tax shopping for a long as I could remember. Until the pandemic.)

I was on the mortgage papers for my wife's new house, which was in Delaware, and I kept them on my front seat as I traveled the backroads to various liquor stores.

My friends thought that was hilarious as well. I didn't really drink. The only time I did was when my neighbors made me a pitcher of their famous Blood Mary for something or another I had picked up for them. Now, on any given day, my Outback was filled with cases of vodka, rum, various wines, and anything else someone would text me for. Captain Morgan became my co-pilot.

But it was always an empty SUV in the garage at night and me sitting in front of the fireplace in silence. Wondering. Thinking.

I did not like the new reality. The silence. The echoes of my footsteps in my home.

My life was supposed to be in motion towards some far away beaches, not on pause.

I wish I could pause some of the songs in my head though. Don Henley was pissing me off in particular. Whether it was a midlife crisis, an intervention by the universe, or Murphy screwing with me, it was Don Henley's song, "New York Minute" that had created the prelude to all of this.

"New York Minute" had been released back in 1994. I loved the song but it had also scared the living hell out of me. Even in 1994, when I was junior in college, it had felt like a foreshadowing, a self-fulfilling prophecy. I was a writer, trying to balance two worlds. Harry, from Henley's song, hadn't done so well. He had gotten lost, found himself too much in this world, and they found his clothing scattered down the train tracks.

I had been on the verge of finally escaping this world to scatter my clothes somewhere along an Italian beach. Looking for balance as I dove into the surf. Trying to reach for that other world that had gotten so far that it only felt like a young boy's fantasy. Wondering if the Italian police tased naked beach goers coming out of the surf.

Now, the universe had put up a "no entry" sign on that other world, along with countries and US states. I toasted Harry as I sipped coffee and stared into the crackling flames.

A Surge of Music; May 7, 2020

I really didn't do well today with the stay-at-home order. I'm not quite sure where I am, but I'm not home. I'm somewhere in northeast Pennsylvania? Everybody who knows me – including former teachers, drill sergeants, and employers – know I don't do well with staying still. But all of this is a bit different.

It's clamping down on me, particularly at night. I had felt the music back in me for a while, the music that surges when I am driving. It is like life has a soundtrack. The playlist fled when Covid rounded the bend as if seeking to escape a head on collision. I can only do so much electrical work and landscaping and that just gets me through the days. At night, the depression is clamping down on me again. From what I am reading on Facebook, it is clamping down on everybody.

A couple years back, in the span of four years, I lost the three people I was closest to in high school. In between, I lost my mother, aunts, and uncles. And then there was the decade before that when I lost a lot of people who still walk this earth. Life gets overwhelming at times and, in a blink, chunks of it are gone.

I've always said the greatest gift of youth is immortality. I had all the time in the world and was invincible. I shed that protective shell as I got older until I was left staring at something incomprehensible. Now, I'm staring at the walls of the house that I was supposed to sell, at the map of Italy where I was supposed to finally be at rest and maybe recharging, at the credit cards I'm using to refurnish the house I just unfurnished.

As the depression clamps down, and clouds perception, I'm staring once again at a bleakness.

The music tells me the bleakness is not real.

I think the opening sequence in the movie, "The Rundown," is the greatest opening of any movie. The Rock, Dwayne Johnson, enters a club where his target is with his crew, a pro football team. He tried to be polite about it but the quarterback wasn't playing nice with his crew around him and refused to give up his super bowl ring as collateral.

"You can give me the ring or I can make you give me the ring."

Johnson had to beat the hell out of all of them but got the ring. Outside of the club, one of Johnson's collection competitors, some old, fat guy, shoots him with a beanbag gun and steals his prize.

Man makes plans; God laughs.

I think the Universe's sense of humor is worse than mine.

I needed to go for a drive, and not just to the big box stores.

Quarantines, lockdowns, and shutdowns. Social distancing. Stay six feet away from everybody. Even the stores have "one way" aisles. Stay as safe as possible.

I don't. I can't.

I see pods forming, family units, safe circles. Everybody trusts everybody in their pod to be safe so they can still socialize. Others are ignoring Covid and creating "super spreader" events. I read a story from Texas where, despite all the warnings, someone threw a surprise party. It turned out to be quite the surprise: someone killed grandma and grandpop.

I sit in my empty house. It's ironic, really, because I probably see friends, family, and acquaintances more than I ever have. But I made decisions. I go to stores regularly, mingle with the other scavengers for goods and that makes me a welcome sight for a hello—from a distance. Hugs are out. I miss my hugs. People are afraid and I don't blame them.

Maybe if I had stuck with the quarantine and the stay-at-home order I'd be allowed into somebody's pod? But I didn't. I made the decision. I hung the bell around my neck and now walk through the world. "Unclean, unclean," the bell tolls. Maybe. Who knows? Covid-19 is a novel virus, and the scientists and CDC are still trying to figure things out. Do the masks even do anything? How long and how much of Covid-19 do you need to be exposed to to be a carrier? As much as loved ones don't want me too close, I don't want to be too close to them. The CDC is explicit on one fact: you can be a carrier and not show any symptoms. I'd rather not kill anybody accidentally.

Masthope, up in the mountains of Pennsylvania, is about two and half hours north of Philadelphia. One of my oldest friends, Mike, Papa Bear, has been inviting me to his family's vacation home there for years. A lake and fishing for warm days; sledding, skiing, and bonfires for cold nights. With work and life, I could never make it up there. Now, I am not welcome.

Their family is in quarantine and I would not think about intruding on it. Mike's wife, Liz, is a special kind of person, always welcoming, giving, warm with an easy smile. But now, with the pandemic, she is a mamma bear on patrol protecting her three cubs. I respect that. But I needed a destination, and my sense of humor got the better of me.

So, I took pictures of the Masthope sign, sat and wrote in what I imagine passes for the town center, and sent the pictures to Liz.

I would have stopped by and waved from their front yard but they wouldn't give me the address.

My sense of humor gets me into trouble all the time. Has my entire life. The depression gets me into worse trouble and has my entire life.

No, Mamma Bear, I'm not intruding. But I desperately needed to go for a long drive, for the music to surge and push back the darkness for a little while. It's a long ride back home, to stare at walls in an empty house, the silence echoing ever louder.

I started back with my "Driving" playlist. There's a good three hours of great songs on that one from various genres. I thought about stretching it, though. Two and a half hours or maybe, just maybe, that 10-hour stretch to the Maine/Canadian border with the music urging me onward the entire time.

A new destination is very appealing. I know I won't be welcome in Canada, or in any state I pass through, but, after having been at the southern end of Interstate 95 dozens of times, seeing the northern end would be interesting—in a geeky kind of way.

The Simmering Pot; May 9, 2020

The motto of the infantry is "Follow me!"

Yeah: don't do that. If we are all in the same boat, put me on a little schooner by myself. I see Niagara Falls ahead and am thinking, "this could be fun? Hold my coffee and watch this."

O Captain, My Captain!

But I just thought I'd write a little bit about that simmering pot and how we are all in the same boat. Yesterday, a couple

Facebook posts caught my attention and they reminded me of a conversation I just had with one of my cousins. The basic gist was, "I'm having a really shitty day and I have no idea why."

I know why. The American Psychological Association knows why and my neighbor who owns a string of psych services knows why--as he makes money hand over fist.

Whether that boat is heading towards Niagara Falls, or just down a lazy river, we shouldn't be in the damn boat. It's unnatural. When the lockdown first started, it was like turning the burner on underneath a pot of stew with a lid on it to simmer. Our brains are the stew. My range top shows the effects of what happens if you allow it to simmer for too long—I'll scrub it all up eventually.

I'm an old pro at this. Battle hardened. I've had that flame on high for large stretches of my life. I had one psychologist mention to me that he felt as if I lived my first 30 years in "fight or flight" mode. Imagine what that does to the body? Not to mention the mind. My bad days are a bit different than most. I've learned to adapt and work through this crap. But it's getting to me as well.

Bad days for no reason goes hand in hand with the total inability to know what day it is. Or month. Or hour. Is it nap time yet?

Herb, a friend, psychiatrist, and true battle-hardened veteran with multiple tours in Afghanistan, explained that we have all lost our "anchor" events. Going to work, the weekly get-together with friends, the haircut appointments, and things like that kept us anchored in our lives, in our identity.

Me? I started out this lockdown with absolutely no idea who the hell I was. Last year, I stripped out of my identities with the final piece flying off at the beginning of February as I helped my wife move into her new home and begin her new life. Perfect timing.

O Captain, My Captain!

[Now I see myself in place of George Washington in the famous crossing of the Delaware picture--but with me in my birthday suit, blue eyes, graying hair, and hairy butt, holding a mug of coffee. If that mental picture is now in your mind: you're welcome.]

I'm just tired. A friend once mentioned a long time ago in an apartment in West Philadelphia that it seemed like I lived 10 years for every one that everybody else did. Another friend recently mentioned it seemed like I lived more in half my life than many do in four lifetimes. If you do the math, I think I'm 637?

I'm an old, old man, rocking in my chair, with the stew on simmer as I listen to the hiss of the boilover hitting the hot steel of the stovetop.

A couple months ago, that stew had the smell of an Italian beach, finally getting some rest while I consider if I have anything left in my tank. Not strip away the years but see if I could strip away the toll those years have taken on me. Get back to 49. Nowadays, at night especially, as I sit staring at the walls of this house that was supposed to be sold, it has the smell of an old age home, antiseptic and bleach with the occasional whiffs of the flowers that young people bring to their grandparents on special occasions.

But that's just the depression talking, the echoes. There is a lot it whispers to me at night. Just trash talk. Meaningless. Pointless. Forgotten like the mists that burn away with the rising of the sun. Maybe that's why I'm waking up at sunrise?

We can start to believe anything is normal if we live it long enough. I'm a pro at that as well. But though consciously we think it is normal, our subconscious is that simmering pot. It knows better. We're going to start to grind the hell out of our teeth at night. Bad dreams. Panic attacks possibly. The fun ones for me are the panic attacks, while I am asleep, that leave me sprawled on the floor gasping for air.

Small things, tiny things, even happy things that we have lived with all our lives are going to annoy the living hell out of us. We're going to have shitty days for no reason whatsoever. But there is a reason.

This shit ain't normal.

O Captain, My Captain.

Hell, I guess to be honest, perhaps the boat I was in was already going over the falls and the pandemic pulled it back. In many ways, it forced me into healthier paths. Some of my unhealthy coping mechanisms are locked out in lock down. I'm forced to look at myself in the mirror each morning and make a choice for myself.

I hate the fact that many of those mornings are at 5 am. But I have my breakfast, establishing new routines. Strawberry frosted Miniwheats with vanilla almond milk. Keeping busy, maybe taking a nap, then some yogurt and granola for lunch. —I don't think I've had three meals a day since I was forced to in boot camp in '89.

This shit ain't normal but you are okay. Just a normal reaction to an unnatural situation.

I'm not okay. But that's been a well-established and entertaining fact for five decades now. My psychiatrist friend recommended that people talk to people who are already screwed up. We're good at this shit.

O Captain, My Captain.

Be your own captain. Establish anchors in your lives. You can't use the old anchors so establish new ones. Work out—the endorphins are a hell of a natural medication. I personally recommend yoga and practicing mindfulness. Establish a routine and stick with it. Make it a point to keep a calendar and remind yourself as often as you can what day it is so they don't blend into the next one. And try to change out of your pajamas each day.

Me? I can't. Long story. I tried. It bothers me. Everything bothers me. More and more. That's why I am planning on reeling in my anchor and drifting for a while. The pandemic pulled my boat back away from the falls. Not being in motion, though, is far more terrifying than the falls. Hold my coffee and watch this.

I'll keep writing though and you can keep reading.

O Captain, My Captain: Fun words to play with but not the happiest of poems by Walt Whitman.

Navigate to your safe harbor to weather this storm, knowing that what you feel is natural and that you are part of a huge club, a worldwide club. We should have t-shirts made. "I survived the Great Detention of 2020."

"The Breakfast Club" anybody? Simple Minds? "Don't you, forget about me…"

The Boys of Summer; May 29, 2020

For love of youth. For love of immortality. For love of that single pitch that can define the outcome of nine innings. For love of the game.

I always hated baseball when I was a kid. It was boring. I would much rather watch the lighting fast play of football or hockey. I remember being allowed to stay up late in 1980 to watch the Philadelphia Phillies beat the Kansas City Royals in the World Series. I can still name the starting lineup. Then, I can't tell you who even played for the Phillies for the next 20 years.

But then the world changed. It slowed down and I slowed down as well. Instead of flying through the 18-hour drive to and from Miami and DC, racing for the pole position in traffic groups, I started taking my time. It was then I started noticing things. And started noticing baseball.

Baseball might be slow moving, but it's an intricate game. While I always thought it was just nine athletes taking the field, I came to realize it was more like a chess match, and the pitching mound is where the king sits: called the loneliest place in sports. His troops are marshaled around him like knights, bishops, and rooks, but it's just him against the opposing batter. The skipper, the manager, makes the moves.

Kevin Costner helped. His baseball trilogy gave me insights into the game I thought boring, giving me a new perspective. At the beginning of the game in the final movie of the trilogy, "For Love of the Game," there is a monologue that has always stuck with me. The announcer is talking about Billy Chapel, Costner's character, an aging ace who might be pitching his last game after a long career with one team.

"...you get the feeling Billy Chapel isn't pitching against left handers, he isn't pitching against pinch hitters, he isn't pitching against the Yankees. But tonight, he's pitching against time, he's pitching against the future, against age, [against his career ending.] And tonight, he might be able to use that old aching arm one more time to push the sun back into the sky and give us one more day of summer."

And then we can tumble down the rabbit hole.

The boys of summer will not be here this year. Oh, I heard they will be, in some form, in a stunted season with everything changed and empty stadiums. We'll be watching our boys take the field from our air-conditioned homes without even the opportunity to head down to the ballpark.

The rabbit hole can go even deeper. The 1972 book, "The Boys of Summer" by Roger Kahn, about the Brooklyn Dodgers moving to Los Angeles. Then there is the Dylan Thomas poem that gave the book its name. The Don Henley song that borrows from everything about the regrets of youth.

"After the boys of summer are gone..."

They are gone this summer. What will summer even look like? What will it look like in the fall when playoff baseball comes round the bend?

But there are other boys of summer. I was one. With the Georgia ground the anvil and the summer sun the sledgehammer. 1988 and then continued in the summer of 1989. Ft. Benning, Georgia. I think the anvil, sledgehammer and drill sergeants were supposed to tear me down and shape me into something else. They didn't. And that's why I did a lot of push-ups. Lots and lots and lots. My stubbornness became the rock that broke the sledgehammer.

A lot of people say boot camp is the hardest time of their lives. For me, it was one of the easiest. Two summers where I did not have to think. I was told when to sleep, when to eat, when to train and even when to use the bathroom. What could be easier?

The hardest thing about boot camp was staying up late. I was part of the last training battalion to go through Harmony Church, barracks that had been built during WWII. No air conditioning. I would have to wait until everybody fell asleep so I could turn the two fans directly on me.

Advanced Infantry Training (AIT), 1989. Where I would eventually graduate and earn the baby blue cord of the infantry. In a very full life, I still consider it one of my finest achievements, one of my proudest moments. There was a shaping that was done by that anvil and sledgehammer. A bad attitude. A cockiness and confidence. Yeah, I'm from SW Philly. Now add Infantry to that.

A shaping and a tangent. A tangent that can become its own story. Brian. I met Brian at Ft. Benning. He was from the Scranton area and was heading to Philadelphia for college after he graduated high school. He would do his one weekend a month up in Scranton with his mortar battalion and I would do mine in Philly with my mechanized infantry battalion.

Things like boot camp bond people. It's supposed to. Companies pay thousands of dollars for the kind of bonding experiences they can get for free by enlisting. The fastest of friendships are born and then they pass into autumn, a wisp of memory without the Georgia summer to keep hammering you closer.

Autumn of 1989 found Brian and I in his dorm room at the University of Pennsylvania. A few autumns later found us in a cockroach infested apartment in West Philly with a cat playground built along the walls and up into the loft for his two cats. It would also include trips up into Scranton, long drives up a turnpike that has been under construction since it was first built.

A short story, "Fishbowls, Tequila and the Meaning of Life," came out of one those long nights in West Philly. Peter would eventually come along with kendo and karate. Their lovely girlfriends--who would become their wives--would follow, Tanya and Kathy. Friendships that would span decades with little contact for years at a time.

"Doctor, lawyer, Indian chief" is from some long-forgotten nursery rhyme?

Fishbowls have stuck with me and so has that. Brian became the doctor. Pete became the lawyer. That left me to become the Indian Chief.

I did my best, boys, but no tribe would take me in, so I became a tribe of my own.

I'm thinking it's time to be the boy of summer again. This 49-year-old body is old and achy. I'm lazy and out of shape. But I'm still SW Philly. I'm still Infantry. I still have that bad attitude. And I am still wondering about fishbowls and the meaning of life—not so much the tequila.

I want to see if I can break that sledgehammer again.

Finding an Anchor; May 31, 2020

The plan was to run to the grocery store and pick up some desperately needed essentials: cream and sugar for my coffee. Then, I was going to return home and do some desperately needed weeding and cleaning. It was such a gorgeous day, I said, "the hell with it" and ran away from home. To childhood.

More precisely, I ran away to North Cape May. It had been the only extension of my world as a child outside of SW Philly. Grandmom's house. Going back there is always like diving into memories and splashing through childhood. What is the saying? "Your cousins are your first best friends."

Dana was closest to me in age, just a couple months older than my older brother. It was the three of us, to be joined occasionally by her older brothers: Dave, Doug, Ken and Mike. But it was mostly us three, with the freedom denied us in SW Philly. Did we even have a curfew?

North Cape May was a small, slow moving little town where the ferries would leave for Lewes, DE. My grandfather bought a house there in 1972 and my Coci ("aunt" in Polish) would later buy one as well.

In later years, when I started driving and before GPS, getting lost was a given. I still can't figure out the streets, a maze of houses with three-foot chain fences and sun-scorched lawns. The tall, blue water tower was my point of reference. Both grandmom and Coci lived on streets off the tower, so I would drive somewhere close to the ferry, hang a right, look for the tower against the skyline, and eventually find it.

It was a huge playground for children. Everything was safe and quiet. Days filled by lathering up with suntan lotion and then making the long walk down to the bay. "Saving the horseshoe crabs" by dragging them back into the water. Walking out on the wooden bridges to the piles of massive rocks, the jetties. Sitting on them with the waves crashing against them, wondering if the incoming tide would leave us trapped. Walking along the almost empty beaches to the channel, where the boats and ferries would come and go.

The older cousins would take me on longer adventures. Bike rides, crabbing in the inlets and maybe a drive to get ice cream at night.

Peaceful, cool nights with the breezes coming in from the ocean. Trundle beds making one huge bed in Grandmom's room. Or sleeping in "Grandmom" Gladys' enclosed front porch across the street.

Away from the city. Away from traffic and sounds. Away from time.

There are more people there now, with the beaches fuller, but kids still play on the jetties or walk out with their parents to fish for flounder along the channel.

One of my oldest memories is splashing in the bay with Coci on the beach. I might have been six? I stepped on something slimy and it came up to stare at me with its one eye pointed upward.

Terrified, screaming. "Coci!" Running up to her. "That was a flounder. You should have grabbed it. It was dinner."

Coci's house. The house of smells. And sounds: Uncle Becky snoring away in the recliner while the Phillies played and the best cook in the world cooked for the army that would descend. Somehow or another, a live crab would always get loose to chase after little kids' toes, only to be scooped up by Coci right before the crabs found them.

I drove out to the ferry and walked along the inlet. The smooth boulders make it like hopscotch at times, skipping over the fissures. Unlike in other places I had been since the lockdown, there were more people here than I remember. The parking lot was almost full. The beach that had been almost empty in my childhood was now full of people and umbrellas.

A drive along Beach Drive, finding a parking spot and walking out to where "my" beach was. Many more people there as well. I had thought to make the trek out onto the jetty but it was filled. My balance isn't what it used to be and the wooden bridge out to the jetty is narrow. I would have ended up in the water if I had had to pass somebody. I got back in my car and drove to the water tower.

Both my grandmother and Coci had passed away and their houses sold, but another aunt had bought my grandmother's old house, tore it down, and built a new one. I arrived and slipped into the backyard to find my Uncle Richie repainting the swing set for the new generation of grandkids. We were talking as he painted and then my aunt saw me from the back sliding doors. That's when the argument started.

"Get inside here and give me a hug and kiss!"

"No!" Didn't she hear the bell clanging from my neck? Unclean, unclean! My Aunt Diane was in the highest risk category. Her age and recent health issues made Covid a death sentence for her.

"Christopher," she said, "don't make me angry. Come give me a hug and a kiss. And I'll make you something to eat."

My uncle nudged me. "You better listen to her." He rolled his eyes.

I looked at her. I tried explaining Covid.

"Oh, piss on that," she said. "If it gets me, it gets me. Now come give your aunt a kiss."

I tried arguing to sit outside. She just looked at me. It was much like walking the jetties. You have to keep your eyes down so as not to step into the empty space between the boulders. I went inside with my uncle, gave my aunt a hug and a kiss, and sat down at the table for her to feed me. We talked about various inconsequential things.

It had been a couple months since I had had a meal with someone. It had been years since I had had a meal in North Cape May.

As comfortable as it was, it was also terrifying. There was no real way to know if I had Covid or not, no real way to know if I was giving my aunt and uncle a death sentence. And she just smiled, happy I was there. She wanted me to stay the night, but I begged off, wanting to get back home during daylight.

I think it would have been nice to stay the night in North Cape May one last time. Despite the changes, the undertow of the place was sweeping me out towards childhood. But I said my goodbyes, with another kiss and a hug, and made my way out of town and back towards the present.

In Absentia; June 2, 2020

It has been about four months since my last day of work. About three months since I helped Tracy move into her new home. About right now, I should have been settling into my apartment in Milos, Greece.

It is about the absence of things. The absence of things can be as powerful as the presence of things.

I miss touch. I come from a family of huggers and kissers. Yes, I still kiss my father every time I see him. Well, not now. I wave him a kiss as I see him through the glass door when I drop off supplies.

My years in Miami were ideal for me where everybody kisses everybody.

I remember one time when I moved back up north to DC after one of the times I quit college. I went out with a female co-worker after our shift for a drink. It was just an innocent drink after work with no intentions or expectations. As we left the bar and were about to part ways, I tilted forward for the Miami double kiss on the cheeks. She recoiled from me.

Too many of my friends had thought it funny to send me the same meme on Facebook:

Me: I think I'm finally ready to start to date again...just waiting for a sign from the universe.

The Universe: *releases a world-wide plague preventing all human interaction*

Me: Well played, Universe. Well played.

But they don't know. Well, most don't.

As I sit in front of my fireplace at night, I look at the VIP card I was given by the owner of Cheerleaders, a strip club in South Philadelphia, one of the few bars you could have a drink and smoke. Believe it or not, they also had a great menu. And cheap. I could get a damn fine NY Strip for $15.

Like I mentioned, the lockdown locked me away from some of my unhealthy coping mechanisms.

Strip clubs had been my escape for a long time. A strip club in Essington, Lou Turks, was the first bar I could get into without ID. At 17. The interesting thing was I had never gone to a strip club when I was in a relationship, only when I was single. Touch had been my escape. Beautiful, naked dancing women were not that bad either.

I missed Justine. After I separated from my wife, I returned to Cheerleaders. I met her as "Paisley." She was a tiny, little woman but an explosive dancer. We had started talking and I found she also had an incredible mind, an openness, a certain comfortable "vibe" as they would call it these days. After being alone in my marriage for so long, it was wonderful to engage with someone again, someone who seemed interested in me, and someone who would touch me.

And then she kissed me.

"No," as Chris Rock said in a stand-up routine, "there is no sex in the Champagne Room." But in all my decades going to strip clubs, there had also never been kissing. There had been the playful pecks, the teasing brush of lips, the hovering of a mouth so I could feel breath on my lips, but never any full-on kissing. Making out. Then, one night, Justine was on my lap, pecking and teasing me. Then, completely unexpectedly, her lips were on mine. A deep, long, sensuous, passionate kiss.

My mind…shredded. It was as if a dam had been blown apart and feelings and dreams and the other world exploded into my reality. It shattered the hardness of who I had made myself become.

I was hooked. Cheerleaders, and Justine, became part of my weekly routine.

"Chris," my one friend said, a former high-school classmate and a former stripper, "she's playing you. It's not healthy."

"Chris," my other friend said, Papa Bear, "If it is what you need and makes you feel good, it's okay."

It all became something more with Justine. A connection. It was not just the lap dances and the kisses. We would talk, have dinner together, and text each other late at night. With Justine, I could be a part of me that I had long forgotten, locked away long ago. It was that rush of the honeymoon period, of getting to know someone and someone getting to know me.

The absence of Justine was keen. The strip clubs were closed, she had joined her pod, and I was alone in my boat.

Alone is not a terrible thing. I had as much interest in dating than I had in drinking heavily. I felt a keen loss of the absence of touch, but I know, for many, there was the debilitating loss of the absence of money.

Justine was okay. Dancing was her second job. Her main source of income was as a crafter and artist. I'm sure she took a hit, but she joined the ranks of the new industry making masks. I even bought a few, handmade and embroidered. Aye, if you are going to wear as mask, you might as well wear one with style.

Justine was one of the lucky ones, as I was. Aye, I was sitting on a pile of cash and far too many credit cards. But I began hearing stories.

For many strippers, along with many other occupations, it is all cash and all under the table. Waitresses and bartenders, nannies, and maids. No access to unemployment or any type of government help.

Things may have gotten tight for many, but an entire segment of the population became instantly desperate. Overnight.

"Closed for business" became a sign on every bar, restaurant, home and strip club in the world.

The absence of everything. Voids must be filled. Certain websites and sketchier dating sites exploded. Sugar babies looking for sugar daddy's. The sex trade exploded.

I was an electrician, bootlegger, landscaper and scavenger. Why not try being a writer again? I started researching it. I spoke to Justine about her friends who she had worked with and jumped onto sites I had no right being on. I asked a former editor about the idea and she loved it--but I ran into a problem. The only women that would talk to me wanted me to pay them for their time and that's a big "no no" in journalism.

I remember seeing all the memes and complaints on Facebook about being trapped at home, that they were prisoners. They bothered me. At least they weren't being forced into selling their bodies.

Weighing Anchor; June 4, 2020

I was just lying there, a 49-year-old version of Huck Finn. Stretched out in a boat, with a cigarette hanging out of my mouth instead of a corncob pipe. Somewhere on the Mississippi—that sounds far better and is easier to pronounce than the Schuylkill River--just gently rocking in the soft, easy current on the side of the river with the boat tied to a tree on the bank.

Just bobbing in my boat, relaxing in front of my fireplace. Doing nothing. Aye: I was way ahead of all of you. I was supposed to be taking this year off. This is not quite how I planned it though.

That first bump of wood on wood had me waking up a little bit. The bumping of all the other boats got to me. Anybody want coffee? Will you people get back to work and your normal lives so I can gloat a little bit? Oh, you can't?

And then I sat up, looked around me, and realized I was part of a massive flotilla. I knew what I was doing here but so many people didn't. And a storm was coming, blackening the horizon. But I just lay back down again, lit another cigarette, and, like the sun dreams of beach days, time was stolen away from me. The Great Detention of 2020 had begun.

Cause and effect: quickly on the heels of the Great Detention of 2020 was the Covid Hibernation, where days turned into weeks and then into months, all meshed together. Time compressed. A day ending before you even knew it had begun. Not knowing if it was Saturday or Thursday.

"I've lived through a lot," said one 97-year-old woman in an elderly community, a prisoner in that community by government mandate, solitary confinement. "The Great Depression and wars and riots and change. I saw a man land on the moon, old Tricky Dick forced to quit, and a host of other things. But this. This I have never seen. Not that I get to see much, being locked in this fucking room."

With the storm coming, and more boats joining the flotilla, more voices and masks and people not wanting my coffee, I knew it was time. So, I weighed anchor, casting off from the gentle current on the side of the river, to bump my way through the mass of boats. Some of the boats were as simple as mine, some huge yachts, some just simple plastic tubs—and everything in between.

"We're all in the same boat," I wrote. I was wrong. "We're all in the same flotilla" is closer.

"Sleep, sleep," said Covid. Just nap for a few more months. And it's hard not to heed its lullaby. I've lived through a lot as well but I ain't never seen anything like this. My mind can't wraparound it, can't grasp the enormity of it or the new reality it is creating. It's as if the old ways are back, fight or flight. But with the inability to do neither, my mind just wants to submerge in the sunshine.

It was time to get into the quicker current. Time to take the tiller and steer my way into the center of the stream, to force myself into action. Or at least reaction. That storm is a comin', I knew, as I crossed from the lighter blue of the river's edge into the deeper blue of the center. Maybe I could outrun the storm? Or maybe I could head into it? Maybe I could find someone who would like a cup of coffee? I just needed to get the hell out of here.

Governor Wolf had finally lifted the restriction on buying and selling houses and I took one of my first offers. It wasn't my best idea, but I had few good ideas left. I started to pack my Outback.

Plan A, Poland, Italy, Greece and a walkabout was a dimming fantasy. Europe was locked down even tighter than the United States.

I decided on a long drive. I had paged through Hemmingway's "Travels with Charley" over a few of the long, lonely nights. He had gone in search of America. I had nothing planned that was so grand. I thought that maybe I could find the thing that I was looking for along the highways and byways of America. Or maybe just see all 50 states.

With the house finally under contract, a closing date set, and the weather getting warmer, I made a trial run up into New England. Packing is an art, as is preparing an SUV for a long journey. I was scribbling outside the lines. After thinking long and hard about it, planning and shifting things, I ended up just tossing a bunch of stuff that I thought I might need into the back and headed north along I495.

First, something old. Up through Pennsylvania to Scranton. Safer waters. Comfortable. Childhood friends and things I knew, like the everlasting roadwork on the Northeast Extension. Meeting with anchors from my past, Brian and Tanya, in their new home outside of Scranton.

I hadn't seen them in a long time. Years. A decade? I remember I was on my back down from a business trip to Buffalo, NY and swung east to say hello. It was our way. Or maybe it was just my way? Brian had come a long way from bootcamp and then that roach infested apartment in West Philadelphia while working and studying at the University of Penn. He was now a radiologist.

I called ahead. In the past, I tended to just show up at doors. With the pandemic, I didn't want to put people in uncomfortable situations. Brian told me to stop by.

Lockdown and precautions are nothing new to Brian and Tanya. Many of the precautions we are being told to take are precautions they have taken since the birth of their son who is immune compromised. Brian had been working from home for years, taking shifts from five hospitals. With technology, he could do what radiologists do from his basement.

I drove up the long, circular driveway to the immense house Brian and Tanya had had built. Oh yeah, we were a long way from that efficiency apartment in West Philadelphia. I met Brian with the now customary elbow bump after getting out of my car and donning my mask. I waved to Tanya. There was the whole Momma Bear thing going on but her smile was as warm as ever.

Brian and I went for a hike through his dozen acres. Our conversation drifted from topic to topic, some catching up and some reminiscing. He was proud of his place as he pointed out various things to me like the fruit trees he was trying to grow and the pond. I was proud of him. We chatted, had a drink on his back porch but then it was time to move on.

Brian and Tanya stood together while I was getting back into my Subaru Outback. Another wave, another one of those warmest smiles, a little bit more chatting across a few yards that felt like miles. Tanya had always given the best hugs. Her tiny, petite frame seemed to enfold you as if you were tiny and she was four times your size.

From something old to something new: West from Scranton to Ricketts Glen State Park. There was a bustling corner store, on a crossroads with nothing else on it, serving hoagies, trail mix and sodas to visitors. A lot more quiet than usual I was told. Masks slipping down under noses. "I hate this damn mask."

Ricketts Glen State Park was the scene of a different kind of kiss a year ago.

Murphy's Law: Anything that can go wrong, will go wrong, at the worst possible moment. Some of my friend's think that I am Murphy. But Murphy has a baby sister and I think she has a crush on me. I don't know what her name is or what her Law is, but every once in a while, I will feel the soft, fluttery brush of her lips on my check and the extraordinary and sublime will happen.

Ricketts Glen State Park was Justine's favorite place. I had stopped here the year before to see what she saw in it. To me, it was just another state park in Pennsylvania. Pretty enough but I had never really been a PA state park kind of guy. Walking through the park, I looked down and saw a piece of jewelry lying on the ground. I reached down and picked it up, instantly knowing it was Justine's, feeling the soft, fluttery brush of lips of Murphy's sister.

"What's this," she asked, a few weeks later, picking it up from where I had placed it on the bar at Cheerleaders.

"It's yours," I told her. "I found it when I went up to Ricketts Glen."

"It can't be. I haven't been there in a long time. But it does look like a belly button ring I lost." She put it in her purse, and we forgot about it as we chatted.

A text later that night; "It is mine! I looked up the serial number. But how could that be?"

Murphy can be an SOB. But the Universe can be funny at times. Tender.

I sat for a while longer in Ricketts Glen State Park, a year after I had first been there, feeling the soft smile of Murphy's sister as I explored a bit further into the park. I wanted to do some hikes, explore some of the other things Justine had told me about, but I needed to get on the road.

I sat on the hood of my car for a while, in the sunshine, with Murphy's sister cuddled up next to me. Remembering. It was enough.

North into something borrowed. Borrowed memories of cousins, and cousins of cousins. I was there once? A long, long time ago. A farm with a pond and a dock to jump into the water? Upstate NY, after taking the wrong "north" out of Ricketts Glen and ending up 45 minutes from where I started--after four hours. Who knew there could be so many norths?

Then, even further north, up the byways and highways to Lake Placid. Home of the 1980 Winter Olympics and the Miracle on Ice. Up along roads with rivers rushing along them into a small town nestled in the mountains. A different feel to the air and the sunshine. Empty streets in the middle of the day, a closed museum, but knowing the forests teemed with hikers. All along the approach to this mountain town there had been lines of cars parked like a sandbar between the river and the road. I wonder what it had been like before the pandemic? Had the streets and town been as empty and had the sides of the road been so full?

But further north. A highway. There were strange signs that I had never seen before. Montreal: 40 Miles. Unseen but known. At the border there will be a "forbidden" sign.

"For the safety of our people, you are not welcome. Go back to your virus infected land!"

To finish the old saying, I traveled east, into the blue. Something old, something new, something borrowed, something blue. The blue of Lake Champlain, the waters both reflecting the sunlight and soaking it in so it scintillates. I brushed against Canada and then drove back down a highway after crossing into Vermont, knowing I missed something. Finding a hotel.

Yes, I was essential personal. Didn't you notice my "Live Aloha" mask? Justine made it for me. Aloha is essential during these times. Aloha is so much more than a simple greeting, a hello and goodbye. When you say, "aloha," to somebody, you are offering them love, compassion, peace, and mercy. I thought that was essential. Thankfully, the hotel desk person thought so as well, and I got a room for the night.

I would later find out I stayed in the largest city in Vermont: Burlington. It had the feel that it could fit into a suburb of Philly and rattle in it.

But I had missed something, so I headed further east the following morning, by going northwest--you sort of had to be there. I might never be there again, so with the morning sun and a full cup of coffee, I made the drive up through the islands on Lake Champlain that I had missed coming down.

GPS can be a fickle thing. It doesn't understand the current of the river. Yeah, that center path might get me there quicker, but quicker is not the point. So, I drove north from Burlington, over bridges and a different type of sunlight, the morning sun, to South Hero, then to Grand Isle and then to North Hero. Isle La Motte was not too far away and then into Alburg and almost bumping into Canada again and the "keep your virus infected ass out of our country" unseen sign. But then I was finally east on a beer run.

John Steinbeck, when first starting out in "Travels with Charley," wrote about the immensity of the country and wondered how he could ever hope to traverse it? My first two days had me thinking how small it was and why had I never been here in New England? In 1961, Steinbeck had road maps and atlases that showed the crisscrossing highways of an enormous country. I had GPS telling me it was only "this many" hours. And I was taking the long route.

10 hours and 35 minutes straight through from Philadelphia to the northern end of 95 if I chose to take that route. I have to find the other quote where he wrote about how you need a destination, even if you never make it there. But the quote everybody knows and uses is:

"A journey is a person in itself; no two are alike. And all plans, safeguards, policies and coercion are fruitless. We find after years of struggle that we do not take a trip; a trip takes us."

For me, it was just nice to be in the middle of the river again, with the anchor nestled in the boat, prepared for temporary moorings, landfalls to make forays into Covid America.

The X [Ambassadors] Factor; June 5, 2020

"Renegades," by the X Ambassadors, off their freshman album in 2015, VHS, is a song that found me on the radio a few years back. New music sucks. But I liked this one. I bought the album—or downloaded the electronic thingie I guess. I hate sounding like a high school kid making mix tapes. The scene in the movie, "Almost Famous," where Kate Hudson gives her brother the album and tells him, "Listen to the words" makes me squirm. But I'll be damned if the album wasn't talking to me. There was something about it that was connecting me with something bigger, something I had almost forgotten.

It was the antithesis to Don Henley's, "New York Minute," that had scared the living hell out of me for decades.

It's our time to make a move
Our time to make amends
It's our time to break the rules
Let's begin

And I began. Other new music found me. Florence and the Machine. Mumford and Sons. Keleo. ZZ Ward. The newer music was talking to me in ways music hadn't spoken to me in a long time. I was enjoying it too much to just brush it off as anthems to the X, Y, Z or whatever generations.

Two years ago, I found myself at an X Ambassadors concert with my wife filled with kids, quickly being escorted upstairs to watch from balcony seats. My stepdaughter had bought me tickets for Christmas. Good show, but something was still tugging at me.

Okay: most new music sucks.

Then, the X Ambassador's new album, Orion, came out in 2019. That one really screwed me up. It came at me with an attitude. It was like entire album said, "okay, you ignored us in 2015. This is your punishment."

Hey child, hey child
We were born wild
Let your neon lights
Keep shinin' bright

I found myself in Chicago last year with a concert ticket for the House of Blues. Alone this time. A travelin' man. What the hell was I doing here? Traveling alone, for pleasure, for the first time in I don't know how many years. No business conference, nobody to stop by and see.

I had seen the X Ambassadors were playing at the House of Blues so I bought a ticket and booked a flight and hotel room. It was just a few months after asking both my business partner and my wife for a divorce.

Nobody knew who The Blues Brothers were! I'm wandering the streets of Chicago, following an online Blue Brothers walking tour. Street sweeper, cabbie, cop, random people. Nope, no idea. In the friggin' bar across from where Jake and Elwood were blown up by Carrie Fischer. Chicago Black Hawks but no Blues Brothers. Nothing!

So, I toasted them anyway. Outside of course, having a cigarette on a rooftop bar with Plexiglas separating me from the non-lepers. A Belgian blond beer. A blond guy came out to join me. He was South African, traveling the US before heading to Hong Kong.

"I have no idea why you are taking a selfie while saying cheers," he said, "but do you want me to take the picture?"

Young guy. Edward. He didn't know who the Blues Brothers were either but promised to watch the movie as soon as he could. We smoked in our leper colony and sipped beer as we talked.

He shot straight up, sloshing beer all over himself. "You're kidding? The X Ambassadors are here? That's my favorite band!" —young guys are very excitable. Was I ever that excitable? But he was immediately hitting buttons on his phone. In a few seconds, he looked up and smiled, asked the waitress for another round, and said, "I have a ticket."

Edward and I exchanged numbers, parted, and I continued my walking tour of the blueless Blues Brothers city, to see where the epic ending occurred, telling Edward I would meet up with him at the show.

I hadn't even told my business partner I was taking an extended weekend—he wasn't talking to me and I had had enough of him.

I was still living with my wife. I had gotten a brief, fierce hug as I was leaving for the airport. There was a heaviness, a sadness, things left unsaid as they were unexplainable. But we were still living together. Friendly. Amicable. With neither of our families understanding. I don't think Tracy and I really understood either.

I arrived at the House of Blues early. Finally! The house built by the Blues Brothers. Statues, t-shirts, memorabilia! Someone in Chicago knew who the Blues Brothers were! A friend had hooked me up with the premium package: early admission, open bar and a meet and greet with the band. But there was a surprise. I received two passes instead of the one I was expecting. I called Edward.

"Edward, where are you at?"

"I was going to be leaving in a while."

"Get here," I said, "now. I have an extra pass. Do you want to meet your favorite band?"

"You're shitting me," he replied. You could hear it in his voice. He knew I wasn't. Knew he had to run immediately.

"It's 6:05. Doors close at 6:30. You lose your pass at 6:28."

I wasn't in any rush. Meeting the band? Eh. But I did want to hit that open bar. Check the venue out in an intimate, private setting before all the people poured in. Sip a beer and take it all in before I headed up to the balcony seat I had purchased before I knew my friend had gotten me the pass.

6:17. Run, Edward, run! A squat, blond, bull like South African guy huffing and puffing his way over the bridge.

We were the last in line. I was the oldest. The young women in front of us were positively gushing. "I'm telling Sam Harris I want to have his babies," the one young lady said. What was I going to say to Sam? Or Casey or Adam? I hadn't even known their names until Edward and the ladies told me.

My turn. Everybody had to go in pairs and Edward let me lead the way. Fist bumps only we were told. There was a young lady being drug away by security, screaming something about beautiful babies. I stood in front of Sam.

A pause.

"Thanks for teaching me that all new music doesn't suck," I said.

He laughed, we chatted, and Edward gushed a little bit. We had our photo op and then went to explore the place. The girls had been drug inside of the building instead of being escorted outside and they were nice enough to get us the first round. The one lady was still discussing the very real possibility of having Sam's babies.

The crowd of kids started to pour in. What the hell was I doing here? I started to scope out the balcony seats, wondering which one was mine. Edward saw me and handed me a fresh beer.

"Look Chris, you did me this awesome favor so let me do you a favor. Don't take the balcony seat. You don't understand. Look at where we are standing. This is where we'll watch the show. Right in front of the stage."

The girls were more than happy to share their electronic cigarette, Edward was more than happy to keep bringing me beers, so why not?

What an awesome show! Edward had been right.

And then the X Ambassadors got me again. Later in the show. The song, "Hold Me Down," off their new album. The album was really beating me up for some reason.

I couldn't get my mind around the song, couldn't push it away and just enjoy it for the good song that it was. Maybe it was all the beer, maybe the loneliness of being in the crowd. Something was bothering me about it. I had been the savior archetype, holding everyone down, all my life. Holding everyone down helped me hold it together. Now, I was on the verge of flying apart. It wasn't until the next song that I could push away the tears that were welling up and shimmer back into the moment.

I set things in motion. I own that. Maybe I can blame Sam and the band? My identity was stripped away. A choice. A difficult choice. But a necessary one. Business owner and husband. Dog walker and cat caretaker. Son, brother. What was left to hold me together? Who would hold me down?

Fast forward to May of 2020, in Vermont.

"Breaker, breaker, Papa Bear, this is Bandit. Or Renegade. Or Foolish Wandering Irish Cap Guy (I need a better call sign). The package is picked up. I repeat: the package is picked up."

I really did make a beer run to Stowe, Vermont. It was the only place to buy Papa Bear's favorite beer, Heady Topper. Papa Bear and his wife Liz still wouldn't give me the address to their place in Masthope, but he had me on the phone every day, holding me down.

What an amazing area. The ride up and down the mountain with the switchbacks and waterfalls now that ski and snowboard season had passed.

Then down the mountain, across Vermont and into New Hampshire. There was an entire column forming in my head as I made my way to Mount Washington, where you can drive to the peak. Drive to the peak! The words! The ideas! I could feel the wings unfurling. Great and mighty pinions made to catch the thermals to take me to the high winds, the powerful winds. Far above the lowlands where I was slowly threatening to fly apart.

Mount Washington, like everything else, was closed.

43

Maine or bust?

Papa Bear: "I gotcha, brother. I gotcha. Always keep in mind: though me and Momma Bear love you, you're the only person my kids like."

Reverse back to Chicago in 2019, two evenings before the concert. High above the city on a rooftop bar at the Virgin Hotel, sitting with an old friend of mine from the University of Miami. Regina had always asked me the most excellent questions.

She interrupted me as we were discussing life. "Why do you refer to yourself as a person who stutters (PWS) and yet you also refer to yourself as a depressive?"

I didn't have an answer for her. As I sipped a beer with a coffee chaser, I knew it was not a matter of semantics, that the word choice was deliberate. It would not be for months before I began to finally understand the reasoning.

Deer Isle (not Island) was the first stop on Steinbeck's journey, his first "destination." It was mine as well, along with someone to hold me down. I had a feeling Deer Isle would be easier to find.

Compass Points; June 9, 2020

Go West, young man! So, I did. Another excursion before the pandemic. Just an airline ticket and a hotel reservation. East to west, but first I had to go north. And then back south. The bus took me to the Golden Gate Bridge in San Francisco in early September of 2019. I let it pass. What's the point? I'll get off on the other side and walk back.

The perils of winging it and not researching anything. There is no bus stop at the park on the other side of the Golden Gate Bridge. The bus went right past it. I watched it pass with my anticipation of an upcoming "beginning" deflating into a "what the hell?" As we slowly started climbing into the hills, I'm looking around. More than a few miles along, I'm thinking to myself, "I'm screwed and this hike is going to be far, far longer than expected."

A tap on my shoulder. I turn around and an elderly gentleman had a smile on his face. "Happens all the time. You wanted to go to the other side of the bridge?"

I nodded.

"Just tell the bus driver. We'll be pulling into a station in about 15 miles and he'll be able to direct you."

With a free bus pass, a bus number, and directions to tell the next bus driver exactly where I wanted to go, I was heading south again.

After the second bus wound through a marina and I jumped off in what seemed to be the middle of nowhere with directions of a short walk to somewhere or another, I finally made it to the starting point. Sitting there and looking out across the bridge, at the suicide prevention signs, and the bay, I realized it was also an anniversary. Or close enough.

It was early September 2019. In late August 1989, almost 30 years ago to the day, I graduated Advanced Infantry Training (AIT) at Ft. Benning, Georgia and earned the baby blue cord of the infantry. To commemorate the anniversary, I posted on Facebook:

"To all those who think I am lazy and out of shape, I am. But I can still walk all of you 'in shape' people into the ground. Once Infantry, always Infantry. Hoo rah, my ass. "Follow me" is our motto."

I started walking.

The drive east into Maine, well, sucked--My apologies to all of you Mainers out there. I was absolutely sure there was a beautiful, scenic route to take, but going from Mount Washington, New Hampshire, following GPS for the quickest route to Bangor, is like you enter a dilapidated and dryer New Hampshire, where the colors are fading along with the towns. There was an unwelcoming heat along the byways I was following. Sunlight that had been so sparkly through the leaves of trees with hints of great mountains in the backdrop turned into a depressive weight. It annoyed me. Where the hell was Maine?

I trudged across the Golden Gate Bridge. To trudge. "To walk slowly and with heavy steps, typically because of exhaustion or harsh conditions." Bikes were whizzing by, joggers jostling for lane space, couples and families almost skipping. I trudged. It's the way I walk. A purposeful gait that can carry me anywhere, far after the non-lazy and in shape people would drop.

A destination? I tried to find Steinbeck's quote on it again that I liked, but I couldn't. But I knew it mirrored my own thoughts. You need a destination but don't have to actually reach it. A destination could be a mid-point or an end point or somewhere way off the map and beyond compass points. My destination as I trudged across the Golden Gate Bridge? Technically, it was where I had been the day before, at Rodin's "The Thinker" at the Legion of Honor Museum. It was about a five-mile hike across the bridge, up along the coastal trail to the park and then I would see if I had enough gas left in my tank to continue.

My destination? I was already there, trudging across the bridge, out on the west coast. Away. And inward. Aware of the cars and trucks rumbling across the bridge, making way for bikers and joggers. Aware of the boats passing underneath with Alcatraz far off in the bay. Aware that to my right was the great Pacific Ocean, a seemingly endless expanse, that lay beyond a wall of clouds.

I was exhausted. Strung out and pulled so thin I didn't think I could stretch anymore. And I knew worse was coming. My office manager was about to go on maternity leave. My partner and employees would do what they had always done: nothing extra. I would be forced to work even longer hours. I should have let the place die years ago. A decade ago. But I needed to hold it together for a few more months while I sold it and got the hell out.

I learned long ago that I could trudge my way through and towards anything, long past where all others would fail. But that day, it was about the coastal trail in San Francisco.

The byways finally ended in Maine and I was on a highway towards Bangor. I would have stopped to see Steven King if I knew where he lived, and if he had invited me—I only like to go where I am invited. I'm funny like that. I was NOT invited into Canada. I really wanted to go further east into Nova Scotia. But I would settle for as far as I could go: the beginning of 95.

As a student at the University of Miami, the southern end of 95 had been a part of my life for seven years. 95 ends, or begins, in the middle of Miami. Just south of the airport, past the causeways that will bring you to Miami Beach, it ends and you merge onto Route 1—where you can follow it another 150 miles to Key West.

Stretches of 95 had defined and anchored my life between Philadelphia and Washington DC and between DC and Miami. But I had never been to the northern end of 95. I wanted to see that. Does it just end like it does in Miami, forcing you to merge onto a lesser road? Or does it remain a highway with a name change as you enter Canada?

At Bangor, I merged onto 1A to Trenton, Maine, a pitstop. The gateway into Bar Harbor. It was out of the way, but home is where family is and my cousins were waiting for me there.

A pitstop along the coastal trail in San Francisco. It's the oddest thing. The bridge is far behind you, as are many hills and beaches. Then, the path takes you into an upscale enclave of houses. You see hikers with backpacks, water bottles and walking sticks walking along sidewalks next to multi-million-dollar homes. There was a granite bench a little way up from China Beach, so I sat, spread my belongings on the bench, and stared at the house across the street. It was massive and beautiful, but rundown. Empty.

I knew I could walk another 20 miles at that point if not more, but I wasn't in any rush to get anywhere. My exhaustion had nothing to do with my feet or legs. It had to do with my soul and spirit. In the sunshine, on the cool marble, I felt a little less tired.

A well-dressed gentleman was passing by and stopped. He had to be from the neighborhood.

"Do you know who's house that is," he asked, motioning to the abandoned home across from where I was sitting.

"No, sir, I don't."

"Look at the bench you are sitting on," he said with a smile. "Have a good day." He tipped his head and continued his walk.

I moved my stuff to look at the inscriptions on the bench. And then I looked at the bench next to it. The two benches were dedicated to the memory of the parents of Robin Williams and his wife. I was sitting across from the former home of Robin Williams, whose exhaustion had gotten the better of him.

"I always thought that being alone was the worst thing that could happen to me," Williams is attributed to saying, "but I realized that the worst thing was being surrounded by people that made you feel alone."

When Robin Williams died on August 11, 2014, I wrote a tribute to those who had lost the battle to depression. The tribute began percolating in my head as I gathered my things and continued my trudge up the hill and back into the forest.

A trailer park in Maine, a gateway to Bar Harbor and Arcadia National Park. The park was closed due to Covid. How, and why, do you close a park? My cousins, Dana and Adam, who had first shown me the area at the other end of 95, took me down to the town where they would be working once things reopened. This was the Maine I was expecting.

The coast of Maine is like the fjords of Scandinavia. Please excuse me as I get a bit geologically geeky. It has to do with the ice age. When the glaciers receded, they gouged the earth. So, instead of the straight, sandy coastlines in New Jersey or Florida, you have "hands" sticking out into the ocean. Think of a spread palm. The "palm" is the starting point, like Trenton. The "fingers" are the islands and isles. It creates a beautiful landscape of inlets and islands, of sandbars and deep channels, where the tide creates entire new landscapes.

I had two "destinations" in mind when I made the trip up into New England. The first was the end of the US portion of 95. I always wondered why I had never been there. It is only 10 ½ hours from where I lived and yet I had made the 22-hour drive to Miami a few dozen times. With the border to Canada closed, though, I decided to make my way to the other "destination," Deer Isle, Steinbeck's first destination in "Travels with Charley."

Deer Isle was as different from Bar Harbor as Maine is from Miami. Bar Harbor is where the cruise ships come in. It was odd to me, but I couldn't even smell the sea there. With Deer Isle, you knew you were going to experience something different when you first drive across the beautiful bridge. It's a sleepy little place, made narcoleptic by Covid. It was deserted. The smell of the sea is pungent in the air. Causeways bring you across inlets.

I got lost. No big deal. It was an island--or isle. And not a very big one. I didn't even put a destination into my GPS, just looked and saw that the main road takes you on a circuit around the isle and back out to the beginning. The drive had a relaxed feel, with the harbor filled with lobster boats and backyards filled with lobster traps. Steinbeck was essentially bullied into making Deer Isle a destination on his way up to northern Maine. I'm glad I made it one of mine.

I reached my destination in San Francisco: Hero Legion, home of "The Thinker." I got there at an ideal time as well. It was closed.

I wish I were a better photographer. It was just...perfect. The massive monument of a nude of heroic proportions sits with his chin resting on his hand. It is argued that it was originally made to represent Dante Alighieri, author of the Divine Comedy, but it has come to represent thinkers and creative types, at rest but never at rest. With the park closed, The Thinker sat imprisoned behind a black iron fence.

On the previous day, I had started here and then hiked the coastal trail south, winding down the cliffs to the old public baths and Land's End Lookout. I'd eventually have a very expensive cup of coffee--that was not very good--and then walk down along the beach. I then made my way to the beginning of Golden State Park, through the park, and eventually back to my hotel.

Today, I walked down the hill from the museum to the park and ambled along the edge until I found a place that served coffee, just a corner store wrapping up for the day. It turned out to be a damn good cup of coffee. I sat outside drinking it—they were kind enough to tell me that I could use their outdoor seating as long as I wanted, as they had a lot to do inside. I sat thinking of the "The Thinker." Imprisoned. It was the end of another day in San Francisco.

It was tough leaving Deer Isle. I stopped at the park before the bridge and just sat there for a while, thinking about things with the massive arch my backdrop, that smell of the sea wrapping me with the cooler winds. But I finally set out along the backways and byways. I had a date at a biker bar.

I arrived at the recommended biker bar right at sunset. It was closed due to Covid.

Route 1 is definitely the way to take up or down through Maine. It is more relaxing and scenic, connecting all the "palms." As nice as 1 is, though, I needed speed after the biker bar, so found my way to 95.

Rolling through the Maine forests at 80mph is picturesque. I had only planned on making it into Massachusetts and find the first hotel. Bar Harbor to Massachusetts was pushing it. I had called ahead. Hotels were accepting travelers, I was told, if you were an essential traveler. Isn't having a place to set up my coffee maker essential? I thought so.

After dark, I arrived at the hotel. I told them I was an essential traveler.

"Where are your travel papers," I was asked. "I can't give you a room without them."

Massachusetts, it turned out, was, indeed, closed.

"I left them out in my car. I'll be right back."

I sat in my car for a little while cursing. Then, I finally made my way back onto the highway.

Safe Harbor; June 11, 2020

...I have a need of wilder, crueler waves;
They sicken of the calm those who knew the storm...

Traveling through the night on a Massachusetts highway, I had a need of a better road, a hotel, and a decent cup of coffee. The way things were looking, I was ready to settle for any motel and a hot, coffee like substance.

I'm not sure why, but everybody has it in their heads that the journey that I am planning has something to do with campsites, living off the land, and dying at the hooves of a caribou. No. My Outback is outfitted to serve as a camper with an air mattress, sleeping bag, sheets, pillows and even a battery-powered fan. The last thing I am expecting to do, however, is use them.

I'm a snob. I like hotels. I like nice hotels with turndown service. I like hot showers and fluffy towels to pat my bottom. For me, "roughing it" means making do with the in-room coffee maker instead of my own. At least one of my suitcases is packed extremely well. I packed and unpacked it a dozen times before I had it just right. Inside of it is my "kitchen." Coffee maker, coffee grinder, Hawaiian Kona beans, a mug and the sugar. —my Carnation Non-Dairy Liquid Creamer is in my cooler.

My journey is about exploration, America and myself: not mosquitoes. But who knows what is going to happen?

I did eventually find a cup of coffee somewhere along the Massachusetts Expressway. The coffee was lousy and I did consider making use of the camping gear, but then I finally found a motel that would take me in. It was about an hour away and about three minutes away from another cousin's house. I think my cousin kind of likes me, but I doubt he and his wife would have appreciated me showing up after midnight.

The next morning, my cousin, Doug, handed me a plate of breakfast as soon as I walked in—I guess he does like me? I had a nice morning of family time in Westfield. Chatting, coffee, teaming up with their son, Jacob, for an epic comeback cornhole win and then I was off for my final "destination" on this trip: Newport, Rhode Island.

I went south and then east through Hartford, skirting Providence. Going through these "main" cities is always anticlimactic for me. If you blink your eyes too fast, they are behind you. On a map, Philadelphia looks like any other dot. Driving through it, though, with no traffic, takes a good 45 minutes. That's what I'm used to: the massiveness of Washington DC, the long stretch of puzzle pieces that make up Miami or even the super sprawl of Dallas/Ft. Worth.

It was a nice drive on a gorgeous day, off the main highways and onto the access roads and bridges to take me to a boat-building town in the smallest of states. And traffic. I had completely forgotten it was Memorial Day weekend. What the hell had happened to the stay-at-home order? I mean, I was ignoring it but I'm special—those on a quest are always afforded special status. What were all these cars doing on my road?

I drove into Newport and immediately thought to myself: virus spike. I don't know if the lock down or the gorgeous day had gotten the better of people, but the place was packed. Taking five changes to get through one light took me to the center of town and

I just wanted to turn around and leave. The virus doesn't bother me; crowds do.

The restaurants and bars were still only serving take out, but the outside seating was packed. The wall along the cobblestone street had no more room for another butt. The parks were jammed as well. I made my way down to the wharf, a safe harbor, far less crowded. A very nice security guard let me in and I wandered around.

It was closed to traffic, much more quiet, and I could walk out on the piers. Yachts were lined up in the water and I watched a guy and a woman take a self-propelled surfboard out for rides. It was getting a good few feet out of the water at the highest speed. I could only imagine how cold the water was.

In the boatyard was something I had never seen before, only read about. A boat, easily three to four times the size of my house, was in a cradle on a transport. The transport's tires were over 10 feet tall. I had always said if I could just pick up my house and move it a mile northeast, it would be perfect. Here I saw a way to do it. Can I get a loaner? Finally get away from the ridiculous taxes and equally ridiculous HOA?

But it was time to head home. Part one, the trial run, was over. What awaited me was the worst part of the entire trip. Massachusetts roads might suck, but they were nothing compared to crossing the George Washington Memorial Bridge in New York. Down through the Bronx like a Formula 1 speedway and then choosing to go over or under the bridge. I went under. Wrong choice. Water pouring down on my car, no lanes, weird turns and construction. Never again.

One interesting thing is the uniqueness of the comparison: GW Bridge to New Jersey, from driving hell to driving heaven. After crossing into NJ, I encountered six travel lanes, all well paved, straight as an arrow with gentle hills diverting me back southwest, back towards Philadelphia.

In a short time, I was back to the known. I had spent many weekends over the past decade making this drive to and from this part of New Jersey, where my wife worked craft shows. Soon, I was back to a safe harbor and home. Back to the calm. Back to fair weather, knowing it would chafe at me soon enough.

Some kind of wrap? 2,000 miles taught me a lot.

1) I suck at packing and organizing and need to get better.
2) 6-8 hours driving each day and take my time, 4-5 hours if I just want to stop and see something. It's not like I'll be in any rush.
3) Making coffee from the car plug-in outlet is impossible.
4) Wilder and crueler waves is the calm.

Fair Weather
by Dorothy Parker

This level reach of blue is not my sea;
Here are sweet waters, pretty in the sun,
Whose quiet ripples meet obediently
A marked and measured line, one after one.
This is no sea of mine, that humbly laves
Untroubled sands, spread glittering and warm.
I have a need of wilder, crueler waves;
They sicken of the calm, who knew the storm.
So let a love beat over me again,
Loosing its million desperate breakers wide;
Sudden and terrible to rise and wane;
Roaring the heavens apart; a reckless tide

That casts upon the heart, as it recedes,
Splinters and spars and dripping, salty weeds.

Once Upon a Home; July 1, 2020

It is sunset at Fells Point, Baltimore Inner Harbor. With the nicer weather, businesses are beginning to adapt to the new reality with outdoor seating. It was nice to just socialize with a friend and see people out and about doing the same. And I had some damn good oysters.

And then the ride back north to Chadds Ford along Route 1. A nice relaxing drive up through Maryland and into PA, a route I had taken hundreds of times from the time when I first started driving when I was 16. Bonnie Raitt on shuffle. I think I have most of her albums. Bonnie Raitt, considered a master of the slide blues guitar, has been a favorite of mine for a long time, especially on long drives. Or for drives where I don't need or want the music to surge. Her music makes me feel like a kid again, with my girlfriend in my car and her arm wrapped around my shoulder.

At Fells Point, I had felt uncomfortable. Too many people without masks. Too many crowded bars. I feel better being outside, safer, but? The calculated risk. I need to get used to this.

There is a spectrum with attitudes towards Covid, from completely cavalier (scamdemic) to completely paranoid. What's the right answer? I think my situation and the realities of my life pushed me into a 5-6? I'm aware, read a lot, believe it's there but also know I need to be on the road, so I do what I must.

My friend is closer to 9-10 on the scale, completely paranoid, which isn't an awful thing. We don't know enough about this virus yet, or the true implications of contracting it. Everything that I read points towards potentially bad outcomes, like the 17-year-old, with no underlying medical issues, that just had to have a double lobe lung transplant.

After my friend and I ate at a crowded outdoor seating area, where neither of us felt comfortable, we went and talked on the pier. We sat a few feet away from each other as the sunset set fire to the harbor in a spectacular display of reds, oranges, and yellows.

What can you really do? The person that I get all my information from is the only person I trust on the topic. Chuck Thompson (YoD–Your other Dad) has been in healthcare for over 60 years. A retired Colonel in the US Army, he's been a nurse, leader, educator, researcher and is now retired so has the time to really research all the information coming out about Covid–and he knows how to read the medical journals. He's been a resource for me since I met his son in the 7th grade. I'd love to go see him before I leave, but I can't. Montgomery County, MD is a hot spot, with regular new cases and deaths. YoD and his wife are both immune compromised and older. They have essentially barricaded themselves in their home. It is an option that is not totally unappealing, but also impossible for me and most.

The closing date on my house is quickly approaching.

The home of my dreams is no more. I'll miss the koi. I'll miss the beautiful landscaping that my wife created over the last six years. I won't miss the weeding.

I realized an interesting thing since the lockdown began: it was never really a home the past six years. It was only since I sold my business in December that the house felt like home. Without the long days, weeks, months and years of dealing with a business partner who was never really a partner, forcing me to carry the place into the new technological paradigm, the house was just a place to sleep and make coffee. After the lab sold and Tracy moved out, I became a willing caretaker instead of a chore doer. A house became a home.

Then, the terrible spring came, the Great Detention of 2020. Lockdown. Locked inside a…home. A trip to Poland, an apartment on the coast of Italy, a friend waiting for me in Greece, and then a walkabout became a scramble for all the things I had just given away. Spoons. Plates. Lamps. Something, anything, to put inside of the fridge besides coffee and coffee creamer. I even bought beds in case I could rent rooms.

A long winter. It seemed to cling to the land far longer than usual. Sitting in front of the fireplace, attempting to fight off the Covid Hibernation. I got busy on my home. I worked on the projects that I could not do for years. When warmer weather arrived, I started working on the pond.

I had hated that damn pond. It's an ugly thing in the winter. Hibernating fish. Murky water. Overgrown weeds and a forest of horsetail around the edges. No running water with the basin, stream and tiny waterfalls closed for the winter. Just something that was barely alive.

Then, it began to awaken. Looking out at the pond, with the fish more active on warmer days, I began to get the feeling of a child the week before Christmas, waiting my turn for Turpin Landscaping to open the pond—opening a pond with the stream and waterfalls is much like opening a pool for the summer.

The pond I hated became my new project.

After Turpin opened the pond and got everything running again, I really got to work on it.

Then, I broke the pond. Tearing out a 10-foot long, 3 foot wide, 120 pound "weed" shifted all of the rocks in the main pool out of place. The call went out to Turpin again. Kevin came out to fix it.

"While you are here…" A new light for the waterfall, a new light for the pond, a new pump, and then tackling the eyesore of the basin that fed it, covering it with slate and rocks. The final touches, water lilies, would have to wait until Turpin got them in stock, after winter finally released its grasp on the land.

With the house up for sale, it was pointless, wasted money. But it wasn't. I would sit by the pond every night, just taking in the evening and my home. Even as I emptied the house —again— in preparation for the buyers, as everything was sold and given away —again— I'd sit outside with my koi.

I sold a shell, a blank slate, to a new family of four to make into their home.

I hope they remember to feed the koi.

It's time to begin the next chapter.

I had writer's block so I just started driving.

Part Two: Drifting in the Current

By the Bays; July 16, 2020

Closing day. It was the oddest closing I had ever experienced. My wife and I sat in our cars in the realtor's parking lot with the notary in her car. We signed papers, handing them back through windows.

Tracy went to her home and I made my way to my house to pack up my traveling home, a fairly new Subaru Outback with 12,000 miles on it. I packed a little bit better. Instead of unorganized chaos it was organized chaos. But it was everything I would have for my time on the road. I'd figure it all out eventually.

My first stop was to get the hell out of the Northeast. Covid was affecting various parts of the country differently, just like with people. The Northeast was on the "paranoid" edge of the spectrum. Things seemed more open south and west. I drove down my driveway one final time, made a right onto one of my bootlegging backroads, and drove down into Delaware.

Before leaving, I made the first of many phone calls that were all the same. My cousin, Ken, lived a few hours south on the eastern shore of Maryland.

"I'm headed your way, planning on driving to Norfolk, but wanted to know if I could stop by to wave? Don't feel bad about saying, 'no.' I completely understand."

A pause.

"We'd really like to see you. Stop by and we'll have lunch outside on the deck."

"GPS has me at about 2 ½ hours. I'll see you then."

2 ½ later, I was knocking on his door and taking a few steps back to allow him the courtesy.

"Oh, get the hell in here," Ken said. "Joyce is making dinner and you are spending the night. Let's go fishing."

It's an out of the way little spot on a creek off the Chesapeake Bay. It is my cousin's piece of the American dream. His home reminds me of his mother's, my Coci. A place of warmth and food and welcoming. My Coci's home was in North Cape May, a nice walk to the bay. Her son's is on the creek that leads to the bay, with a dock for his boat. To get to the bay, you cast off from the dock, travel down the inlet, into the channel and then finally into the bay.

At his brother's wedding, I gave a speech, talking about the Zborowski's. The five of them, Mike, Ken, Doug, Dave and Dana, grew up a block away and taught me what it means to be a man. Not by telling me what to do, but by showing me. You want something? Work hard. Plan. Own your mistakes. Move on. Oh, and learn how to take a joke.

Ken joined the navy after high school and then the Philadelphia Fire Department after that. 24 years ago, he bought a piece of land in Maryland and started building a house. He finally retired about a year and a half ago, after 30 years, and now the house is his piece of heaven, retirement. Ken and his wife, Joyce, live there full time now, with a daughter and son-in-law an hour away and a son, daughter-in-law, and two grandchildren making their way from his son's previous duty station—a move that has been held up by Covid.

What is a piece of heaven? What is home? For Ken and Joyce, it's a little spot on the creek, complete now with a chicken coop and enough room for a lot of guests. He enjoys taking people out fishing. He enjoys sharing his piece of heaven with anybody and everybody that wants to stop by.

"It really does break my heart," he said to me. "You know how my mom was. I always wanted people to stop by. Now that we are here full time, I can't with Covid. I have to turn people away."

Every travel story I read talks about the "sleepy little towns" the writer passes through. I either have to come up with better phrases or this is going to get very repetitive. The drive from Wilmington, DE to Princess Anne, and then on to Norfolk, is a long drive through small towns along Route 13. I just don't know how sleepy they are.

Nicer people, a slower lifestyle, a hello and a thank you. Many people awake at dawn to fish or go crabbing. Each town can fit into a suburb of Philadelphia and is much like a suburb, complete with the McDonald's, Lowe's, chain restaurants and chain gas stations. The differences are the lifestyles, and the people who enjoy those lifestyles.

Bait and tackle shops line the roads. In Philly, you see the billboards, "donate your car for charity." Along this stretch, it is "donate your boat."

They know about the tides and the seasons, about when what fish are running and where best to catch them. They talk shop with the older fishermen to learn. They know how to tie ropes in a certain way and how to string lines.

And Ken is kind. He knows enough to know that I don't know anything about fishing. I'm not big on fishing, but I enjoy spending time with Ken on his boat as he talks about fish and tides and casting and lures. I enjoy spending time with Ken and Joyce as they talk about their piece of heaven. It's calm and peaceful, with laughter and great food. It reminds me of my Coci.

And then there are the life tips, the "pearls" you pick up and take away, much like from business meetings. With me on the road, there were a bunch of things that I would never have thought of. Why buy ice for the cooler? Use the hotel. Hotel points? Yeah, go with Hotwire. Like a big brother, he's giving me the inside tips on traveling light and traveling well.

While I was there, Ken's older brother, Mike, was texting me along with his wife, Dawn. Dawn is a dear, so much so that she is in my phone as "Dawnie Dear." Mike wants more than updates— if I'm okay with it. Just in case. This is how you set up the iPhone to permanently share your location. Mike is a trucker and knows a lot of other truckers all across the country. Just in case. They're worried.

The baby brother and baby sister chimed in as well. Places to go. Do you know your new cousin is in Norfolk? Great stops here and there and everywhere. --I'll be looking into a lot of places.

But the bars they recommend? I just don't know. No, I know. It's a "no."

It's the age of masks and staycations. Of not seeing family and friends. Of people feeling guilty for saying, "no." Of uncertainty. Of a virus I could have and transmit without having any symptoms. Of understanding people and their desire/need to have others in their life, to have company, to hug. Of my desire/need. Of my calculated risk and not wanting to inflict that risk on others. Of a new reality that we all do not understand yet and are frustrated by, the misunderstanding and frustration forcing us to take risks that we should not.

I still think the government screwed up everything from the start with semantics. With "social distancing," they used the wrong phrase, and the phrase became the reality. No. It's not "social distancing." It should be "physical distancing." But this is our reality.

I need to keep that in mind or this trip could possibly be cut short by a ventilator. Aye, it's basic science. I'm a two pack a day smoker which means my lungs are shot and I'm constantly touching my mouth and eyes. I might not be in the "highest" risk category, but I'm close to it.

Norfolk and West; July 15, 2020

Down along 13, along ways that I know and populated with people that I know, still by the bays but crossing over towards the unknown. The Chesapeake Bay Bridge-Tunnel is, to me, an awesome feat of modern engineering. It stretches across the mouth of the Chesapeake Bay, a 17.6-mile combination of bridges and tunnels, one of only 12 like it in the world.

I have a thing for bridges and tunnels? I also have a thing for avoiding the Washington DC loop. Into the unknown, a new "known" was waiting for me. Lisandra, my newest cousin who I had never met before, had agreed to meet me for dinner. I was nervous meeting her. She had been excited to meet me but what did that mean? It would just be me and her as her husband, my baby cousin, was out to sea.

She was a tiny little thing and a great big hug was waiting for me.

I really miss hugs.

Lisandra is a truly incredible young lady. I think we forget how old we are and the passage of time. Wasn't Adam, her husband, just rolling around in my Miami apartment in his walker? And now he is married, in the navy, and out to sea? I'm the same age as Lisandra's parents, who I think should be very proud of such a capable woman—I can't wait for the rest of the family to meet her. And did I mention how damn adorable she is? To top things off, she had a bumper sticker: "Me and Coffee are a thing." A woman after my own heart.

We had dinner at an open-air restaurant on Virginia Beach and then took a stroll along the boardwalk. Lisandra is Cuban American, and it was nice to catch the turn of phrases, accent and little quirks that brought me back to my time in Miami.

The next day, I went out to explore Norfolk. My timing, as usual, was impeccable. Everything in Norfolk is closed on Monday and Tuesday and I missed my cousin returning to port by a couple days.

Norfolk: where all of the streets have names but the people don't have faces. It was deserted. Traffic was still zipping by on the highway but there were very few people in the streets. The few people that were wandering the deserted streets were wearing masks except, oddly, the older people. I personally didn't appreciate people getting on the elevator with me without masks on. I'm wearing it for them. Can't they offer me the same courtesy? Some of the places of business had signs: "Masks are strongly encouraged." They were right next to the signs that read, "No shirt, no shoes, no service."

But the battleship was awesome. You don't realize how big a battleship is until you walk around it. The USS Wisconsin was the last battleship to fire on enemy targets, during the Iraq War.

But now I am off west, to Charlotte. Then? I seem to be getting a lot of tips of where to go after the plans are made so I need to be more flexible. But I am also wondering what's open? Where will I feel safe going? Who is practicing the prescribed precautions?

I crossed the line on the map! I finally crossed over 95 as opposed to the dozens of times I've traveled it to and from Miami.

Just a lot of driving, with some interesting things that I find interesting, but others may not. Most may not. Like crossing that point on 95–where I think I spent the night once a long time ago at a Red Roof Inn. Stopping at the rest area in North Carolina. Watching the heat climb to 97 and then plummet to 75 with a storm, along with visibility. Passing through all the cities I knew by their college basketball teams.

Packing for travel is an art. I'm still scribbling outside of the lines, sort of like a first grader's try at Picasso. Trying to whittle down what I need to bring into the hotel. A part of me wondering what the hell I'm doing in Charlotte? Still trying to figure out this new computer. Definitely have to stop making hotel reservations until I get to where I'm going because I really don't know where I'll end up. Just shaking off the dust, working out the kinks and creaks and snafus.

Wait. Stop. I lied when I wrote that I had no idea why I went to Charlotte. I did. Herb Harmon. The psychiatrist/old friend/war vet. I wanted to see him. We met for coffee.

One of the things Herb and I discussed was the social media effect. We hadn't seen each other since college. 1995? But it felt like it had been a few weeks. He's been a good friend to me as I battled depression. He tossed out a lifeline and I grabbed on to it. The truth is I wanted to make it convenient for him to say he'll meet. So, I was down in Ft Mill, SC for a cup of coffee and great conversation. And a real connection.

Covid sucks. Handshakes are out, as are hugs. We did the elbow bump. And then he made it a point to pat me on my back. It's an interesting time when a pat on the back becomes a "memory," a "thing." We are all missing the sensation of casual touch. It's part of the new reality.

But that is one of the fears we spoke about. The need, the loss, will drive us to do things we shouldn't do. Is Herb positive for Covid? Am I? So, we sat outside, sipped coffee, went and got his dog, and then talked politics, family, medicine, Covid, psychology, trauma, UM, and a host of other things. It was well worth the drive.

Next stop: Back tracking to Winston-Salem. Gail is a new friend I met through the professional association I founded a few years back. Lab owners LOVE to show off their labs. Walking into her lab, I itched to sit down at a bench and bend some wire. There is a lot to be said for just allowing muscle memory to do its thing and create something intricate. There is a satisfaction involved.

Winston-Salem was going through a lot of changes even before Covid. I mean, Winston-Salem? Can you guess their main source of revenue? As tobacco sales waned, tobacco fields transformed into wineries and microbreweries. Krispy Cream, of course, still has its roots there. Good food, good people, and a wonderful time, but it was time to head back to Charlotte to pack up and get ready for the next day.

Civil Engineers Who Drank Too Much; July 19, 2020

Well, I didn't know what the hell I was going to do after Charlotte but everybody else seemed to know: Asheville! So, I went to Asheville, NC.

I got the name of a highway wrong in a Facebook post and my uncle reminded me that north/south highways are odd numbers and east/west are even. He's from NC so he knew exactly where I was–I even passed his boyhood home. So I asked him: why was it when I left Charlotte, my GPS took me on 85 South but my compass most definitely said NW. Asheville is most definitely NW of Charlotte. Along 85 South.

Asheville is amazing. Nestled along the Blue Ridge Mountains (Appalachians), it boasts a week or more worth of activities. My first trip was to Chimney Rock State Park. 74A straight to it. Well, you drive 74A to it; straight is in question. My cousin, a motorcycle person, told me of a road nicknamed something like the "Dragon's Tail" in this area with more switchbacks than any other road. I think I found it.

The Dragon's Tail made me think some civil engineers were drinking on the job. Heavily. It's roads like that, though, that make me dream of my Lexus 360 F Sport. It would have been a hell of a ride—or I would have died. Or it would have been a hell of ride until I died? In a straight line, it is about one mile. You travel five miles of road.

Chimney Rock boasts some stunning views and the largest waterfall east of the Mississippi. I pulled up, parked, and bypassed the bus that takes you up. Hiking seemed like a good idea at the time. I trudged. With a few breaks at the steeper parts. One very large man had his family around him, fanning him, and made him takes sips of water while they checked their cell phones for coverage in case they had to call 911. But it was a nice hike with some awesome views.

One shirt I saw in the gift shop said it best: "The Mountain Called: I Gotta Go!" But maybe the mountain called for a bus ride? A man must know his limits. This one pushed me to mine. I remember a quote by a writer. I forgot who. It was about how we don't know our limitations until we exceed them. I guess trying to climb a mountain is one way of finding out.

I couldn't find the author or the actual quote but looking for it I ran across this one by Claude Chabrol. It seems as apt as the other one: "Stupidity is infinitely more fascinating than intelligence. Intelligence has its limits while stupidity has none."

I do love the mountains, though, especially knowing the hike down will be much easier than the hike up. I encouraged a few people on my way down that were just starting out: "I'm lazy, out of shape and unhealthy; if I can do it, anybody can."

After the hike, I stopped in at a coffee shop. Why do people insult me by asking if I want cold coffee? It was lousy anyway. But in the shop was this old picture that showed Chimney Rock before they built everything. I loved the contrast between the natural and man's attempt to blend his efforts into the natural. Man typically fails but the alternate would be far fewer people making the trek and seeing the incredible views.

The drive back to Asheville took me along the Dragon's Tail, making it very difficult to sip coffee and light cigarettes. Then, my one-man University of Miami reunion continued as I met another old friend and his husband at the Biltmore Estate, the largest residence ever built in the United States.

I don't know what to say about the Biltmore Estate. Nothing I have ever seen can compare. I can't even imagine living there. It would take an army of staff just to maintain the place and a game of hide and seek could go on for months.

On one hand it was majestic, opulence in full bloom. On the other hand, why? A separate room for just about everything, including the former slave quarters. It was wealth vomited that made the opulence obscene. It was for a single family and yet it was larger than most apartment complexes that could house thousands and had a kitchen that was far larger than all of the restaurants I've worked at.

I'm not knocking it. I'm of the opinion that if you have the cash to spend, you can spend it on anything you want. But I also think there is a line between having what you want and garish displays of wealth.

And now it's time. A drive up the Blue Ridge Parkway awaits and then, for some reason, I feel a pull to go into horse country.

Blue to Smokey to Blue; July 20, 2020

…and then I came down out of the mountains onto the plains, following the path blazed by Daniel Boone, through the Cumberland Gap and three states. I had no idea where I was, how I got there, and I'm still not sure what time zone I'm in. But let's back up a little bit…

I could have stayed in Asheville for a week. It's a beautiful, scenic town nestled against the Blue Ridge Mountains. Which are also the Smokey Mountains from the Tennessee side. Which are also the Appalachian Mountains. I had heard about the Blue Ridge Parkway so headed north along it. My uncle, from North Carolina, warned me and he was right: you can spend a long time on the parkway and not get very far. It took me most of the morning to travel about 30 miles.

The Blue Ridge Parkway is a beautiful road that winds its way down from Roanoke, VA into Georgia. It's two, well-built lanes seem tucked away from everything. It's amazing in the summer, I was told, but spectacular in the fall with the changing of the color of the trees. Amazing views, like the clouds below me, are everywhere. It felt unreal to me, as if I was traveling on a road between realties.

I left the parkway in a tiny town called Little Switzerland. There was an incredible bookshop. I could have spent a day in there alone. But it was time to head to Kentucky. Somehow or another, I started in North Carolina, went to Virginia, then to Tennessee, then back to Virginia, then back to Tennessee and finally into Kentucky. A rainstorm hit and smoke could be seen rising off the mountains.

I got into an argument with Siri, my navigator. SHE wanted me to take the quickest route. I didn't. Unfortunately (typically), this argument with Siri took place while I had Pappa Bear on the phone.

"You are the only person I know," Mike said, "that doesn't want to take the quickest route."

There is a reason. You know what you'll get on the quickest route: big highways, trucks, and whizzing through without really seeing anything. When you take alternate routes, it's a roll of the dice. There is the chance of not seeing anything. But there is also the chance of seeing the extraordinary in the ordinary. Like in Kentucky.

It was only much later I would figure it out after crisscrossing the country a few times. The country is a huge place, but also small. It is the scenic byways, lesser highways and state roads that make the country the imposing vast expanse that Steinbeck experienced. The interstates and superhighways compress the country and make it smaller.

My first stop was Fort Boonesborough State Park, southeast of Lexington. My next stop was my hotel in Georgetown, just north of Lexington. Siri wanted me to take the quickest route, a 35-minute drive through Lexington. The longer way was an hour drive circling around. It was just ordinary Kentucky I was later told by the hotel clerk. Just lots and lots of horses and lots and lots of horse farms. It was an amazing drive through neighborhoods. It was just like the neighborhoods in Philly, but each plot was the size of a city block enclosed with fences.

North on 627, northwest on 1958 to 64, then came the fun part: North on 859 (Haley Road), left on Briar Hill Road, right on Houston Antioch Road, left on 68, then right on Iron Works Pike to Mt Horeb Pike to Lemons Mill Road and then to McLelland Circle.

There was something about it all that enthralled me. Horses. It was like a drive through a neighborhood where all the homeowners have their dogs in their front yards. Here, though, it was horses. You could see one or two here and there or a half dozen to a dozen.

The only thing I had ever known about Kentucky was bourbon. I enjoyed the more intimate view.

Horse Lovers; July 21, 2020

You're not going to Lexington, Kentucky. You're going to Georgetown, a suburb just north of Lexington. And if you don't love horses, you have no reason for being there.

Old Friends Thoroughbred Retirement Farm. I found out about it when I was talking to the hotel clerk. I read the brochure and picked up the book but couldn't do the tour as they are only accepting a few private tours per day, down from 20,000 people per year, due to Covid.

Just the idea of it. $25 per person, $15 for the regular tour when it is offered again. It reminded me of James Earl Jones' monologue in "Field of Dreams." They'll come to Kentucky without even knowing why. $25? Sure. They'll hand it over without even thinking about it because it's money they have and peace they seek.

You get up close and personal with past racing greats like War Emblem, Silver Charm and Game on Dude. There are over 175 former racehorses. Thoroughbreds. I just can't wrap my head around that. Horseflesh unlike anything else you will ever find with the horses you rent for trail riding.

Next, I traveled a little way to The Kentucky Horse Park. Of course, me being me, it is closed on Mondays but I got to wander around which is what I wanted to do anyway. Empty parking lot and nobody there.

"Dedicated to sharing Kentucky's love of horses with the rest of the world," a sign read. A few bucks and I could wonder around as much as I wanted.

I'm really starting to think that a thing being closed is not an awful thing. Everything becomes more intimate and I hate crowds anyway. I've always loved horses, always wanted to be around them more, but the opportunity was just never there. Though I've always had a love of horses, my interest in horse racing began with watching the movie, "Secretariat."

The Kentucky Horse Park can satisfy all your horse loving cravings. Man O War is buried there and his monument stands proud in the park. A bronze of Secretariat, being led by his jockey from his unprecedented win, is there as well. What would it be like with the crowds and shows and fanfare? I don't know.

What is a tour for horse lovers without a trip to Churchill Downs? About an hour west of Georgetown, just south of Louisville, is the impressive stadium that houses the Kentucky Derby. It will be run this year, rescheduled and only 125 spectators. The normal capacity is 150,000 with the record from 2016 170,000.

But then we have to discuss the fear and uncertainty. Kentucky just mandated the wearing of masks. Things are just starting to reopen and people are returning to this new version of normalcy. The people I spoke with think everything is about to be shut down again with the spikes in cases in the US and around the world. They are happy to be working again. For a while at least.

After visiting Churchill Downs, there was the 2 1/2-hour drive to Nashville where I'll be settling in for a few nights to unwind, get my car serviced, repack and check out what is called by locals, "Nash-Vegas."

The Road to Me; July 23, 2020

One of those new bands, an Icelandic band, Keleo, helped me with the trip to Nashville from Churchill Downs. Driving down that long straight open highway through the heart of Kentucky, close to 100mph, it was fitting. Nashville is where the band calls home now. I believe they got stuck there for Covid.

Their freshman album, A/B, is named after the A and B sides of old 45 records. The A sides were the hits; the B sides the sleepers. Keleo is a rock band that spent time before the pandemic opening for the Rolling Stones. There are softer songs on the album, though, and even one in their native tongue.

None of the songs from A/B ever made it on my expanding play list. I always liked to listen to the entire album from start to finish, sometimes playing it a second or even a third time. Like "X Ambassadors," something in the lyrics and the soul of the songs spoke to me.

A restlessness put to rest by staying in motion. Speeding from town to city to suburb. Hitting the A sides but finding sleepers on the B sides, like that wonderful drive around Georgetown through a neighborhood of horse ranches.

One of the lyrics from a song pulls at me and I can sometimes hit repeat a few times. It asks the question: Are you going to break?

I'm wondering if I already broke? If there is more breaking to do?

The question has been asked a dozen times if not more: what the hell are you doing? The question has been answered the same way, with a half lie. It keeps things interesting, entertaining, and, for lack of a better phrase, in motion.

Is it a midlife crisis or just a man in crisis? Was I running away from something, running to something, or looking for something?

All of the above?

I always thought a midlife crisis was a man trying to relive his youth. There was an accidental part of that to the trip: the dumbass mistakes I made after I graduated college. I graduated with a degree in journalism, with tons of clips and recommendations, but I could never quite put all the pieces together. I was stupid, arrogant, and swinging for the fences, sending my resumes and clips to the publications where first year journalists don't even get interviews. I had just wanted to be a writer and instead I would eventually buy an orthodontic laboratory.

In many ways, I was swinging towards the fences again. Posting online, reaching out to editors, keeping my website updated in the hope that an orthodontic lab would not be waiting for me at the end of all this.

I even sent out letters and emails to many of the publications that had never gotten back to me before. "You turned me down 15-20 years ago but look what I've accomplished since then and look what I am doing now." I didn't get any replies.

But being in motion was helping keep the depression at bay. The constant stimulation of all five senses was helping. The music was back, after being locked away inside of my silent home for so long. I was fighting against exhaustion.

I'm hearing it from around the country now, from social media to newspaper articles. Depression and uncertainty. I had chats with a psychiatrist and a psychologist. The lockdown, isolation, cut off from what we know as normal: it's trauma. It's just not like the normal trauma we think of, the quick hit, the lightning strike that can release the powerful chemicals in our brain that can help protect us and get past it. This is a long, drawn-out trauma. How are we supposed to react to this?

I compare it to taking hammers to a boulder, with the hammers, trauma, and the boulders, our brains. Break out the ten-pound sledge and you reduce it to rubble in no time. Or, you can take out the small ball-peen hammer and start tapping. It might take years or decades, but the result will be the same.

That ball pean hammer has been in motion on my brain for a very long time now, with more than a few swings of the that 10-pound sledgehammer.

Some people think I already broke, but in a different way. While many see my journey as an epic adventure, the once in a lifetime opportunity, there were family members who thought otherwise.

"It's a fair enough question," my brother had said, referring to my aunt's question.

"No, Joe. It's not. I'm not like mom. I'm not manic. This is not a manic episode. All that you have to do is talk to me."

My mom had passed away a few years ago. That's an entire other story, another book. I knew mania far too well, or its current classification, "bi-polar disorder." I could know within a few minutes of talking to her if she was manic or not. My stepfather would know just by walking in the door.

From the outside looking in, my actions and history did beg the question. No, it wasn't mania, and my psychiatrist agreed with me. It was the other end of the spectrum if anything. I found that interesting. Pushed into what could appear as a manic phase by an almost violent reaction to a depressive phase.

But there was Nashville in the distance. A city rising from the road and the mountains. Through a time zone and across a river and then coming to rest somewhere. Experimenting. Three nights instead of two. I finished the drive with the song, "I Can't Go On Without You."

I can't go on without me, so I'm driving, looking for myself, staying in motion to keep the depressive hibernation at bay. I'm feeling good. There's a purpose. Maybe even a home run. All the pictures, sharing on Facebook and Instagram, maybe piercing through other's hibernation to give them glimpses into a world beyond the trauma.

Experiencing, living, questing, sipping coffee. With the exhaustion lifting. Damn but I was tired. Old, ancient. I know what I am good at and what I am bad at it. I'm good at reacting, awful at acting. Something is missing. Always has been, and the reacting exhausted me. The only things to react to now are the mile markers.

Yeah, I have no idea what the hell I'm doing. But Nashville awaits, and then Memphis, home of the blues. A swing through Arkansas, Mississippi, and Alabama back to where I was, before I push further outward.

Covid held up the release of Kaleo's sophomore album. What the hell have they been doing for the last three years, besides touring and opening for the Rolling Stones?

I'm looking forward to what comes next.

Nashville! July 22, 2020

"Only you," a friend texted me.

It is something I get a lot.

Yep, only me.

I use Hotwire and Priceline to find deals on hotels. I go by reviews but never know what hotel I'll get until I pay for it. I ended up in a very nice--but very pink-- Dolly Parton themed hotel, the Graduate, by Vanderbilt University.

The entire hotel tells her story: a young girl making her way to Nashville, hoping to hit it big. The first floor is filled with sofas and fast-food signs, representing her couch surfing and early trials. There is a karaoke bar/recording studio (closed), coffee bar, and did I mention how pink everything is? I think my room could have been decorated by Ms. Parton herself, more like a bedroom than a hotel room. The top floor is a rooftop bar/restaurant/pool: the White Limozine.

A mile and a half walk from the hotel brought me to storied "Broadway" and the "Alley." There were a few live bands here and there, but most everything is closed due to Covid. It's not what it used to be/will be. I did find a nice little place in The Alley to have dinner and listen to some live music. I was talking to a group of people from the table next to me, with all the tables spaced out. After yelling for a few minutes, I joined them.

They are in Nashville often. I ended up doing my mentoring thing with a young lady fresh out of college and considering the military. She wants to travel, and with everything going on, sees the military as an option. I think it's a pretty good option, these days especially.

She was telling me about Nashville before Covid and told me New Orleans is the same way. It's usually packed with crowds, with an energy pulsing through it. They both are not the same. That's both good and bad, though. I don't see the things most would, but there is a certain intimate perspective seeing things slower, almost empty. I'm now very curious to see New Orleans.

I would say the city has a different feel but I'm only making assumptions.

The following day was the long walk. It was about 10 miles and 18,000 steps according to my iWatch. I wanted to see music row and find a coffee shop. I found one. The coffee was...well, not mine. But I loved the place itself. Another young lady was there as I sipped my bad coffee and had some breakfast. She just lost her job due to Covid and was applying for one at the coffee shop. She had been a personal assistant.

Nashville reminds me a lot of Miami. It's where the young and beautiful people come with dreams and struggle to carve out a piece of the place for themselves. The young woman was telling me how she has plenty of contacts in Denver, but with a new life and boyfriend here after four months, and how much she loves the place, she wants to try to make things happen. I wished her the best and headed on my way.

I walked back down to the river and then turned around and walked towards Centennial Park, where they have a full-sized replica of the Parthenon. I had been to the original but, well, I like walking and wanted to see the park.

"Only you" happened at Centennial Park as well. I'm used to things being closed. There, it wasn't closed but the entrance I was trying to use was closed. Under construction. I was standing at 6 o'clock to the park. Of course, I walked in the wrong direction, counter clockwise, looking for another entrance and found it at 8 o'clock. Figures.

Walking the wrong way turned out to be a good thing. I ran into Jeff and Pee Wee, his French Bulldog. I can see why Steinbeck made it a point to take his dog with him. It really is a great way to make introductions. Pee Wee took care of it for me, being the clown that Frenchies are known to be. Then, Jeff and I got to talking.

Jeff is not one of those young people trying to find their big break. He's a cosmetic dentist in Nashville (Smile On for the shout out, Dr. Jeff Trembley). Of course, we talked shop. He's doing some amazing work with the new technology. I'm still just mystified and dumbfounded by the whole thing. There are so many opportunities for the right companies, so many possibilities. But nobody is looking outside of the box, still trying to jam square pegs into round holes. Jeff is way outside of the box. I don't think the box even exists for him anymore.

Our conversation also turned to Nashville, while Pee Wee was happy playing with me or chasing after other people in the park to make friends. There's a battle going on, Jeff told me, between the mayor and the bars. The mayor is making it harder for bars to reopen than other places, while he puts millions of dollars into public works projects like two new helicopters for the police and adding a 25% tax (or something like that) on businesses.

But Jeff likes Nashville, the energy that I'm missing.

But then it was back to the mundane. I enjoy walking in the heat but it crushes me. I went to the White Limozine and looked out over the city. When they brought me my drink and water, I told them to leave the pitcher of water.

That's one of the differences between the nicer hotels and the cheaper ones. I got a great deal on the Graduate but everything is far more expensive. In the cheaper hotels, they usually have a laundry room. Just five bucks or so to do a load. Here at the Graduate, I think it would cost about $100. $3.50 for a pair of underwear? C'mon. I went and found a laundromat.

Tomorrow, I leave for my appointment in Memphis to get my service done on my car (Covid makes things like that harder and the earliest appointment here in Nashville was Saturday). But then I'll be in the home of the blues, where B.B. King, Elvis, and Johnny Cash got their start. And I get to see the Mississippi River. I might even cross it just to do it before heading back east towards some people I need to see and a place I must go.

Walking in Memphis; July 24, 2020

Of course I was listening to the song, "Walking in Memphis," on the way to Memphis from Nashville. I made it through three Marc Cohn albums as I drove the three hours down Route 40 and then around the beltway to my first destination: Subaru! –I needed an oil change, tire rotation and have everything checked out. Then, I was back on the loop and arrived at my hotel, just a few blocks off the Mississippi River.

Route 40 was unlike any highway I have ever traveled. It was a nice enough highway as highways go, but there were more trucks than I have ever seen. An endless line of 18-wheelers barreling towards the Mississippi River and West Memphis.

West Memphis--which is actually not Memphis or even in Tennessee--is in Arkansas across the river. It is a trucking hub and became known as the "crossroads of America" in the trucking industry–hence the volume of trucks flowing towards it. It is also known as one of the most dangerous cities in America, which is why I won't be flowing to it. Well, maybe just for a peak?

I met a friend for lunch. I had put out the word on Facebook, "I'm coming!" Some people responded, many didn't. Many couldn't meet. It's the Covid thing and I understand. Zach was one of the people I had met through the professional association I founded. He saw me on Facebook and invited me to meet him.

"Memphis is gritty," he told me, as we sat and ate lunch.

That's the word I was looking for: gritty. Nashville is all shiny and new, with construction going on all over the place as new high-rises go up.

"Memphis," he said, "is like a combination of Detroit and New Orleans. It has the grittiness of Detroit mixed with the weirdness of New Orleans." Other people I have spoken to like the place. I know I liked it.

The plan after lunch was to walk and look out on the Mississippi River, go and grab some dinner and then head back to the hotel for nap. As usual, Plan A didn't go well. I finally got to hear my blues here in the home of the Delta Blues, sitting in BB King's Bar at the beginning of iconic Beale Street.

It was weird, uncomfortable. The south is handling Covid very differently than the north. It's more on the "cavalier" end of the spectrum. Both lunch and dinner were inside of restaurants. I guess at lunch, I could ignore it by chatting with someone, but in BB King's Bar, I was alone with my own thoughts. The place was far from crowded and the waitress was wearing a mask but?

Not too far from Beale Street is the Blues Hall of Fame. I walked there. Closed due to Covid.

Memphis is known as the birthplace of Rock and Roll, with Soul to Blues to Rock. Just another two-mile walk is Sun Studio. I checked this time: it was open.

At Sun Studio is a great picture of the first "super group," nicknamed the Million Dollar Quartet. One night, Jerry Lee Lewis, still only a session player, was playing with Carl Perkins. In walks Elvis Presley. They started chatting and Sam Phillips, the owner, called Johnny Cash—along with every newspaper reporter he could find. The quartet would do a long set including their favorites, mixed in with soul and Christmas songs. Phillips illegally recorded the entire thing—Presley was then under the Epic label—but waited over 30 years to release it.

Amazingly, Sun Studio is still a working studio and has never been updated since the likes of Elvis, Cash and BB King recorded there. Newer artists have gone there looking for the sound like U2, Bonnie Raitt and Maroon 5.

Back in between Beale Street and the Blues Museum is one of the other facets of Memphis: the home of the Civil Rights Movement. Just past the Blues Hall of Fame is the Civil Rights Museum and the infamous Lorraine Motel where Dr. Martin Luther King was assassinated.

It was eerie. The motel has been kept intact with the cars still in the parking lot and the museum attached to it. I've seen the sight in countless movies, documentaries, history books, and articles. But to stand underneath room 306?

There was a strangeness to Memphis, though. A hushed silence away from Beale Street. There were more boarded up windows than people, more "business space for rent" signs. On a weekday afternoon, when I walked about eight miles instead of napping, I could not feel the "downtown" of a major city. A quiet day or Covid? Like other places I am finding, it is just not like it was/will be. But the grittiness just made it seem more stark against the July sun.

Not Driving in Memphis; July 25, 2020

Live aloha. Live aloha. That's what I kept telling myself the next morning after finding out the valet left my car unlocked overnight. What came out before I got a better grip on myself was "SOMEBODY TOOK A CRAP IN MY [edited] CAR!"

Nothing was stolen but everything was rifled through. And I was left a "gift" on my front passenger side floor. How would someone even position themselves to…

Friends don't know whether to be horrified or laugh. Live aloha. I finally laughed my ass off.

"Only you," I was told. Again. "They need to rename Murphy's Law to Gajewski's Law."

I don't know why, but, if they had stolen something, it would have made me feel better?

The detective told me that I was not the only one. Three of us were hit by Memphis' first official serial shitter. –The detective couldn't help from laughing either. So, the "only me" was sort of correct.

But that was my second day in Memphis. The valet manager called everybody he knew and finally found someone that could get my car detailed quickly, scrubbed inside and out. I had to empty my life all over the sidewalk in front of the Sheraton. My fully packed car was unloaded—after just throwing away the front passenger floor mat with everything on it. I'm not quite sure what I lost but I was not about to sift through it. Then, I had to spend the next eight hours moving stuff to the room that I was about to check out of, doing laundry, and then repacking.

The hotel had not offered me any help with the unloading or the laundry, but they had offered me a free night. They seem perplexed that I asked to use the industrial laundry machines instead of sitting through multiple loads that never seemed to dry. I was perplexed that they expected me to stay there again.

But it's about living aloha.

It's hard being me sometimes.

For the sake of mental health–and because I'm planning on hitting the hotel and the valet company with the bill–I made quick reservations at the Peabody Hotel, the grand hotel of the South. It was only a couple blocks away from where I was and it had the most secure parking lot I could find. A parking garage with security and cameras seemed very important at the moment.

Dinner (and all food for the day) consisted of a slice of pizza and two pints of Guinness on an eerily empty Beale Street. I walked there after checking into the Peabody.

Beale Street was like every other place in the city; it shuts down at 10. Once used to staying open and hopping until 3-5 am, last call was at 9:30. I arrived at 9. Last call got me another round of Guinness, but it seemed like last call had been a couple hours before. On a Friday night, places were empty, everybody was wearing masks, and there was a wide berth around people. If you go into any bar, bouncers are placed strategically and they get your name and phone number. I know that at any time, I can get a phone call. It's part of the tracing efforts. If I get a call, it means somebody got the virus and I'd need to bunker down for 14 days or get tested.

I was not expecting a call. Ever. The Covid precautions and tracing efforts seemed shallow to me, for show, just like the cardboard cutouts they were using to fill up stadium seating for baseball games. The USA was lousy at Covid. A friend from Greece remarked that Americans had too many freedoms. I agreed.

I'm really starting to not like cities. It's not just the incident with the car, but just the oppressive feel of them. Panhandlers are multiplying and getting much, much younger. It's not just the old crazies asking for a smoke or a dollar. Things are closed, hours cut, and people that made their money as bartenders, waitresses and such just don't have jobs anymore. Many were working under the table before the pandemic so had no access to unemployment. Saying "no" or just ignoring them bothers me. But saying "yes" opens a floodgate. And many are not wearing masks when they approach me.

The evening ended on a better note at the Peabody. One more beer before bed. In a mostly empty grand sitting area. There is something I enjoy about the five-star hotels. You're away from things. They create a getaway, an oasis, if they are done right--and the Peabody was done right.

I started off Saturday in a much better way. Close by the Subaru dealership, north of the city, where I had to go to replace my floor mats and get something fixed on my Subaru, I found a little piece of Memphis that not even many locals know about. Crystal Shrine Grotto. It's the heart of the Memorial Park Cemetery. Built in the early 1900's, it is based on a new style of cemetery, "The Cemetery Beautiful" movement. It is a departure from the 18th century style of dark and depressing. The Cemetery Beautiful is a place filled with parks, art, open spaces and gardens, a place to be at ease and celebrate life.

I made it back to the Peabody Hotel in time for the daily Parade of the Ducks. I just love the story:

In the 1930's, the GM of the hotel went duck hunting with two of his friends, one friend being a bottle of Jack Daniels. They didn't get anything but came back drunk and thought it would be a good idea to put the decoy ducks (live in those days) in the fountain of the grand foyer. The GM woke up the next day and ran down, horrified at what he might find. What he found was the ducks still swimming in the fountain and a crowd of visitors stopping by to see the sight. The rest is history.

In Need of Crayons; July 26, 2020

The country needs crayons. That's the thought that came to me while walking to the Big River Crossing. Vibrant. Vibrancy. I want to come back to Memphis again when it regains its vibrancy. Everything is duller now, with a lot of shops closed and crowds missing. I look at myself and know some of the things I do are not the smartest things to do. Going into a bar, even with social distancing rules? A restaurant, where I know how the virus is spread?

I know better, but I long for the simplicity of having a beer with other people. I miss it, and I'm not even a drinker. I think businesses are the same way and the people who work there. There is a forced feeling about it. Some don't want to be there but they have to be. The bars must be open and making money. They need to pay the rent.

Riverwalk is a great stroll along the Mississippi River, filled with parks and views of the river and riverboats. I started close to the pyramid.

Yes, Memphis has a pyramid. Zach, the friend I had lunch with, told me it used to be a sports arena but when they built a new arena, Memphis needed to do something with the pyramid. It was bought by Bass Pro Shops and made into--as he called it--a monument to red necks, and he said he's enough of a red neck to enjoy it. There is a lodge inside, shooting ranges, fishing, and even a bowling alley. I'm not enough of a red neck so walked in the other direction, south.

The bridge called me. The Big River Crossing is the longest walk bridge across the Mississippi River, nearly a mile, connecting Memphis to West Memphis in Arkansas. Did I mention I liked bridges?

One of the first short stories I wrote was, "When Bridges are Torn Down." Long ago at the University of Miami, it was the first time I tried to not only write a short story but to craft one. All my short stories are me, just as much as the personal essays. Scratch at the surface, I once wrote, and B negative will seep out.

"Bridges" tells the story of an older man, older than the boy who wrote it in college and younger than the man I am today. He lives in an apartment in Philadelphia by the Schuylkill River within walking distance of the Walt Whitman Bridge. He is a failed writer working in a factory. He tries walking across the bridge one night in an attempt to make it down the shore. Midway across, he turns back, and the bridge disappears.

There is a certain symbolism I enjoy about walking across bridges. Riverwalk led me to The Big River Crossing and I set out at sunset, making my way into Arkansas. I was extremely disappointed that there was no "Welcome to Arkansas" sign. I sat, stared across the river at Memphis, and then made my way back.

Night is when Memphis breaks some of the crayons. The bridges begin to light up at dusk. As I was walking back across the Mississippi River, I could hear surges of electricity and sunlight was replaced with neon colors to light my way.

I got back after full dark with no idea what to do. It had been a long walk and a long day. It felt good to be only physically exhausted. It was getting late.

First, I turned my back on the illuminated bridge and walked into a part of Memphis I did not know well, around apartment complexes, basketball courts, groups of kids and looked for cell phone reception to call an Uber. No luck. After a few blocks and not knowing how much longer I'd have to walk in unknown territory, I turned back towards the bridge and walked the way I came. I eventually found Riverwalk and began to trudge my way back towards my hotel.

I needed some water and food. I also knew I would get back long after kitchens were closed with the new hours due to Covid. I had forgotten something else. Mississippi River? Marshy and wooded land? The mosquitoes paid no heed to the stay-at-home order and they were feasting on me. I was looking at a completely miserable walk with little expectations of a fruitful end.

Then, I ran across one of those electric scooters that are becoming popular in many cities. Me? On a scooter? My balance isn't what it used to be. Every time I tried paddle boarding, I would end up face surfing. But I was desperate. Underneath the trees in total darkness, the mosquitoes had invited their friends to the dumbass just standing there, looking at a bright green scooter. I figured, "what's the worst that could happen?"

It took me a few minutes to figure out the controls, slapping at my ankles and wrists while I danced around trying to get enough cell phone reception to download the app to pay for the scooter, but I was soon speeding through the evening. I wobbled a few times at first but managed not to hit any trees or park benches. Aye, it worked out okay for once.

I sped along Riverwalk and back to my hotel, where I made it just in time for last call and a meal.

Part Three: Ghosting Through the South

Following a Young Man's Ghost; July 28, 2020

Go west, old man! But a young man's ghost pulled me east.

I drove southeast from Memphis, down through Mississippi and across Alabama into Georgia and then battle traffic around Atlanta. The seemingly nonexistent traffic I had been experiencing in other cities was in full force in Atlanta.

One night in Alpharetta, a nice suburb north of Atlanta, became two nights. I needed to just take a day and think. With the virus surging in Florida, everybody was telling me not to go. But can it really be as bad as anywhere else I've been going or will be going?

Alpharetta is a beautiful little town, built with European architecture. It's odd to me. Everything looks on top of each other like in any American city, and yet there is a feeling of openness and space. My friend's house was simply amazing. Magical. From the outside, it looked tiny, squeezed in between two other houses. I walked in the door and it was like one of those fantasy fiction books where the inside is far larger than the outside.

With the virus, I wonder how many places are like Alpharetta. It seems like the people in charge are doing all the right things. Signs on doors, sidewalks and in windows say everything that you are supposed to be saying. Maintain six feet distance, wear masks, and even the sidewalks in Avalon, an enormous outdoor shopping area filled with stores, restaurants and coffee shops, have the sidewalks directional so people aren't passing each other. The kids ignore it round the clock. The adults at night. The bars and restaurants are socially distant but not that distant. Lines form. Masks come off inside. Someone got after me for smoking (Avalon is a non-smoking area in its entirety) but nobody said anything to someone about not wearing a mask.

I needed to stop for a bit and think of the days ahead. Of tomorrow, and the few days after it. Of where a young man came and made decisions that altered his course in life. 32 years ago, on this date, I was about two hours away in Ft. Benning. 29 years ago, on this date, I was preparing to go away, down to Florida, to the University of Miami.

The depression continues to nag me some nights, though not as bad. Sometimes it is like the pull of a current standing ankle deep on a beach. Sometimes it is like a wave crashing into me. Always at night. There is something there about loneliness and a disconnect. That isn't real. I shake it off and do what I need to get done. But there is the feeling. Is this what I am doing out here? Trying to find a release from it? Wondering how much of my life has been determined by it?

Last year in Chicago, I had lunch with another old friend from the University of Miami. Regina asked me, "Why is it you refer to yourself as a person who stutters but as a depressive." I didn't know the answer then, knowing only it was not a matter of word choice and semantics.

I know the answer now.

To me, "a person who stutters" is not being controlled by the stutter, it is just something that is a part of them, something they must deal with. It influences choices but does not make decisions. "A depressive" imprisons themselves within their depression, allows the illness to dictate their decisions.

At Ft. Benning, it was easy and the depression never touched me. In motion continually, constantly reacting to commands and schedules. Miami was much harder. It was like standing in the ocean waist deep, sometimes shoulder deep, and that powerful undertow, sweeping me out at times. That's why I think of the two times very differently.

In 1989, I earned the baby blue cord of the Infantry and still consider it one of my proudest moments, one of my finest achievements.

In 1997, I stumbled across the finish line in Miami, having to take two courses in my 13th semester. Not really knowing what to do with my degree, never having been able to put the pieces together, I went back up north and started working in an orthodontic lab.

From boot camp, I came out with pride and purpose. From college, I stumbled away with exhaustion and uncertainty.

My family makes jokes about my time in Miami. I was a professional student, on the extended plan. 6 ½ years, and a summer semester, to get a four-year degree. I laugh with them, joke about the beaches, the bars open until 6am, the siestas and the senoritas. The truth is very different. I battled depression and lost many semesters to it. I quit school a few times to retreat and regroup. I even quit when I had only two classes left to earn my degree, spent some time in DC, and then finally forced myself back down to Miami to finish what I started.

I sat in Avalon's "smoking section," far away by the parking garage. I was thinking of demons. Those suckers couldn't keep up with my car. But it got me thinking about one semester in particular at the University of Miami. My junior year? The year I considered my junior year? I had lost track.

My demons were big, ugly awful things. Soul eaters and life destroyers, scaring away the sharks while they waited for me in the night surf. It was the fall semester so I was doing well. I think I typically got a 4.0 during my fall semesters and it was the spring semesters when things went sideways. This semester was not going to be a 4.0 semester. I was struggling with Symbolic Logic and had the final exam the next day, my first final of five.

A knock came at my door. That was odd enough. Nobody knocked at my door. They usually just walked in. The two guys I was closest to were standing there with tentative looks. Attila and Ben were only a couple years younger than me but it seemed decades at times. This was one of those times.

"You have to go see Joe," Ben said.

"No, I don't," I replied. "Go tell Herb." Herb was the Resident Assistant. Each floor had one. They got free room and board for this kind of stuff. Joe was another dormmate. A nice enough guy but I had begun keeping my distance a few weeks prior after I saw him sneaking out from the electrical closet.

I knew mania from life with my mom. I knew crazy. Joe had been well on his way when I saw him. I didn't want to deal with it. I had a tough exam to study for and I knew my demons had come out of the nighttime surf and were awaiting me in Joe's room. This is what Resident Assistants do. They go to the Resident Coordinator who would then go to the Master. This was their job, what they got paid to do.

"We can't reach Herb," Ben said. They also knew my personal history.

Symbolic logic, or predicate logic, is about arguments. Every argument, every single one, can be broken down into symbols. Then, the equation can be proved or disproved. An oak is a tree. Trees grow. Therefore, oaks grow. $X=Y$, $Y=Z$, therefore $X=Z$.

I knew the logical progression of events so went and saw Joe. I closed my symbolic logic textbook and walked down the four doors to his room. I didn't bother knocking.

Joe looked up at me from the floor was he was studying his long, jagged fingernails. He mumbled something.

"Chris, don't you see? There are universes in the atoms in our fingernails. So, if we cut them off, we are destroying entire universes. We shouldn't do that."

Then, he turned back to his contemplation and lit another cigarette.

I cracked the door open. Ben and Attila were there. "Get Herb or any RA. Go downstairs and bang at the RC's door until she answers. Get people up here now. I don't care how late it is."

I sat down and started talking to Joe. You must be careful. You can't spook them. I asked about his meds and found empty bottles in his drawer with pills scattered everywhere.

"I didn't like them," he said when I asked softly. "They make me feel bad."

A demon started giggling.

I waited. Herb finally knocked and stepped into the room. He took in the situation. "I'll go get Sheila." The RC.

I kept talking to Joe.

An hour passed. Sheila eventually arrived. She took in the situation. "I'll go get the Master."

"I think we need to go for a ride, Joe," I started preparing him for what was about to happen. "I think we need to go to the hospital."

His eyes opened wide and his entire body tensed. "I don't like it there."

Attila was still standing by the cracked door. He was average height and gangly thin but incredibly strong. Joe wasn't particularly strong and he had lost a lot of weight but I knew what could happen. As the story goes, it once took eight police officers to restrain my tiny mother.

The Master finally arrived. He took in the situation. It was about 3 am. He mentioned something about psych services and the police. Joe shot up and pushed himself against the wall. I glared at the Master. "Let's step outside," I said. I turned to Joe and made my voice much softer. "Aye, buddy, I'll take care of this. Relax. I'll be right back in."

The RA and the RC were in the hall.

I made my voice both soft and steely. "What the fuck are you people doing? Yes, get the police. Plain clothes. I've been talking him down and think I can get him in a car. Haven't you ever dealt with this before? Things can get very violent very quickly. Do it my way."

I went back into the room. They didn't do it my way. Two uniformed officers showed up with vests and batons. I've never spoken so fast in my life. To Joe. Ignoring the officers.

"Aye, look Joe, a police escort. What an honor! Just for us. I guess all the taxis were taken by all the drunks. You know how Miami is. Free ride—they don't have meters! Yes, of course I'll come with you. C'mon, buddy. Yes, I'll take care of you. No, they won't lock you up. My promise, buddy, my word."

I got him down in the elevator talking constantly, lying through my teeth. I knew what came next. I didn't want any parts of this but knew how the other arguments played out. I got him to the hospital and then the police were nice enough to give me a ride back to my dorm.

It was sunrise. The symbolic logic textbook stayed closed. I let the tide sweep me out. Another semester gone, another semester of late drops and incompletes.

The Master's wife, a psychologist, would call me later. I had done a good thing, she said, got Joe to the hospital just in time. They were working on his meds while he was in five-point restraints.

Sitting in the smoking section in Avalon, I could still hear Joe, as if underwater, screaming my name in hatred. I could see him, struggling against restraints in tears.

But I had done a good thing. X=Y. Symbolic Logic would be one of the classes I would make up during my final, two class semester at UM. Both the professor and textbook were much better. I'd get an A in the class.

I'm stopping at Ft. Benning tomorrow and then heading to Miami to follow a ghost around. I don't want to dwell in the past or think about regrets and decisions. I just want to brush up against that past, that past that followed me into the future. Maybe dance with it a little bit.

And there are some old friends to visit. And a new friend. I'm ignoring 95. I've taken that dozens of times. But I'd like to do another trip down into the blast furnace that is the Florida summer, speed across Alligator Alley once more time. Before Covid, I had planned on seeing more of Miami and its surroundings, explore the things I never allowed myself during college.

The Ft. Benning Bounce; July 30, 2020

I thought I was following the ghost of a young man. As I wandered the empty museum grounds, I felt like the ghost.

Like everywhere else, Ft. Benning and the museum were closed. I was not allowed on base, so I went to the closed museum and my car was the only one in the huge parking lot. I stood underneath the larger-than-life sculpture in the entryway, up on a pedestal, and wondered what I was doing there. The sculpture was of the Infantryman in the classic pose, surging forward with his rifle in one hand and his other hand lifted and curved ahead. Follow me.

The Home of the Infantry. Home. A great sadness welled up inside of me underneath that statue and I was close to tears in the shade of the Georgia sun.

It's tough to describe. The sadness was very much for the ghost of the present. Not the past, not the regrets, just…something. I need to consider it more, allow it to ferment and take shape before I can describe it better. Learn its texture and taste, its smell and see the entire field for what it is.

I was 17 when I enlisted. I was living in Maryland at the time, attending Rockville High School for my junior year. I'm still not sure why I walked into the recruiter's office that I passed every day to and from school. Me, with my issues with authority. People took bets on how quick I would be kicked out for not being able to keep my mouth shut. But I signed on the dotted line and took the

ASPHAB test, scoring almost a perfect score, offered any job training. I chose infantry.

Bounce

"Are you sure about that," the recruiting sergeant asked. He handed me the thick MOS book, the book that listed all the jobs I could pick from. I pushed it back. "I'm sure. Special Forces. Airborne." Special Forces was the best of the best, the elite with the most rigorous training. At the time, I didn't even realize you couldn't sign up for it; it was by invitation only. So, I was assigned as support personnel to 1st Special Forces group Airborne out of Ft. Meade, MD.

I was in Maryland again, during my bouncy days, years. Bouncing between Philly and Maryland when my mom had a manic episode. My aunt and uncle always took me in. And then they always threw me out. I was going to settle down. Stop running. Stop bouncing. I committed to something larger than myself. So, in June of 1988, the night after seeing the Monsters of Rock concert in DC, the recruiter showed up at my door saying I was invited to Ft. Benning. That day. I left.

Bounce

I really wanted to go on base but it was closed due to Covid. I had been part of the last training battalion to go through Harmony Church, barracks that had been built in WWII, no air conditioning, and would be torn down after I left. I think the story of boot camp is unimportant. I don't know why. All summer long in full fatigues doing lots of extra push-ups because I was a smartass. Couldn't keep my mouth shut. Walking in the sun and heat still doesn't bother me at all.

I finished at the end of August and took a plane back to DC. My uncle alone picked me up at the airport. Nothing had been said or written but I was informed on the car ride to the house that I would be moving back up to Philly. I just accepted it as a matter of life. I packed up my stuff, again, along with my new fatigues, and was driven the 2 ½ hours a couple days later, past Ft. Meade, knowing I would never see the inside of it. After moving back to Philly, I transferred to 1/315th Mechanized Infantry Battalion located in North Philly. Years, decades later, I would realize the car I bought with my pay from bootcamp could have just as easily brought me to Ft. Meade.

Bounce

Summer of 1989, I was back at Ft. Benning to complete my Advanced Infantry Training (AIT). Again, not much matters. It was hot, I marched. I did well, even though I did even more push-ups for being an even bigger smart ass with the West Point Cadets that arrived to help with training as they were being trained. Brand new barracks. Air-conditioned. Shower stalls and toilet stalls. Luxury. Earning the baby blue cord of the Infantryman. I arrived home in Philly and continued my one weekend a month, being promoted to the rank of corporal around my 19th or 20th birthday. In 1991, two years after I graduated high school, I was both accepted to attend the University of Miami and invited to go to Iraq. I chose Miami.

Bounce

Leaving from Maryland to go to Miami.

That was the end of my infantry career. When I arrived in Miami, counting on the monthly paycheck to pay for my new car, I was told no reserve unit would take me in due to cutbacks and I was transferred to Inactive Ready Reserve. No paycheck. No Montgomery GI bill to help with tuition. I would eventually quit school in the spring and drive back to MD, wondering what the hell I had just done. Where the welcome was cold. So, I continued my way up to Philly, where I moved into my Coci's house in SW Philly, going to work for my cousin and a mason who urged me to go back to school after kicking my ass each day. I lost my car, giving it up. I went back to Miami in the fall to the surprise of everybody there.

Bounce.

Underneath the statue in front of the Infantry Museum, I did my 22 push-ups as part of a Facebook challenge. 22 push-ups for 22 days to raise awareness for the 22 vets that commit suicide each day--about 6x above the national average for the non-vet population.

Empty and alone, I felt like a ghost as I wandered the area, the parade grounds and through the monuments at the Home of the Infantry.

"Follow Me" is the motto of the infantry. Where should I follow? Where should I have followed? Hindsight is not 20/20. It was a blurry vision that day, like seeing someone through a cloudy window with the sunlight behind you. Distorted and ghost like.

Should I have gone to Iraq instead of Miami?

I know that I wanted a home.

Home is where you hang your hat? I think a soldier's cap looked pretty damn good on me, felt pretty damn good. I looked into it. Maximum age to reenlist is 35.

Bounce.

Still in Florida; August 1, 2020

When you drive to Florida, you really have no idea what you are getting yourself into. I remember the first time I hit Jacksonville on my way down to Miami in 1991. After a long drive down the Eastern seaboard, I was excited. Driving straight through from DC, though, Jacksonville is just a bit south of the halfway point. There is a whole bunch of highway in Florida.

Out of all the states I've driven through, I think Florida driving is the most stressful. The three-lane highway confuses most people: it's too many choices. Then you have the one lane highway that allows for the possibility of a 20-minute trip turning into a 40-minute trip.

You really need to drive differently in Florida. When I first moved down, my cousin's then boyfriend, now husband, insisted on taking me out for a driving lesson.

"But I know how to drive," I told him.

"Not in Florida," Adam told me. And he was right.

People hate my driving. "You drive like your father is a cop," I hear a lot. He is, but that's beside the point. I drive like I was trained to drive in FL. You must be aggressive. The best defense is a good offense. The entire point is to stay the hell away from the other drivers.

Instead of 95, I came down the other way, along 75, with my first destination family in Kissimmee and a friend who lived close by, in the center of the state close to Disney World. It was my first time back in Kissimmee since I was there five years ago for when my mom passed away while she was living with my uncle. He had since passed as well but my aunt and their daughter were still living in the house.

It rained more in the sunshine state than any other state. But even rain is different in Florida. You can see the clouds in the distance. With the flatness of the state, you can see the clouds being pulled down to earth. A torrential downpour is not uncommon with nothing but sunshine 10 minutes away.

There are a lot of things I forgot about Florida.

No matter how hot it is, no matter how beautiful it looks, do not leave your windows down. I came back from a trip to a dog park 15 minutes away, under a clear sky, to find my seats soaking wet from a deluge.

And the heat. It's just not like other heat. July and August especially. A friend once said the heat in FL is "like hearing the sound of something big coming at you." Early morning, late at night, in the water, the only escape from it is in air-conditioned rooms.

Then there are the critters. Wildlife everywhere. Bugs. I remember my cousin telling me a long time ago that when she came down to Florida for the first time, she was mortified. From Pennsylvania, with a father an exterminator and a mother who cleaned the house daily, bugs were a sign that something was wrong. It took her years to accept the fact that bugs are just a part of living in Florida and cleaning it eight times a day won't stop it. All food must be kept locked away. The sugar bowls that are a part of everybody's kitchen? They get put in the refrigerator.

And then, of course, there are the hurricanes. You just never know. My second year at the University of Miami, there was a tropical storm coming towards us with an expected path east into the Atlantic Ocean. I, of course, ignored it and went and got drunk with friends. A frantic phone call from my cousin the next morning, with me trying to listen through my hangover. "There's a hurricane coming!"

"The tropical storm," I asked, "that was projected to turn east into the Atlantic?"

"How drunk are you," she asked.

"A bit."

"Turn on the news," she said. "No, don't bother. We're coming to pick you up. Now."

Hurricane Andrew made landfall as a Class 4 / Class 5 hurricane with the eye passing a mile south of campus. School was closed for the next month as Miami picked up the pieces.

But I did enjoy Florida. A college student in the 90's in Miami? You get used to the heat, humidity, critters, rain and hurricanes. You just adapt and move forward. I was there for seven years.

I had been in Ft. Myers right before the shutdown to visit an old friend. It's always a wonderful time visiting Myra, a former professor of mine, and her family. This time around, I stayed out on a little island called Captiva, close to Ft. Myers, and I got to meet her son, Ben, who I had not seen in 20 years. A man grown, with a beautiful wife and teenage daughters of his own.

The hustle and bustle of Ft. Myers seemed odd to me. Was it this way the first time I was here so long ago? It now seems to be in competition with Texas for sprawl, with traffic lights seemingly miles away from each other and traffic, even in the off-season, racing between them.

The plan was to go to Miami and visit another old friend and former professor. A tropical storm that changed track and was upgraded to hurricane status nudged me, saying, "I think it's best if you postpone this trip and get out of Florida."

For once, I listened. A virus hot spot, Miami, I can deal with. Virus plus curfew plus hurricane with up to a foot of rain? It was time to start making my way out west, but not before the daylong drive north. After stopping to see another old friend in Tampa, I made it about 20 miles west, still in Florida, headed into the panhandle, before I stopped late at night.

Still on the road, have to get back on the road: 6 ½ hours to New Orleans.

There is so much to write about and discuss. Politics and pandemics and plagues and everything in between. But "between" is narrowing and the people there are slowly being forced out with a combination of forces. There is no middle ground anymore. No compromises. No civility. Worse to me is the extremism.

Depending on who you talk to or what the topic is, I'm either a conservative Democrat or a liberal Republican. It seems I'm not allowed to be either anymore. I must be on a side, Democrat or Republican. There doesn't seem to be room anymore for "moderates." Everybody is being squeezed into the far left or right.

Or at least that is what social media is telling us. For myself, I think most people don't care. The people that I talk to from red and blue states are moderates of both parties that just want to be left alone and live their lives. Their murmurings, though, get drowned out in the shouting from the far left and the far right.

Two last quotes before I start packing up.

"A plague on both your houses!" –Shakespeare.

"Clowns to the left of me, jokers to the right, here I am stuck in the middle with you." –Stealers Wheel.

New Orleans, here I come.

West, here I come.

Closing the Southern Party Triangle; August 2, 2020

Still in Florida! No, not really. But Florida is such a huge state. It even has a second time zone as you drive across the panhandle. You really don't know what you are getting into driving it. Routes 95, 75, and 10. I almost get the feeling that it has size envy from Texas so it makes its highways longer to make up for it.

But I'm just sipping my coffee in a courtyard in a hotel on Bourbon Street in New Orleans. Quiet and peaceful. A fountain in the background. I did the coffee and beignets thing when I woke up and then came back to make my coffee. Apparently, New Orleans is the coffee capital of the US so I have a feeling I'll be well caffeinated today. But first, some writing. Catch up on a few things. And find a laundry mat.

A lot of the journey is just about the road. Pushing 7,000 miles so far. Some people I know hate driving. I don't understand them. Driving is annoying at times. White knuckling through idiots or downpours where you can't see–I prefer the downpours. But driving is also like yesterday when I first drove from 75 north to 10 west. 10 started out a very civilized highway, two lanes, with people doing what they were supposed to do. The scenery passing with the miles. Tallahassee to Pensacola. Then out of Florida and into Alabama.

A route change when things got uncivil through Mobile, Alabama. I passed right by the USS Alabama before heading back onto 10 and through a tunnel. The roads and bridges interest me. The tree lined highways that pass at 90mph. Watching the clouds in the distance. Being in motion on the road. Playing my music as I pass through Alabama and Mississippi to enter a new state: Louisiana. Route 10 taking me right across the Mississippi River and into downtown New Orleans.

It's crazy when you first arrive in New Orleans. I was immediately in downtown, a tight network of one-way streets. No time to see anything except to follow the GPS and try not hit anybody. Bourbon Street. Underground parking. And then a room in a newly reopened hotel with everybody trying to figure out the new normal. Exercising patience. And then a little walk.

Bourbon Street is the southern point of the Southern Party Triangle. You have Broadway in Nashville with country music. Beale Street in Memphis with Blues and Rock. Bourbon Street is all that jazz.

Broadway in Nashville had the feel of a dispersed crowd with small, tight pockets of people clinging to an old reality. Beale Street in Memphis seemed forced. Bourbon Street in New Orleans has the feel of a somber jazz tune, a mournful dirge, an ache for when times were different and will be again.

I arrived on a Saturday. I was told that it should have been packed. It is just reopening. Bars are still closed except if you serve food. Strict regulations are in place. It was a ghost town during the day and it didn't get much better at night. Saturday night had the feel of a block party two hours after the block party ended.

It is an interesting place though. I'm okay with the somber music. It allows me to explore and wander without the crush of crowds. People have referred to the area as dirty. Well, what the hell would you expect? If I went to a frat party, it's not like I would expect to sip wine on a $1,000 sofa. Know what I mean? It is so eclectic and varied, though, it is well worth the crush of crowds-- when they exist. Posh boutique hotels and 5-star restaurants cozy up to strip clubs (closed) and souvenir shops. Coffee houses and fine antique shops are next door to dive bars.

At night, the peddlers come out. Snakes and parrots to wear as your picture is taken, live music, actors and magicians, tarot card readers, and, of course, the traveling apothecaries. The apothecaries have updated with technology so you can now buy edibles or your joints from Segway scooters. Are joints still called joints?

During the day, I walked a little, still exhausted from a very long drive. I was shocked. Being in the neighborhood, I forgot that New Orleans is so much more than Bourbon Street and the French Quarter. In some direction or another, you find the trolley tracks and the riverfront that opens up beyond the tight little one-way streets. In another direction, it opens up onto Canal Street with Downtown and the Garden District across the way.

I went back into that ache, that mournful dirge, the waiting for when more souls will fill the block party as it was meant to be.

But now I'm off to be overly caffeinated. There is a lot of walking to do. Louis Armstrong Park, the WWII museum, Riverwalk and the Garden District. Oh, and a laundry mat. I'm running low on shorts and underwear.

Dawnie Dear; August 3, 2020

Dear Dawnie Dear,

Yeah, your daughter telling you not to visit New Orleans because you'd hate it because it is so dirty? She was here on business so probably got drunk—although she denies it. The first thing I was told by the valet when I checked in was to take a picture of my valet ticket because EVERYTHING gets forgotten on

Bourbon Street. I think one of the biggest things that gets forgotten on Bourbon Street is, well, New Orleans. It's not as hard as it sounds. Some people come just for Bourbon Street, whether to throw themselves into the fray or people watch along a balcony. Myself, it took me a while to figure out how to get out.

It's weird. All evidence to the contrary, I have a very good sense of direction. Bourbon Street, for me, has this uncanny quality that nullifies it–without even drinking. North, south, east, west? Nope. Not happening. Even with the help of my GPS on my phone it took me a long time to orient myself. The weirdest thing, though, is that it should be easier, much easier. The French Quarter, and much of New Orleans, is laid out in a grid. Just like our Philly. One-way streets and everything. I finally did get out and quartered the French Quarter.

New Orleans is called the Crescent City because it lays on a crescent in the Mississippi River. The French Quarter is on a loop in the river (I just typed "liver in the river" which fits just as well.) But you have the Mississippi and Riverwalk on one side, southeast. North Rampart Street to the northwest, with Armstrong Park. To the northeast is Esplanade Avenue with the Jazz Museum and the Marginay District beyond. To the southwest is Canal Street and Museum, Downtown and Garden Districts.

I'll never stay on Bourbon Street again. It is just a bit too grungy for me and I feel like I'm a bit too old for it. A bit too snobby? Warning from a street tap dancer: keep your wallet in your front pocket, always keep an eye on your drink, and do all your solo walking during the day and stick with the crowds at night. But I'll hand it to the police: at night, there is a strong presence here, even during Covid.

Just a few blocks from Bourbon Street, you'll hit Riverwalk, The French Market and some more NOLA landmarks that has nothing to do with drinking (except coffee). I'm still getting far too much of a kick out of seeing the Mississippi River. That's where you'll see Jackson Square and St. Louis Cathedral, the monument to Joan of Arc, Maid of Orleans and the Cafe Du Monde, a NOLA landmark coffee and beignet staple. Lunch, I had the New Orleans sampler: Gumbo, red beans & rice, crawfish etouffee and jambalaya. Of course, trying to take the picture, my sunglasses ended up in the gumbo.

Three blocks away the transformation is awesome. At Canal Street, you move from the French Quarter to Downtown and the Museum District. Past that is the Garden District. At the edge of the French Quarter is the French Market and Riverwalk. It really is beautiful. So many pictures to take, so many pictures that won't upload—I hate technology. So, me being me, I just walked. I went to the Riverfront and the Cafe Du Monde. I walked the river and then headed down Canal Street, making a left to see the WWII museum and then Lafayette Park.

Lafayette Park was puzzling. There is a monument there. Why did a guy from Chicago give the people of New Orleans a statue of a guy from Philadelphia? But there you have it. Ben Franklin stands tall with one of his many quotes inscribed on the pedestal.

"Save while you are young, to spend while you are old, one penny saved is better, than two pennies earned."

An interesting way to get around is the trolley cars. I was planning on walking, but a storm hit the same time a trolley car was at the stop right by me. The trolley was going in the wrong direction, but I jumped on anyway (it does a loop and storms in the south are heavy but brief). By the time we made the loop (Canal Street and then all the way through the Garden District) the sun was shining. I jumped off the trolley and started walking.

Magazine Street is the place to walk back. Filled with shops and authentic New Orleans, it's just a nice place to stroll. It takes you out of the Garden District and into the Museum District. Then, back onto Canal Street.

Back down Magazine Street, you run into the Museum District (and Harrah's Casino). Just a bit beyond that you are back on Canal Street. Up Canal Street, you run into North Rampart Street and along it, Armstrong Park, with the statue of Louis "Satchmo" Armstrong.

On the statue: "His trumpet and heart brought everlasting joy to the world, embodying jazz as the pulse of life."

I thought about it as I walked down Esplanade Avenue back to the Jazz Museum and the waterfront. I'm not a big jazz fan. I don't get it or it doesn't get me. Trumpets (sorry Mr. Armstrong) always sounded shrill to me. A sax is more my style. BB King said something to the effect that the Blues is the little brother to Jazz, that the worst jazz musician is better than the best blues musician.

But there is so much to write. Did I mention that? Talks with locals, talks with other travelers, the small things and something that somebody wrote to me: it is like I am getting a personal tour of America with the virus shutting everything down. It's true. It is like being in the museum after hours. At times, I feel like I am just running through the museum taking pictures of the emptiness. Which is why after I write my columns, I tend to just throw all the pictures together, huffing and puffing, quickly uploading them to my computer, to get ready for the next run through a hallway. I also think it will take me months to figure out what is what. And lots of coffee.

Nowadays, I'm seeing mostly couples, hand in hand as they stroll down the parks and avenues. There is a longing. But that is why I am out here. Just trying to stay free of the drama and the simmering pot, examining the outward while reflecting on the inward. Wondering how twisted I got with the lab. Trying to untwist.

I have been thinking that maybe that is why I long for the west? Beyond the cities and the Mississippi River. I realize it sounds weird, but I just get a feeling, a call, that the west is where a person can/should be alone. With Alaska or Hawai'i the ultimate place to be alone and reflect on things before I travel back east towards the known and cities and couples and families.

Morning coffee brought me another acquaintance who asked me to have drinks later with him and his wife. I think I'll take him up on it. There are so many lessons to be learned. He and his wife are traveling west as well. He just received a bad medical diagnosis so closed up shop and went driving. He was asked at his retirement party what one thing he wanted. Anything. And it sounds like he has done well for himself so he could have anything. His reply puzzled the person who asked, who didn't take him seriously, so he had to repeat himself: The one thing he wanted for retirement was his wife.

But I think you'd love New Orleans. Just don't stay in the French Quarter. –but I would check it out and wander and people watch. Maybe do what I plan on doing tonight: getting a balcony seat at an upstairs restaurant to sip a drink, sip some coffee, have a meal, and not think too much.

Love,
Me

Part Four: Beyond the Mighty Mississippi

Texas! August 5, 2020

Some days, it's just all about the driving. The drive from New Orleans to Texas was a nice long drive through a pretty state. The transition from Louisiana to Texas on Route 10 is noticeable and stark. Louisiana is a state filled with bridges over waterways. It felt like I was on a raised highway through most of the state. I passed through towns and cities with unmistakable French sounding names. Baton Rouge. Lafayette. Lake Charles.

Then, I hit Orange, Texas–with Beaumont right down the road.

The first exit is the Welcome Center. I've done a lot of driving. I used to count down the exits north to south and east to west. Route 10 counts down by state east to west. The Welcome Center is exit 880. 880! I texted my friend from Austin: I think you Texas people take this "everything is bigger in Texas" way too far. 880? But I was in Texas, driving west and then northwest towards Austin.

I like Texas. I've been saying that since the first time I was here in Dallas about six years ago. They get over the fact I am a Philadelphia Eagles fan quickly. I hate making generalizations but I haven't met a single Texan yet who wasn't nice. There is a just a way about them that speaks of manners and civility that can be lacking in other places. It's almost –almost-- comparable to the Hawaiian "Live Aloha" or Bill and Ted's "Be excellent to each other." Outside of the Eagles thing, people just don't seem to care who or what I am. My eyes are met and my "good morning's" and tip of my head are greeted with a "good morning" and a smile. "Please" and "Thank you" are common. Like I said: a civility.

I do joke that I guess you must be civil in a state where open carry is taken very seriously. Where most trucks can run over my SUV like you would a speed bump. But I do wonder what influences it? A shout out to the moms of Texas?

But it was about the drive after pulling out of exit 880 (exit 1 is El Paso). You quickly come upon a sprawling metropolis, Houston, passing an oil refinery that looked like a Borg Cube from Star Trek. The four-lane highway went to a six and then an eight and then a ten, with bridges, bypasses, floating roads and a glut of traffic. Civility does go out the window on the highway there. And it seems like it goes on forever.

In the Northeast, outside of the big cities, most are small towns that you pass through quickly. I felt like I was in the Houston Metropolis for two hours–and I wasn't even going all the way around it. But I was finally out and away, with the eight-lane highway narrowing to a six and then back to a four and then you are just in Texas Country, back to civility. Cattle farms are reminiscent of the horse farms in Kentucky, large spreads with cattle grazing.

The speed limit ticks up from 70 in Louisiana to 75 in Texas. Gas prices drop, from the average around $2.15 per gallon to as low $1.60. Just outside of Texas, gas prices hovered around $2.50. With Covid, gas prices, along with oil prices, are bottoming out. For the first time on record, oil prices went into the negative. On April 20th, the price plummeted from $18 a barrel to -$37 per barrel. Of course, with demand so low and nobody traveling, one person mentioned it was like a bald man winning a comb.

The further inland I went, away from Houston, the heat ticked up, with 100 common and 100+ even as the sun began to set. All those people who talk about the humidity, about dry heat versus wet heat? They are right. I went for miles and miles with the windows down and no air conditioning. Northwest and then north through Austin, the state capital, before making it a little more north to Leander where friends live.

Leander would be a suburb of Austin if Texas admitted suburbs existed.

I was nervous when I pulled up. Jason and Crystal were friends I had met through the orthodontic lab association and I had been there a few times. Right before the pandemic hit, I had flown down in January for Crystal's surprise party. They had invited me this time. But there was the Covid, the traveling, and they had three young kids.

The door was open and a drink was waiting for me along with hugs. There was the soft hit about the Eagles. Something about six rings as opposed to one. And then. Texas. I'd eventually sleep for 8 1/2 hours, the best night's sleep I've had in a long time.

Now it's time to relax for a bit and regroup. Take a drive down into Austin to finally see the bats.

A Hush in Texas; August 8, 2020

Wandering through downtown Austin, I was thinking of Paula Abdul. "Hush, Hush." Then, finding out Paula Abdul's song was, "Rush, Rush," I turned to Deep Purple. Now that song is "Hush." But nobody was calling my name. Nobody was anywhere. So then how can you not think of "Tush" by ZZ Top when you are in Texas?

I said, Lord, take me downtown
I'm just lookin' for some tush...

But all that I found was hush.

I've been in Austin a few times. I like Austin. I was down there on a Thursday afternoon and there was a marked hush to the place, so different from the hustle and bustle I've seen in the past. Congress Street is the main road that starts at the capitol building. It is like Broad Street in Philadelphia or Broadway in Nashville.

I was able to stand in the middle of the street, in the middle of the day, to take pictures of the capitol and down away from it. Other streets were the same. There was no traffic. None.

But what is a trip to Austin without seeing one of my musical heroes? I was told that Stevie Ray Vaughn had been vandalized. They tried to pull him down! Failing that, they spray painted "FTP" across him (Fuck the Police).

Steinbeck set out into an America, in 1961, on the verge of the Vietnam War and the Civil Rights Movement. It would be two years before Dr. Martin Luther King's "I Have a Dream" speech. Unfortunately, today's America didn't seem too much different.

"FTP" and things like that were becoming more and more common even before the pandemic. Protests and violence were becoming more and more common as well. Covid didn't help. There was a backlash against police brutality. One incident had occurred in Minneapolis and protests had spread across the United States. Portland, Oregon, I heard, was burning. Many cities were experiencing rioting and looting.

In Memphis, while standing outside of the hotel where Dr. King was assassinated, I met a black family, a mother and her younger daughter and older son. I approached them.

"Do you mind if I ask you a question? I'm a writer."

The mother nodded.

"It's a simple question. Here, at the monument to Dr. King, and everything going on in the country, do you believe his dream is dead?"

The older boy, about 15, was quick to reply, "Yes."

The mother looked thoughtful for a moment and then replied, "Yes."

The younger girl, about 12, looked at her mother and brother and then looked at me. "I think it is hard right now, but I also think there is hope."

As the son of a cop, and seeing everything I had growing up, and experiencing things through the racial lens of Philadelphia, and then evolving in the racial mixing bowl of Miami, I didn't know what to think except that it is pure ignorance to lump all groups by a few. I respect the police and what they do. I also know there are bad apples.

I am firmly against rioting, looting and vandalization. But I was also aware that people were being pushed to extremes on both sides. There was that boiling pot. We needed leadership. We didn't get it.

I had even had a run in with a bad cop before. Young buck. Must have been straight out of the academy. I was allowed to be in the strip club. As he was on duty, he wasn't. And he definitely wasn't allowed in the ladies' dressing room. He was also harassing a friend of mine who worked there, pushing himself on her and getting far too friendly. She was scared and had told him. He ignored her. She told me and I didn't ignore her.

It wasn't much of a run in. After the place closed, I kept putting myself between him and her. Outside, he pulled his cruiser up to block her in and me away. I just waited. He tried to be threatening but I ignored him. He eventually left.

"He won't be bothering you anymore," I told her as she hugged me. "Promise."

I had tried to explain to the cop but he had ignored me as well. The next morning, I made a phone call to my father. What I had tried to explain to the young buck was my father was his former sergeant and his current captain had known me since I was a baby.

"What's his name and badge number," my father growled. My father's nickname was Sergeant Rock because he was a hard ass. That hardness came out as he grilled me. I didn't remember the name or badge number, but did remember what he looked like, what time he was there and his cruiser number. Then dad grilled me on exactly what happened the entire time the cop was in the club.

"I'll call you back in ten minutes." He didn't like the fact I went to strip clubs or my friend was a stripper but he hadn't mentioned either.

He called exactly 10 minutes later. "He won't be bothering your friend anymore. He won't be bothering anybody anymore."

And that was that. But it was easy. I'm white. Having an FOP (Fraternal Order of Police) courtesy card helps as well.

My conspiracy theory of the day is that it all has to do with television. I, like most of my generation, grew up on police shows.

NYPD Blue is still a favorite of mine. But there was everything from Barney Miller and Miami Vice to Hill Street Blues and Law & Order. Two common themes that ran throughout them were "The Blue Wall of Silence" and "IA (Internal Affairs) was the enemy." We grew up seeing the house keepers as the bad guys. Things need to change.

But I was ready for my time with Stevie. I wore a special shirt, though my friend told me it might not be prudent to wear it. My Fraternal Order of Police shirt. I also brought rags and cleaning solution. There was no need. Somebody had already cleaned Stevie up.

Stevie Ray Vaughn came up in Austin in the Texas Blues tradition. I made the trek along Ladybird Lake, the riverfront that runs through Austin, to see Stevie Ray. His shadow is a part of his statue. He was a short man, who couldn't even read music, but he cast a long shadow. BB King said of SVR: "To play the blues, you need to be black twice. Stevie missed both times but I never noticed."

Ladybird Lake is a part of downtown Austin but it is not a lake, just a lazy part of the Colorado River that loops through Austin. It's a nice waterfront area where you constantly see walkers, joggers and bikers. Even in the hot Texan sun, there is shade. Out on the "lake" you can see people paddle boarding and kayaking. Boat tours are normal–in normal times. Like the rest of Austin, it was hushed.

One of the "not to miss" sights, that I have now missed all four chances here, is the bats. The bridge that crosses the lake along Congress Avenue is home to thousands of them. You can hear them chittering as you walk underneath the bridge on the river path. Sometime around sunset, they'll leave for their evening hunt like a cloud rising from the bridge. I'll get pictures of it. Eventually. It is typically a two-hour window and I just don't have the patience for it.

Austin is an odd city. Its motto is "Keep Austin Weird." The citizens oblige. It's an artsy city with awesome murals and, well, women going topless is legal–they celebrate it once a year. It's an odd little pocket of liberalism in a very conservative state. The state's capitol and Supreme Court building overlooks it all.

Sam Houston, when Texas was its own country and he the president, tried to move the capital and sent troops to get all the official records out of Austin after negotiations failed. A middle-aged woman, Angelina Ebery, saw what was happening, set off a cannon, blowing a hole through a building, and the people rallied and pushed back the troops. There is a bronze statue in her honor where she stood on Congress Street.

Hippie Hollow is a nude beach at an actual lake not too far away. That's Austin for you.

But Austin is an interesting city, smaller than its fellow, nearby Texan cities of Houston (161 miles away), San Antonio (91 miles) and Dallas (161 miles). –seeing my numbers and the triangle the cities form has my Austin friends weirded out, asking what's in the middle?

It's a hushed topic.

PS. I asked my friends, "what does make Austin weird?"

I got the usual answers: the art, culture, music, hippies, nudists, etc. Then, I got a history lesson. "Keep Austin Weird" started out as way of supporting local businesses. Big chains are not welcome and the locals make it known. When MTV did their "Real World" series here, they were chased out of bars and restaurants.

My friend, Crystal, said her first day here she saw something that made her feel good. She was having lunch at a cafe and saw a lawyer (she later found out) on his way to work, dressed as lawyers will dress in a suit and impeccable attire. Next to him was his friend, The Lizard Man, a tattoo artist, inked head to toe. She found out later that they do this every day, walk to work together and then walk home together.

"Acceptance" is what makes Austin weird. Everybody from all walks of life mingle and get along…and are nice to each other. Race, religion, creed, sexual orientation, political orientation and all of the other things that might divide us simply doesn't matter here.

Let's make America weird?

Still in Texas; August 8, 2020

Yep, still in Texas. Aye: it's a big state. From my friend's house north of Austin, I jumped on Route 35 south down to San Antonio. This is where I get into trouble paying attention to the various GPS apps. All three apps told me it was the fastest way. I hope to never be on 35 again. Traffic was cooking down the road, but between the number of cars and constant construction, it is white knuckle driving. I much prefer my open roads.

The trip between Austin and San Antonio is much like any other trip between points. GPS can make it easier or more difficult. Yes, 35 is the fastest route and GPS will push you towards it. Do you have an extra 10 minutes? If you talk to people, argue with the GPS, and don't mind listening to "rerouting, rerouting, rerouting," other, more civil roads, become options.

But down to San Anton'. There was a little bit of business to take care of at the University of Texas. A friend of mine works there in the dental department so I wanted to float some ideas by him about working in a university setting like he does—I might have to start adulting again at some point. With my background, he sees it likely. In the current climate with Covid, he sees it as impossible. Like every other business in the United States and world, schools are hurting. Even with a wealthy state like Texas, the university is looking at an $80 million shortfall. They are not hiring and won't be for a while.

After some excellent company and advice, I went to downtown San Antonio. There is a certain kind of awesomeness in some cities and their highway systems. San Antonio is one of them along with Atlanta, Houston and Dallas. I imagine that as traffic increased, they just decided to go up with the highways. It can be confusing, but there are long, sweeping ramps, under and over passes, and special lanes where you can speed through–for a price and if you know where you are going.

Texas overpasses and on ramps are different than in the other states I have traveled through, which makes the highway systems around cities very different. They are higher. Much higher. It is almost as if Texan engineers looked at something and thought, "well, we'll need 15 feet clearance. Let's do 45 feet just in case." On ramps become these towering loops hundreds of feet in the air. I looked down once. I couldn't see why. But, then, I'm not an engineer or a Texan. I'm sure there is a reason for it.

In the middle of downtown San Antonio, amid the jungle of concrete and steel, there is this tiny little building made of stone: The Alamo. It is surprising both in the contrast and in the size. It's tiny. Even if you include the original structure's walls, it is not the imposing place you might think it to be. It makes you think that Crochet, Houston and Bowie were friggin' nuts! This place couldn't be defended against a few platoons of Boy Scouts let alone against the entire Mexican Army.

Right across the entrance from the Alamo is another attraction. You walk down a set of steps, through a hotel, and enter the underground mini city of Riverwalk. It was 106 degrees topside but underneath was a cooler, beautiful space, with a river looping its way through hotels and shops. At night, I was told, is when it really sparkles with neon lights. Beers and margaritas were offered everywhere, but there was not a single coffee shop that I could find. So, I returned topside. And still couldn't find a cup of coffee. I also couldn't find the usual crowds.

The lack of coffee, the 106-degree heat and with most everything closed, led me back to my car to find an alternate route back to Austin.

I ignored my GPS and headed northwest along a two-lane highway out towards a little known part of Texas: hill country. Yes, there are hills in Texas. Fredericksburg is considered one of the prettiest parts of hill country. There is a beer garden and wineries, and Main Street is lined with all the shops you might think of being there. I stopped to see an old friend of mine.

You can spend a month or longer in every state. I've been back to Austin four times now and there are still things I want to see and experience. Each city I go to, I get recommendations--that I, unfortunately, must ignore. I'm moving and bouncing without a real plan but I do have to finish at some point in time.

I started looking at the calendar. August 8th means nothing in Texas. September may see a drop of a few degrees with cold fronts bringing it into the 80's at night. But there is a definite window for Alaska. Mid to end of September, at best, before the snows and real cold weather begins to hit. That's 4,000 miles of straight driving and I am not very good about driving straight.

Sunset in New Mexico; August 13, 2020

I would spend a week in Austin with Jason, Crystal and their family. Their son, Jaylen, didn't seem to mind that I kicked him out of his bed. As a three-year-old, he just loved helping me set up my coffee maker, grinding the beans and then he would watch it as it brewed. Their daughters, Presley and Tesla (named after the band and inventor, not the car), were about as charming and adorable as an eight and six-year-old could be. Tesla, the middle child and the quiet one, I felt was going to give Jason and Crystal the biggest run for their money as she got older. She just had this sweetness about her as if she was running while twirling red flags. Time will tell.

Many people thought Austin would be my eventual home, but, after a round of hugs, it was a time to move on.

Getting out of Texas from Austin is a day's drive in itself. I made a pitstop and stayed the night in the DFW Hilton, about three hours north of Austin. Four hours if you go the long way as I did to avoid 35.

The front desk person remembered me and I was upgraded to a suite. Something had pushed me north towards it. I was supposed to here at the beginning of April. I had been coming for the last six years, first as a speaker for the Dental Lab Association of Texas (DLAT) and then as the president and founder of the Association of Orthodontic Laboratory Professionals (AOLP) — now renamed the Orthodontic Resource Group (ORG). Our conference this year was supposed to be our biggest ever. We had filled the hotel, booked every exhibitor space, and were working with the hotel to expand for more exhibitors.

The hotel was empty. The bar was closed. I was one of the few guests wandering through the massive entry hall.

I remember waiting those days in February and March, watching each state shut down one by one, with conferences and gatherings cancelled. Texas was one of the last. I had seen the writing on the wall and wanted to start reaching out to guests and vendors, but everybody wanted to wait and see. Maybe, just maybe, we could get in in time. It didn't happen.

Leaving Dallas, I needed a destination. I could have driven straight to New Mexico and shave a few hours off my trip, but, me being me, I needed to drive through another state. Oklahoma was closest. Randomly, I picked a coffee shop on iconic Route 66, The Red Bird Coffee House.

It was about three hours north of Dallas in a suburb of Oklahoma City, Yukon. Completely by chance, I found something I was looking for out here: hope.

I stopped, stretched my tired back, and then went in to grab a cup of coffee and something to eat. I was met by this truly remarkable place. The coffee was good but the feeling was even better. It was inviting and comfortable, a place that felt different than many of the businesses I had been in.

Absence is what I find most. The absence of people, cars, and energy. I find a lot of fear and desperation as the Covid winter threatens to engulf another winter. Flu season is approaching. People are getting restless and lonely with uncertainty fueling the fear and desperation. The Red Bird was different.

My GPS app led me to the Red Bird Coffee Cart. The owner, Rachel Goble, had begun renovating a building to move the cart into a coffee house. Construction had been delayed so I arrived right before the official grand opening.

Something new. Building. A hope for a future. A dream perhaps, becoming a reality. It was a nice change of pace from what I had been experiencing.

Then, it was back to the normal: I got lost. I lost an entire road. On the map, it showed that iconic Route 66 ran west for a distance. Years ago (you can check the history online) Route 66 had been overtaken by Route 40 but stretches of 66 still exist in places. I turned off the GPS and drove west. Somehow or another, I ended up on Route 81 going north. I pulled into a casino, turned the GPS back on, and had to turn around to jump on 40.

As I traveled 40, I soon realized that I really could have driven old route 66. Route 66 is now Business 40. And yes, I saw a sign for the devil's trail, route 666. But by that point, I was looking for speed so stayed on 40.

It was a nice stretch of highway through Oklahoma and then back through Texas. With the winds sweeping down from the Great Plains, wind farms stretched for miles. Empty of most traffic besides a few trucks, the temperature, which had been a chilly 90 in Yukon, ticked back up into the triple digits.

The transition from Texas to New Mexico is dramatic. Even the Welcome Center has a different feel, red stone and gravel. Where the Texas Welcome Center had the sign "watch for snakes," the New Mexico Welcome Center could have had one that said simply, "Bugs."

Sitting down on the wall, I was quickly swatting away ants. Big suckers. So, I made the mistake of taking my break in my car with the windows down. In a matter of minutes, I had more flies in my car than first cousins, which is saying something. It took me 20 miles of driving with all the windows down to get them all out.

But it was back to a different kind of driving. Texas is long, straight, flat roads. New Mexico is hilly with twists and turns. Miles of wind farms and cattle ranches transform into scraggly brush and mesas jutting up in the distance. Reds dominate the landscape.

Then, the sun set.

I had always enjoyed driving at night but I don't like to anymore, especially as I do this road trip, wanting to watch the scenery of each new state pass by. But you have to do what you have to do. At the welcome center, I made the decision, and the reservation, to go to Santa Fe instead of Albuquerque. It's the same distance, more northerly, and is only an hour between each other.

In the new time zone, I knew I was driving late and would get to my destination well after dark. What did I miss heading NW off Route 40 after the beautiful sunset on the mesas? 10:30, Mountain Time, got me to my destination. A hotel that wasn't quite a hotel.

Art Sans Bugs Bunny; August 14, 2020

And then it hit me: maybe this wasn't such a good idea?

I'm standing on top of a mesa in Albuquerque, the temperature about 100 degrees, after hiking up in jeans and my Olukai shoes. The thought wasn't about where I was or how I was dressed. It was beautiful. The western "wall" of Albuquerque is a line of mesas filled with petroglyphs. The thought was about how I got there. Maybe I should have gone counterclockwise through the states, hitting the northern ones during the hotter months and the southern ones on my way back as fall descends? But there I was anyway, a bit too late. If I drove for Seattle right now, it would still be too late. My ass is going to be cold at some point. But anyway...

It had been a beautiful start to the day. The day before ended in Santa Fe at a hotel I picked from a few hundred miles away. La Posada de Santa Fe was like coming home. It is not so much of a hotel as it is a community of tiny homes–built adobe style. I wandered through a warren of low walls to enter my own little patio with a table and chairs. The interior of the room matched the exterior, with white walls and dark brown wood. It had the feel of a comfortable, tiny home. It made me think of a Hobbit hole for some reason, just made taller for humans.

After traveling through the heat for a long time, it was nice to wake up to a chilly morning, low 70's, to sit outside on my patio and sip my coffee. It was still chilly as I made my way down to the central square of Santa Fe to have breakfast.

Someone got after me about not wearing a mask as I walked. I find it absurd. Everybody is wearing masks in this "age of masks"—until they enter the restaurant or bar. Aye, I know at least some of the science behind the masks and the virus, at least what the scientists learn and pass on. If you pass someone on the street, and they have Covid, and aren't wearing a mask, your chance of catching it are slim to none unless they sneeze on you. Sitting downwind from them in a restaurant, though, even six feet away, with improper air circulation? That's another story.

But I had my breakfast (outdoor seating), took my morning stroll, and thought of all the people that would kill to be here. An artist could spend days within one square mile wandering through the jewelry shops, art galleries and sculpture gardens. Broadway, Beale and Bourbon Streets combined, with their countless bars and drinking holes, has nothing on Santa Fe when it comes to art.

But why did Bugs Bunny say to make a left at Albuquerque? And can I finally stop typing Albuquerque as I still haven't learned how to spell it properly so have to keep looking it up because even spellcheck has no idea what I am trying to type? So, I jumped on Route 25 and drove down into the heat of the lower lands. I saw the mesas, went into downtown, or old, Albuquerque, and even got my car washed and did some banking.

An interesting note: 530 miles. Just yesterday, I was at the Red Bird Coffee House. In old town Albuquerque, I found a Black Bird

Coffee House. Of course, I had to go in. The coffee wasn't that bad.

I still have no idea why Bugs Bunny said to make a left at Albuquerque. I still have no idea why that line from an old cartoon is stuck in my head. The truth? I thought Albuquerque might be "home." I was just drifting on my little dingy and I thought something would reach out to me here, grab me with long tentacle arms with little suckers, pull me towards a giant maw, and gently whisper, "this is the place."

It wasn't Bugs Bunny that brought me here. It another television show, In Plain Sight. The show ran from 2008 to 2012. It was set in Albuquerque where US Marshalls would help people in the Witness Protection Program start new lives. I had enjoyed the show but something about the place made me want to visit, to see and experience it. There was the thought that a feeling would well up inside of me. "You are HOME."

It didn't.

I took the scenic route back to Santa Fe. No, I did not get lost. Someone mentioned the town of Madrid and how nice it was. It turned out to get there, and back to Santa Fe, you take an official "scenic route," The Turquoise Trail, Route 14.

It was a beautiful drive through what I am now thinking of as New Mexico. It takes about twice as long (even longer as they work on that road as well) but worth every extra minute. Madrid is a quirky little town with shops lining the main road and quirky little houses to compliment it.

But back to Santa Fe, with the suggestions pouring in from Facebook, what to do and where to go. A couple I met at Petroglyph National Monument, who drove cross country 26 times, said the best place to go in New Mexico was Carlsbad

Caverns National Park. That's a couple hours south, though, and I'm heading north. The simple fact is that I do not have unlimited time and I'll be missing a lot of things. Many places I could wander for days and I'm just doing drive bys. Now that Albuquerque is crossed off the list, something is pushing/pulling me onward, something I haven't found yet.

On to a completely unplanned part of the journey now. Just a little out of the way. I'll finally be getting up into the Rocky Mountains and Colorado soon. I just checked the weather: low 60's at night.

Just a couple last "firsts" that I find interesting that nobody else might.

1) why did the weasel (or mongoose) cross the road with its baby in tow? I don't know but I had to slam on my breaks not to run them over. I've slammed on the breaks for squirrels, birds, deer, dogs, cats, but never for whatever they were.

2) On the way to the place that I will not attempt to type its name anymore, I saw a road sign, "Dust storms possible the next five miles."

3) Road crews are smarter here. Instead of having police cars with their lights flashing to slow people down? The road crew vehicles have the lights.

Silence in Colorado; August 15, 2020

The drive up into the highlands of Colorado was amazing. From Santa Fe, I stopped in Taos and then continued north to Great Sand Dunes National Park. The most amazing part of the day was the silence in the park. There were some crowds there but there are a lot of dunes. The wind carries sound. But if you find the right place, sit in the sand, close your eyes, you can feel why the Navajo considered it a sacred place, the beginning of life and an energy point.

The first stop was Taos, New Mexico. It began as a small artist colony. Like the rest of America, it's being hit hard. They depend on tourism. But I found a pottery shop that just opened. There is hope and, as the owner put it, "you have to keep moving forward."

I bought stuff. I know art and pottery like I know astrophysics but it felt right to buy something. He mailed the stuff for an extra $20. I have no idea what I mailed or who I mailed it to. Did anybody get pottery without a note or explanation? Yes, that was from me.

Then the drive up and up into Colorado. The views are stunning as you travel up into the mountains along a river and through valleys. Twisty scenic roads turned into straight highways as far as the eye could see as I made my way to Great Sand Dunes National Park.

It's not on the "to do" list of National Park goers, but it is stunning. I was going to try to take the "primitive road" out of the park, but, for once, I was smart enough to talk to an expert about it, a park ranger. He said a 4-wheel drive is necessary. I pointed at my all-wheel drive Subaru Outback. He replied, with a laugh, "I pull them out all day long."

There is just so much more to see and do. I need to slow down. But I did hike up into the dunes with the sand sledders and trudged away from the groups to be on my own. I realized a couple things. First, I don't like hiking in sand. There had been a thought in the back of my mind, a story maybe, about just wandering into a desert to disappear like how a mirage bends and shimmers and then vanishes. That was not going to happen.

Second, the heat that everybody else was complaining about did not bother me at all. I did realize I needed to prepare better with water, backpack and proper shoes—I had just gotten out of my car and gone for a walk like I would in cities.

I wanted to try going to the top of the dunes. I am not used to seeing sand dunes not associated with oceans. A wall of dunes spreads for dozens of miles in either direction, with all the dunes climbing up the mountain. There had to be an ocean on the other side. I wanted to find it. If I could just make it to the top, I knew I could find it.

A bit more than halfway up, with no water, the parking lot a tiny spot in the distance, and my Olukai shoes filled with more sand than feet, I found myself settling down to just sit and enjoy the silence. With the winds, it was cool. When the winds shifted to carry sound away, I was completely alone. I breathed it in. Settled into myself. Let go.

I found something beautiful.

It has always been hard for me to shut out the noise, a mind raging in thoughts with the fury and howling of a tempest. Being alone and in silence can be terrifying. There, it was magical. I think it was the first time in 49 years that I did not have to be in motion to find peace. I didn't need music to surge to push back the darkness and quiet my mind. I was not afraid of days, weeks and years compressing into a single moment, into song lyrics. I could relax.

I tried sitting cross-legged but that didn't work. My knees and legs just don't bend the way they need to make it comfortable. So, I took off my shoes, stretched out and arranged some sand into a pillow. I drew the bill of my baseball cap far over my sunglasses.

It was an odd feeling. Quiet. A quiet that went beyond silence. Deeper. I couldn't even hear the far away conversations of others with the drifting winds. I was alone on a sand dune in the middle of the day and that was perfectly fine.

But then it was time to trudge back, empty my shoes of the two pounds of sand that accumulated in them, and return to parts of civilization to take highways up to Colorado Springs.

Smoke on the Horizon; August 17, 2020

It wasn't a red moon I was seeing as I drove to my hotel in Colorado Springs. It was the sun. With a smoky haze blurring it. Most will not find this hard to believe but it was not the best time for me to visit Colorado. Apparently, the state is kind of on fire. There is a massive blaze to the north, shutting down Route 70, the main east-west corridor. The forest fire is doubling in size every day. There is another one just starting, north of Grand Junction in the west of the state.

Walking outside, depending on the way the wind is drifting, can be like walking out into a backyard with a bonfire going. Waking up, I was told residents can find their property covered in ash. It is an especially hard time for business owners as they are just starting to reopen with Covid regulations only to find the tourists chased away by fire and smoke.

The day began at the Garden of the Gods, a city park in Colorado Springs. It's a gorgeous little loop through the park with high cliffs and walking trails. It was a weekend when I got there so the crowds were large. I stayed in my car for the most part.

Garden of the Gods? Everybody told me I had to stop there. Everybody told me it was amazing. Some people said it was the most beautiful place they had ever been. Me? The name excited my imagination but the reality did not live up to the expectations. It was beautiful, a ring of cliffs rising out of a city, but it was just a place for me to check off my list. It was a great place to stop, a "must see" that I'd recommend to other people, but it just didn't give me the feeling of a place I'd want to delve deeper into. It was more of a "been there, done that" kind of place.

The original plan was to head north on 25, swing through Denver and then pick up 70 going west towards an old friend in Snowmass, a bit past Aspen. It is a four-hour drive. Ben, who had been a dorm mate at The University of Miami, moved out here in 2000 and had been inviting me ever since. I was trying to finally take him up on the offer but the fires were making it difficult.

"You picked a hell of a time to visit," he said on the phone. The story of my life. I had planned on surprising him, just showing up at his door, but someone else had mentioned it would be a hell of a surprise if he wasn't there. So, I called him. He was there. Getting to him would be trickier.

The ironic thing about going to see Ben was that for years I had avoided the trip because I didn't want to be caught by snow in the mountain. I had wanted to go in winter, drive from Denver, and maybe ski. Snowstorms forced me to cancel a couple trips. Now, I was there in the summer and still couldn't make the drive I had planned.

"This is a good thing," Ben explained. "You get to do the drive I always wanted to do but never did. You have to go south and it is going to take longer, about seven hours." He gave me directions. GPS wasn't going to do me much good. I went old school. Written directions. Looking for signs.

The typical drive from Colorado Springs to Snowmass was four hours along highways. The drive I took to Snowmass was nothing short of epic. Just…WOW. Canyons and valleys and switchbacks. Going up mountains, through passes, and then down mountains. Lakes and rivers spring out of nowhere and then become your companion for miles. Tiny towns appeared and then disappeared. Signs that read, "No gas or food for x miles."

I passed Pike's Peak and drove through and around national parks and national monuments. I crossed the continental divide as I got intimate with the Rocky Mountains. South towards Carson City and then along Route 50. 50 meanders west and south through cities like Salida and Gunnison. It passes through Gunnison National Forest and the Curecanti National Recreation Area. You travel through fissures in the earth. Then north along 92 and then 133, along Gunnison Gorge National Monument. Finally, you travel east along 82.

And then there was Ben. He didn't look much different from when I last saw him in Miami. My UM reunion tour continued. Though I knew about them, the kids and wife were a surprise. It was so easy to transpose an image of 1997 Ben and a 2020 Ben, but the images also jarred against each other. He was still very much Benny. But he was also Ben.

Ben had been a jazz guitar major. I've seen some of the greatest guitarists live, from Eric Clapton and Pete Townsend to Dickey Betts of The Allman Brothers. I was in the third row for Eric Johnson's 25-year anniversary tour for Ah Via Musicom. Ben is the greatest guitarist I've ever seen play. During college, I got him a weekly gig at a pub I worked at in Coral Gables, The Crown and Garter, and I saw him play at other venues with bands from the music program. With the right musicians pushing him, he was inspired and electric.

It's difficult being a musician, he explained, when you move to a place like this. There is a much smaller pool of musicians than in Miami. Life intruded as well. A wife and kids can create a different reality. It's not a bad one at all, just different. Priorities shift.

We spent the evening just chatting and catching up. The smoke wasn't that bad and the chill creeping up was refreshing after a few weeks in 100-degree heat.

Ben explained what to do with the stuff in my car. I could leave cash or valuables in an unlocked car, but no food. The bears know how to open car doors. If they can't open them, they will get in anyway. He showed me the claw and teeth marks on his outdoor refrigerator. There were also some dents on it from when a bear had tossed it.

Welcome to Colorado: a full wallet was safe but a Snicker's bar could get you into a lot of trouble.

Waking up, it was 59 degrees and I had to dig a hoodie and my slippers out of the car. Then, we took his kids down to the river. The day heats up quickly and the chilly waters of the shallow river were refreshing. The kids weren't happy about being drug outside away from their computer games. Ben and I lounged on lawn chairs in the middle of the river and watched them mope.

I wanted to spend more time in Colorado but I couldn't. I spent that first night at Ben's. The next night I spent in a hotel a few miles away. The smoke was getting worse and I couldn't handle it. Ben had warned me that I might have a problem with altitude sickness. I did. The smoke compounded it. Wind from the right direction cleared the smoke, but something like a vortex would pull it down at night. Standing outside of my hotel room or driving to get dinner was very uncomfortable.

My second night there, I had dinner in an empty restaurant. The owner joined me. The food was excellent. She had opened at the end of 2019, her dream, with her son working as her chef. The restaurant got off to a fantastic start with a flood of people. Covid turned that flood into a trickle of take out. As the people finally began making their way back in when the restrictions lifted, the smoke arrived and chased them away.

"I don't know what is going to happen now," she said.

I had never seen anything like it. The sun hung like a pale disk in the sky. There was an orange tint to the air, like looking through sunglasses with orange lenses. The air was murky.

I spent the day with Ben's family and a friend of theirs, Peggy, stopped by. When Ben had heard of my wandering aimlessly, looking for something, he specifically called Peggy. We talked for a long time. She was a wanderer. She had made four trips to India and multiple trips to many other countries. She explained that she had found something she was looking for at home. She said that being lost is the best place you can possibly be. It is only when you are completely lost that the best destinations are found. Things got a little bit mystical.

I wanted to talk to her more but called it a night and went back to my hotel. Ben later told me that, with my early departure, Peggy thought she overwhelmed me. She didn't. The smoke did. I was forced out of Colorado.

Lost and Found in Utah; August 18, 2020

I took 82 north from Snowmass, Colorado. 82 brought me to 70 which was open going west but the fires had it closed going east. I drove west to the other fire in Grand Junction. I heard there was a good coffee shop. It was a nice little city where I got my first parking ticket. I think I actually paid it? Then I made my way south into Utah.

Snowmass, and the area around it, had a certain feeling to it. Moab, Utah reminds me of it. It's a place to get lost. And maybe found. The mountains in Colorado that leveled out leaving the state were imposing. The features jutting up from the ground in Utah were softer.

Was I about to get lost? Did I still owe Ben money from college? It seemed like it when I took his advice and ignored the GPS. GPS wanted me to take 70 to 191. I exited 70 onto a somewhat paved road running southwesterly towards "Cisco." There was a big sign saying "there's nothing here for 60 miles" —or something like that. It was just...empty. Even when I made a left onto 128 and crossed a set of railroad tracks, I still wasn't sure why Ben sent me this way. I passed what I could only describe as a trailer park graveyard.

What the hell did I get into now?

I later read that Cisco is a ghost town. It was once a thriving town along the railroad. When 70 bypassed it, it began to die. Now it is just a collection of dilapidated buildings in the middle of a desert. I stopped to take pictures but something told me to stay in my car with the engine running. I just had an image of a mob of Quentin Tarantino's gimps (from Pulp Fiction) rushing from the graffitied buildings in their leather body suits and chain link collars to pull me in. Did I still owe Ben money from college? What did I do to piss him off?

A few miles down the road, Utah revealed her treasures and I knew why Ben sent me this way. I guess I didn't owe him money.

It was like the epic drive in Colorado but gentler. 128 encounters and then follows the Colorado River into Moab. Huge red stone formations line the road and then valleys spread out in greenery. With the temp on the car showing 105, the river begs you to jump in. It is the real gem in Moab that most people will never see as they fly up and down 191.

Long beautiful drives is what the southwest is all about. And silence. Being from the hustle and bustle of the northeast, I guess I never really knew silence. There have been quite a few drives where I turned off the radio and just drove through scenery, experiencing it.

I touched upon the silence in Great Dunes National Park. There were crowds clambering up and down the dunes and I hadn't been prepared for a longer stay or a longer hike. At Arches National Park, outside of Moab, I did it right and existed in the silence.

The hotel desk person warned me: "If you don't mind the heat, don't go to Arches first thing in the morning. Do something else. The heat will drive people away in the afternoon." I took her advice. In the morning, I went to a state park, Dead Horse Point and the national park beyond that: Canyon Lands.

As with every other place I visit, you can spend days at any one place. Weeks. Each park has its unique character. Short drives take you to spectacular views that never get old and the hiking trails can be endless.

Some older woman did piss me off in Canyon Lands. There was a nice path that led to a lookout point. It was on the narrow side and there was the whole Covid thing that made many people paranoid. So, when she and her husband were coming up, I clambered out of their way and stood as they passed.

"Stay on the path," she hissed at me.

I exchanged a look with her husband. He rolled his eyes.

"Have a nice day," I said.

It case she reads this book: "I got out of your way and off the path out of kindness and courtesy, you old hag. I guess my mother taught me better than yours taught you. Remember: "look out point" and "push off point" can be interchangeable."

Discourtesy in return for courtesy bothers me. But at least there was nobody to hiss at me in Arches National Park.

Arches National Park is a one-way drive, not a loop. You drive up through switchbacks to enter the park and then the end is about a 40-minute drive north. There are pull off points and short hiking trails all along the way. With the heat at 107, and maybe the whole Covid thing, I basically had the place to myself.

At the end of the road is THE hike. About a half mile in, the paved trail turns into a "primitive" trail. The primitive trail is what takes you to the heart of the park. I was ready this time: plenty of water, sunscreen (70 SPF), the right shoes that had been recommended to me at a store in Moab, and an eagerness to dive as deep as I could into the park.

It is a two-mile hike, four-mile roundtrip. Primitive trail is a misnomer. There is no trail. Yes, I got lost a couple dozen times, wandering around looking for markers that you could barely see. Small piles of rocks, sticks, driftwood, and the occasional sign. I wasn't the only one. At one point, I was looking up a long, sloped, high rocky outcropping saying to myself, "that couldn't be the trail." Then, some guys appeared at the top, calling down, "yep, this is the trail."

At another point, I was completely lost. The trail disappeared. Or I did. I found myself angry at a sign. "Stay on the trail. Leave no footprints." In Canyon Lands, I could see the trail so know that, technically, I was wrong when I stepped off it. Here, I'm wandering through the wilderness looking for a tiny pile of rocks, stacks of sticks, driftwood or a signpost. How do you stay on the trail and leave no footprints when you can't find the damn trail?

The sun was setting. My knee went out rushing down a slope that I couldn't do anything but rush down, stopping my just locking my knee to the side. It was like downhill skiing, black diamond, with no soft snow to fall in to slow down. Just an enormous, smooth boulder about as long as two football fields, 25 yards wide, and a very steep angle. Those 25,000 steps and 63 flights my watch told me I was taking were adding up. Fear? No, not really. Laughter. What the hell did I get myself into this time?

I sat down to massage my knee. I did still have a phone signal. I called Mike, Papa Bear. "Call and order a pizza," he told me, "They'll find you."

There were a few other people on the "trail." Hikers were sparse, but everybody was friendly and laughing about the lack of a trail. I finally found my way to one of the ends: the Double Circle Arch. As tired as I was, there was one more arch a half mile more in, the Dark Angel Arch.

Next time. I turned around and started to make my way back.

One thing I hate is traveling back along a path or road that I have already traveled. I just don't like the idea of a one-way path to and from. With all the times I got lost, however, taking the path back, which seemed a lot clearer now, was just like taking a brand-new path.

I did relax a few times, finding shade and just sitting or lying down, sipping on water, and enjoying the utter silence. It's a reflective place when you are alone. You can even push away the self-reflection and just be. Just breathe. Be so in the moment you forget the pain, the way back, the way in and the world around you.

Eric Johnson is a favorite musician of mine. He has these hard-hitting, jamming songs that speed you on your way. He also has these interludes that I never quite understood until now, tracks like "Desert Sound." In the song, he tries, and succeeds, at capturing the moment of being in the desert.

It felt good to be back at my car. I found myself sitting in the driver's seat and staring. I was parked in front of a post a little higher than the hood of my Outback. On the post was an enormous raven. It didn't move. Its eyes followed me as I stepped back out of the car and took its picture and then it kept staring at me as I got back into my car and started it up. I sat there staring at it and it stared back.

Though I was looking for them, I'm not big on signs and portents. Aye, I'm a guy. We're not good with hints. We need to be slapped across the back of the head. With something heavy.

Was it just a very large raven staring at an idiot that had just made a four-mile hike in 107-degree heat? Ravens signify guidance, partnerships, adaptability, and transformation. A raven sighting indicates you might be in need of some kind of guidance in your life. They also signify death.

It just stared at me. I backed up and turned my car towards the exit to the park. A little down the road, I looked back and it was still there on its perch.

Castles in the Sky; August 20, 2020

"I just kept finding myself coming back here," the waitress said in the restaurant at the end of the day in Moab. "Now, I can't leave."

She gave me some great tips on spending time here. Moab is the "gateway" town to Arches National Park. The waitress explained it is also a Mecca for rock climbers, white water rafters and hiking enthusiasts. She called herself a rock climber first. It's hot here in the summer, with triple digit temperatures. Spring and fall, she explained, were perfect. Winter, with snow and sub-freezing temps, she runs away to Southern California.

"South about eight miles," the waitress said, "and then turn left towards La Sal. You climb into the mountains and the temperature will drop 20 degrees. Then, it loops around into Castle Valley, where the first season of Westworld was filmed."

You have to watch for dogs, though, if you hike any of the trails, she explained. The dogs aren't bad, but they are out chasing the bears. So, if you see or hear dogs while hiking, it can be a very bad thing.

The day after Arches, with my knee slowly returning to its normal size, I started driving south. In a couple miles, I came to a nicely marked sign: Ken's Lake and La Sal Mountain Loop.

La Sal Mountain Loop could easily be renamed "Darwin's Loop." It reminds me of driving in Iceland. The speed limit signs are not arbitrary like they can be out east. If the sign says, "20 mph," you do 20 mph. If you gaze at the scenery instead of the signs, you could end up on the list for the Darwin Awards—those who die for doing stupid things.

Yes, I had one scare. Then, I paid the hell attention. There was a road I took in North Carolina that was called the Dragon's Tail, a snaking, loopy road that took you one mile in five miles of road. The La Sal Mountain Loop was its big brother. If you dropped off the Dragon's Tail, you end up in trees and brush. If you drop off the mountain loop, you end up a few thousand feet down.

There are a lot of cutoffs as you make your way up. Each trail leads to gorges and hikes. I just tried to stay on the road. As the temperature dropped by 20 degrees in 15 minutes, I was up in the mountains.

I finally saw cows! On the road! --It really doesn't take much to entertain me. After close to 10,000 miles of driving, and hundreds of signs saying, "open range," "cow crossing," and things like that, I finally saw some cows and had to stop. Five of them were in the middle of the road. One glanced at me when I took their picture.

What goes up must come down and I made my way into Castle Valley. I drove right past the huge sandstone castles in the sky that give it its name. They had seemed so very far away. Ranches, farms, a winery and resorts grew up from the desert. The temperature slowly climbed back up as I made my way down and back onto Route 128 and the Colorado River.

What the hell is with the Colorado River? It was starting to remind me of Texas: it's all over the place. I think I have crossed it about 50 times.

There is the thought to leave the car go bear hunting. I won't. But the feeling is there and I want to hike down some trails and explore a little bit, on a loop that brings me back to being lost. Maybe next time.

If I do run into a bear? My cousin, Mike, has me on constant locator. Find my phone. The pictures should be epic!

But now it's time to move on. I struggled with what to do next, how to make it to California. I promised Papa Bear I'd stay away from Las Vegas. Do you realize how hard that is? It is as if all roads west pass through Las Vegas.

A joke got me into trouble. Okay, okay: an often repeated joke got me into trouble. "I'm just going to put everything I have on black. Or red. Roulette. Let it all ride. Double or nothing." So now I'm banned from Las Vegas under penalty of getting my ass kicked.

It's not like I would do it. Would I? Covid and my own stupidity did take some massive chunks out of my nest egg--that I'm now scrambling up the rest to go with some rye toast. The idea of going head-to-head with Murphy was appealing, one roll of the wheel, one bouncing ball to determine my fate.

But isn't that what I had already done? The wheel was spinning, a titanic spin, and the ball was bouncing. The wheel is massive, the backways and byways of America. Murphy was rubbing his hands together. I tipped my cap to him and lit another cigarette.

I thought about going south through Arizona but decided to make my way north to Salt Lake City. I always wanted to see the salt flats and then make a long drive through a desert.

You Are Here; August 21, 2020

I hit the 10,000-mile mark on the five-hour drive from Moab to Salt Lake City. It was an interesting drive, but I would need to check a topographical map to be sure–which I'm not going to do. It felt like I was driving up enormous steps, each step 20-50 miles long. Up through mountains and down the other side. Down through one final canyon, and then there was a Walmart, and then Provost, and then BYU, and then Salt Lake City and an eight-lane highway (under construction of course–you'd be amazed at how many highways are under construction).

But 10,000 miles and counting, and I haven't even made it to the west coast yet. I'm not even quite sure why I came to Salt Lake City when the plan was to go south through Arizona. Now, I have a very long stretch of desert to cover, possibly in one long drive– two hours longer to avoid Las Vegas.

I'm reminded, though, from time to time, what I am doing out here. It happened in Salt Lake City.

Outside of the convention center in Salt Lake City is this interesting sculpture, "Point of View," by Maine artist Aaron T Stephan. It is a collection of over 150 road signs, with words on them in black, at various heights and depths. The first sign that jumped out at me was "Lost Found." But then I walked into the middle of the street and more jumped out at me. It is filled with diametrical words like "catch throw," "truth dare," "desert ocean." In its entirety, I see a blending of contradiction, a harmony of opposites. "You Are Here" is at the center of them, within them, so it appears blurred if you don't look at it from straight on.

I made a circle to come back to the signs/sculpture. It was a random route that I took but it was to the center of Salt Lake City. The Temple is the center of Salt Lake City just as surely as William Penn is the center of Philadelphia. The original church, the Temple, the choir and the conference center. The grounds were enclosed yet open and inviting. The city streets were quiet outside as all cities have been, but the quietness was even more pronounced on the Temple grounds.

No, there was no Mormon mob waiting to drag me in and convert me from my heathen ways. Some people on Facebook have the oddest ideas. There was a pair of very nice young ladies, though, that approached me.

"You are welcome here," one of them said. "Come find us if you have any questions. And please, there is no smoking on the grounds."

A friend of mine, Lance, that I'll get to in a few more states, explained the Mormon religion to me. He's a hierarch. In his youth lectures, he explains that it is a religion of "can," not "don't."

"You can certainly have a drink," he said, as he sipped on his water at a business conference. "I tell them if they can't drink, they need to go and see a doctor."

You can do anything, he explained, but the question is "should you?" You can booze it up, do drugs, smoke, have sex, etc. But once you make that choice, go down that path, the question of "should I or shouldn't I" becomes a statement of "I can't." It goes from an open ended path to a dead end that is hard to make your way back from. Choices that we make, he explained, can lead to a loss of freedom.

I think of my 35 year, two pack a day smoking habit and can't find fault in his logic.

Everything was closed due to Covid. I would have liked to have seen the choir. The temple itself was under construction and it was unlike anything I have ever seen. They must have been doing something with the foundation. If the temple itself was a full city block, then they must have dug up the eight city blocks surrounding it, hundreds of feet down.

Right down from the temple is, to me, a contradiction: City Creek Center, an enormous and beautiful indoor/outdoor shopping mall with a creek running through it and multiple levels. It just seemed at odds to me, a contradiction that shouldn't be there, so close to the temple.

And then I came back to the signs/sculpture and stood in the middle of the street. There is no "viewing area." I had to dodge cars. But I needed to see the "You Are Here" at one depth. And see what else jumps out at me. All the other signs are black lettering on white backgrounds. "You Are Here" is in red, painted on multiple signs, with a red circle around it and at multiple depths. You can only see it as one piece if you are standing directly in front of it.

10,217 miles.

Perspective: use it or lose it.

On the drive here, a column was percolating in my head, something about mercy, aloha, being lost and something from one of the original columns. There is an entire other piece being written inside my head with each travel column. The two are a blended contradiction. A teacher/advisor awaits in LA. I've been finding them haphazardly as I go, like a man I spoke to this morning. There is a destination now. At least momentarily.

My destination is being here, right where I am supposed to be.

Antelope Imposters; August 22, 2020

I don't know what most people think of when they think of Salt Lake City, but it was nothing like I imagined.

"First thing," a woman told me told me with a laugh, "we're not all Mormon. I come from an enormous Catholic family."

I was checking out the guidebook and there is also a huge Buddhist community, brought in from migrants. As the Japanese moved east, displaced by the Californian Great Earthquake in 1906, they brought their religion. Now, Salt Lake City has become the epicenter of American Buddhism.

In many respects, Salt Lake City is like every other major city. It has the huge superhighway running through it and a sprawling metropolis where everything is bunching up on each other. It's as slow as every other major city as I have been to with Covid, with empty streets and little traffic off the highway, but you can feel the need to have more people on the roads.

I blew out my knee in Arches National Park so I wanted to take it easy. A friend recommended Antelope Island, about a 40-

minute drive from where I was staying. You drive along a seven-mile causeway across the Great Salt Lake and the city disappears.

You can drive around much of the island, though there are hikes that can take you to the top of the mountain. It was not the best time to be here–go figure. The fires, now from California, cause a thick haze in the air. People are complaining about it but I just keep my mouth shut–it's not nearly as bad as Colorado. I wanted to do the hikes but didn't. I wanted to save what's left of my knee for something else. It was on the hikes, up into the highlands, that you can supposedly see the antelope. On the drive, there are plenty of places to pull over and see buffalo.

There are numerous signs: don't approach the wildlife! I wanted to make friends with them but there was the knee. I know for a fact that a buffalo can run a lot faster than I can, even without the knee bothering me. So, I kept my natural impulses under control.

Buffalo aside, that is one of the things that bothers me about this journey. Random encounters. Everywhere that I have gone throughout my life, I have struck up conversations with people. I've made friends and acquaintances around the globe just by saying, "Hello." I like to talk to people, learn about them, learn about where they are from and what the local life is like. I've even made friends with people I was not supposed to talk to.

"Don't talk to anybody," my wife once told me once in Hawai'i. She was from there so knew the people and the lay of the land. We were on the west side of Oahu. "They don't like your kind here." – "my kind" being white, non-Hawaiian, haole. She had been tortured as a child for being hapa haole, half white.

I started talking to some random guy while my wife wandered around. It's my nature. He invited me to his family's house for a barbeque that night.

It's different with the pandemic. People keep their distance. They want to keep conversations short and to the point to avoid risk of exposure. They don't want to be drawn out. They don't want to engage.

But the Great Salt Lake. I'm a history buff and a bit of a geology geek. I have always wanted to see it and stand in it. One of the things that brought me here is that the drive to California will carry me across the salt flats.

The Great Salt Lake is all that remains of Lake Bonneville that covered much of Utah and parts of Wyoming and Idaho after the last ice age. It's the largest salt-water lake in the Western Hemisphere, called "America's Dead Sea." Because it has no outlets, the only way it loses water is through evaporation, causing a buildup of salinity. The salt makes the water so dense swimming is like floating. I always wanted to stand in it. So I did. It was little bit of a hike. When I got back to my car, my legs were white with salt.

My journey started out on an island (or isle as they say in Maine). I didn't see any deer on Deer Isle just like I didn't see any antelope on Antelope Island. Deer Isle jutted out into the Atlantic; Antelope Island juts out into the Great Salt Lake. Okay. I like islands. And bridges. And causeways. And being places I have never been. The differences between different places and different parts of the country are becoming much more apparent to me along with the people and the way they think and act.

It was a 40-minute drive back along that superhighway (speed limit was 70 with everybody doing 80+). Back in the city, I found an outdoor restaurant with live music! --and social distancing. People are adapting. Businesses are adapting. A thing I noticed is the west is more crowded, with crowded meaning "not completely dead." People go to the outdoors and state and national parks. Escaping the Covid Hibernation. It's easier out here I think.

But off to my hike in the hazy air. The guidebook told me about this interesting little place about an hour away. I'm doing it right this time: sunscreen, proper hat, proper shoes, water, backpack and I'm even bringing a bathing suit.

On the Bull; August 23, 2020

Closed. Again. A mountain was closed to begin my journey. Then an entire state. Down the east coast: closed. Even when I found things open in Virginia and Kentucky, they were closed the day I was there. Broadway, Beale and Bourbon Streets were mostly closed. Here, I drove an hour back the way I came to find something in the guidebook: Fifth Water Hot Springs.

How can you close a hiking path and a natural hot spring? I had had enough. I was going in.

Fifth Water Hot Springs is in the guidebook of places to stop if you are going from Salt Lake City to Moab. Now, maybe the middle of the summer is not the best time to visit hot springs (unless you are in Iceland), but I'll be damned if I wasn't going to walk around the gates and signs after driving through that mess of a highway again.

They say the trail is moderately strenuous, about 4 1/2 miles round trip. It sits about nine miles off the highway (I saw cows again! In the middle of the road!).

I can just imagine coming here in colder weather. As hot as it was, I jumped in anyway. It was beautiful, with the warm to hot waters oddly refreshing in the heat. It's a little piece of extraordinary amid the ordinary.

The return trip was less strenuous with the knee aching only a little bit.

The day started off with learning a few things about bull riding. It's funny what you learn when you talk to people. Outside of the hotel, a guy asked me about the electric scooters--that seem to be popping up in a lot of the cities. I explained and then asked him what he was doing in town. He was from a small town in California and was here for a bull riding competition.

Bull riding always looked to me like a person hanging on for dear life and being whipped around like a rag doll. It turns out, that is the way it is supposed to look. The rules are simple. You hold onto the bull with one hand and can't touch the bull or your body with the other hand. Your free arm becomes a counterweight. A bull rider must guess what the bull is going to do and react. Each move is in counter to the bull's movements.

"Chin down, you always keep your eyes on the bull's shoulders," the guy said. "Where your eyes go, you will follow. So if the bull is getting close to the fence, and you get nervous and look at the fence, you're going to end up on the fence."

That's a life lesson right there.

But I'm about to go out for dinner and call it a day. I haven't been sleeping too well and have a long drive tomorrow through a lot of desert. Salt Lake City is an interesting place. As much as I think the road crews really screwed up the job marking the new lanes for construction, the thing that jumps out at me about the highway is it moves fast and smooth. The streets in downtown are really wide. It is just so much more open than back east. I wonder if that has something to do with it being settled later and having the room to build right at first instead of trying to fit more roadway into an existing plan?

There is a lot more to do and see around here. The great outdoors in all four seasons and just a short drive away, from spelunking to skiing – I wouldn't recommend the two together. But you can: skiing, spelunking and even scuba diving. Seriously. No shit. I'd love to visit in the fall or winter. Or even another summer. I wouldn't mind heading out to the Great Salt Lake again and going for a swim and seeing if I can find those antelope.

People ask me what place I have liked the most. I'm just enjoying the ride, keeping my eyes on the bull's shoulders.

Through the Desert; August 24, 2020

I had to fight with my GPS. I wanted to make it to LA by not going through Las Vegas. It's not as easy as it sounds. It's almost as if Vegas has paid off the GPS companies so all roads go through there—which I would not put past them. I finally managed it, though, and set off on a 13-hour drive. With over 11,000 miles logged in, I finally made the 3,000-mile trip to the west coast.

Driving gives you sights and feels of America that flying just can't. The first was a drive across the Bonneville Salt Flats, just west of Salt Lake City, along 80, before you get to Nevada. At one rest stop, I saw people crunching their way into the whiteness. It was a long, straight highway across what, in the north, would look like a light snowfall with rocks sticking out. It was what I wanted to do.

The road quickly brought me to Nevada and signs of why I did not want to go to Vegas. Gambling everywhere. Attached to chain hotels, casinos with hotels in them, and even slot machines in the gas stations. I was in Vegas in January and found it depressing as hell. I was there for a conference and stayed at the

Palms. The desperation was as palatable as the stale cigarette smoke.

I watched this one woman hit on roulette. She hit HUGE. I sat and watched as they just kept piling chips in front of her. They even had to call over a pit boss to bring more chips. I thought, "good for you." I walked past about an hour later, though, and she was still there. She had a sad and perplexed look on her face and only a few chips in front of her.

Two rules in Vegas, and in life: the house always wins, eventually, and you have to know when to walk away.

I never learned those lessons so drove away, into Nevada, planning to cross the state through the northern end and southwest through the dessert. I didn't stop much. 13 hours is pushing it for me.

I took Scenic 93 and then Route 6 west. Two signs I saw were "no gas for 167 miles" and "no gas for 100 miles." I read these as "no coffee, even bad coffee, for a long, long time." Signs I did not see were speed limit signs. I really don't think there were any. You pass through a few small towns, but it is mostly just desert.

In the beginning of the ride, it was a race. First, when I got off Route 80 at West Wendover, and then again when I jumped on Route 6 at Ely. Trucks starting out along with RV's and cars pulling campers. There were a few miles of high-speed passing to make it around and in front of them. Then, it was just open road. Maybe passing another car every 20-30 miles.

I did make one stop. You could see a long path through the scrub running as far as the eye could see in either direction. It is the old Pony Express route. I just think it's amazing that they could get a letter from the east coast to west coast in 12 days on horseback. It was an awesome idea that needed a different breed of people– and a different breed of horses. I read that the racing thoroughbreds were fine for some of the stretches but, out in the west, they needed half broken (wild) mustangs.

My first goal, after arguing with GPS, was Bishop, California. It's a small town that sits across the border and south. It just looked interesting even from the maps. You drive between two mountain ranges. Going south after you pass into California, on your left, are the mountains that make up eastern California and the edge of Death Valley (I passed by two entrances). On your right are the mountains that make up the edges of a few national parks. I saw the entrance to Yosemite, but it also includes Sierra National Forest and Sequoia National Forest.

After the final mountain pass in CA, you really get moving and start passing through cities as they get bigger and bigger making your way to LA. After sunset, it became white knuckle driving, even on a Sunday evening. But it was a blast! I saw some beautiful views of the sunset on the last set of mountains and then it was all a race downhill and towards the coast. Everything you have heard about the LA Freeway? It's all true.

The road twisted and turned through the passes but then it was like what I learned from the bull rider the other day: keep your eye on the shoulders of the bull (or the car in front of you) and react. I would relax for a while behind the car in front of me and then jump at my chance to pass left and right. I had no idea what the speed limit was or where I was because I didn't have time to look at maps or dashboards. I would not say it was quite "kill or be killed" but it was exhilarating powering my way through the last stretch of an 11,000-mile journey.

And then I was there, pulling off the freeway and finding my hotel in Seal Beach. It was about a mile or two from the Pacific Ocean. I'll make my way along the coast to San Diego to see an old friend–surprise the hell out of him actually. But this part is a wrap, from the northeast corner of the continental US in Maine to the extreme southwest and the Pacific Ocean before me.

Go west, old man. I did.

Part Five: In the Shadow of the Pacific

Across the US; August 25, 2020

After a bit more than 11,000 miles, I finally made the 3,000-mile trip from Deer Isle, Maine to Seal Beach, California. It's been about 52 days on the road. I punched it into my GPS and found I could probably do the cross-country trip in four days. Maybe five.

Seal Beach, I was told, was more for the relaxed crowd. It seemed fitting to be here. It was not a planned destination. My thought was simply "Los Angeles," a city I had been to before for a conference and then as a layover for flights to Hawai'i. I struggled with the right place to stay, finally taking some friends' advice and letting the hotel app do the rest. Seal Beach is officially 22 miles south of LA, and 3,244 miles from Deer Isle, Maine.

I wonder how many steps I've walked in that time? If you go by the daily averages as per my iWatch, it has been about 522,500.

159

The walk to the beach, round trip, was about five miles, with eight miles on the day and over 15,000 steps over level ground. What is there to say about a halfway point on my journey? I said it simply on the video I made standing in the surf of the Pacific Ocean: I made it and now I was going to take a walk into the sunset.

I walked up the beach, out onto the pier, and then found myself (with help) a nice Irish Pub that served a pretty good pour of Guinness and damn good shepherd's pie. Then, there was the walk back in the evening to my hotel with thoughts percolating in my head.

I have walked into a lot of sunsets but I haven't driven through many on this trip. Entering New Mexico and the climb to Santa Fe, and then when I drove down out of the mountains into LA were the only two. Over 50 sunsets since my house sold and I became a wanderer. Or, as one friend put it after showing me the clip from the movie, "Pulp Fiction:" a bum. (John Travolta talking to Samuel L Jackson about traveling the earth.)

…and I find that I am trying to force something here that doesn't want to be forced. The thoughts are still percolating. Something about all who wander are not lost, but I am lost and that is okay. I found that somewhere in Colorado. There is the exhaustion that spurred the trip, the weariness of a man 687 years old. Am I still that exhausted? There are the glimpses of America. The hopes of those opening businesses and the desperation of others losing everything.

There is something about Facebook to write. I stopped. I really enjoyed Facebook. I was able to find friends and family who I had not seen in years. Many are on my list of people to visit as I travel. In San Francisco, I'll see a childhood friend that I haven't seen since high school. But Facebook has become a cesspool of vitriol. The politics and arguments and news just got to be too much so I stopped, asking those who felt the need to tag me to stop or blocking or snoozing them when they wouldn't. Life is better now.

Lessons learned. From the bull rider: chin tucked and watch the shoulders of the bull. If your eyes go somewhere else, your body will follow. Lost and found. Found in the lostness, but not quite lost enough yet to truly be found. Hope and tinkering with tomorrows and possibilities. Do I really want to go back to school to earn my Masters?

But then there is the road, where staying in motion allows me peace and to be at rest.

And there are the seals, and San Francisco and the whole other half of the United States to see, wondering what to do when a chill comes to the air. Mail another suitcase home with shorts or fly in for a few days to trade out the shoes and sneakers for boots and long pants from my storage locker?

I need more socks. Calf socks. I brought mostly ankle ones for shorts, not thinking I'd be out this long, thinking I'd be on my way back by now.

Thinking today to just keep writing about the surface. It's a wondrous country. The surface will do. Diving deep can always wait until later when I find the key to be at rest while at rest.

The Big Kid; August 27, 2020

There is just something about seeing wildlife in its natural habitat that makes me feel childlike with wonder and awe. —thought many would say that acting childlike is not a far stretch for me. I was staying in Seal Beach but there weren't any seals. A friend told me about La Jolle Cove, just north of San Diego, where you can see seals and sea lions on the beach and rocks. I had to go.

I parked my car and heard them barking as soon as I got out and started making my way down. The California coast is littered with great stretches of sandy beaches and impressive rocky faces. La Jolle Cove is a combination of both. There are a few places where people are hitting the surf but many places where the seals and sea lions own it.

I wandered down along the path. Kayaks were out in the water along with some swimmers. The seals and sea lions were sunning on the rocks or coming up on the beach. They must be used to people because they were allowing everybody, including me, to get close. I swear there was this one that was like, "take my picture, I'll strike a pose!"

Even better, I saw pups at play. It was like watching two puppies. One had a feather in its mouth and was teasing the other one with it.

The pups look cute but of course you must be careful. I just wanted to cuddle with one like I would a puppy but mothers will be mothers. I was not about to approach the pups as I knew mom wouldn't be far away. They can't move very fast on land, but I was told they will chase you.

It was great to see another small slice of Southern California. I then made it back up to the LA area to have dinner with my cousin in a part of Disney that is open. Can you imagine Disney with empty parking lots? I saw it.

The following night, I had dinner with another old friend and her husband. Distance and lives separate us but there are still those strings from the past that attach us. I had first met her when we were in high school and hadn't seen her in decades. She and her husband showed me another part of LA, their place, Huntington Beach (which Sunset Beach is a part of). She was telling me how they rarely ever leave the area. Most people just like to stay in their little piece of paradise.

I did finally realize something interesting: I wasn't in Los Angeles, only LA County. I don't think I was ever actually in LA except when I was on the freeway driving down from Nevada. I can see why people love it here and I also can see why people are leaving here. The weather and the escapes to nature, the beautiful beaches and the awesome sunsets capture people. The flip side is the expense and the constant crowds. California goes nuts on taxes. I swear if there was a way for them to tax the cup of coffee I made in my room, they would. My cousin was telling me the property taxes are ridiculous. A long time ago, CA grandfathered in houses so they would only see a 1% increase per year, so you could be living next to someone that was paying what you might have paid in 1980.

There is an attraction to every place I go, with a level of "pull" to return and see more. Los Angeles? I was here for a convention last year. Beaches just are not my thing except for quick walks. There is a slight pull to return and see and do more, explore more, but the counterweight is the crowds, taxes, traffic, and just general noise.

But it's time to start heading north. Time to start part two (or part eight) of the trip.

A Tantric Interlude; August 28, 2020

I had one last stop in LA proper before heading out. It's not what you think! Okay, it can be exactly what you think but this wasn't that. Out of the many tantra practitioners in LA, I picked this one because it specifically stated on her website: there will not be any sex.

When people think of tantra, they think of tantric sex. Tantric sex is a "thing," but it is more of an offshoot of tantra than anything else. As one Tantrika (also called a Daka or Dakini) explained in a video, yes, tantra can teach you to have sex all night long but who has time for that?

When I first got separated, I stumbled across yoga. Cat cow anybody? I found something in it when I first started practicing. Mondays and Wednesdays were my busiest days at work. I made it a point to leave work on those days to go to my yoga class.

I was not the most flexible person, but I found the sessions invigorating and only a little bit painful. I also found that it gave me more energy. I see yoga as a "fake it till you make it" kind of thing. For the first month, it was only about the poses and stretching, of making time for myself. I remember during one session where I assumed the half pigeon pose, with one leg stretched far behind me and the other bent underneath me. My body demanded that the leg underneath me not be at the 45 degree angle the pose was supposed to be, but the instructor always made it a point to say that this was our yoga session and to do what our bodies allowed.

I folded myself over my forward leg and reached even further until my forehead touched the mat. I found something internal. A calmness. A peacefulness that had nothing to do with the pose, the session, the studio, or anything else.

"You got it now," my yogi whispered to me and then moved on to the next person.

It was that internal thing I was looking for and tantra seemed like the next step.

Tantra means "to weave" in Sanskrit and is about reaching spiritual enlightenment through connecting with your energy. Sexual tantra is more accurately described as neotantra. I saw Tantrika as guides.

"There will not be any sex."

I liked that. It set boundaries and expectations. The ceremony is a simple one, sort of like an expanded massage.

The first part of the ceremony is stripping down to what you feel comfortable with and the Tantrika does the same. There is incense and a foot bath in a bronze bowl.

Next, I sat on the massage table and she sat on me, straddling me with her legs on mine. It then becomes about sensual touch, not sexual, exploring each other, allowing touch to become a way to connecting. It gets a bit mystical here. She is touching energy points and guiding my energy. Slowly, we start beathing in unison, matching breaths, matching our energy.

This is the part that I found most healing. Touch. Touching and being touched. Connecting. Easing myself back into that web of connections that create our lives.

Then, it was the massage. There were a few twists. There is a sound bath, essential oils, and incense but it was your basic massage.

Much later, I would take personality tests. One of them was clear that touch is my love language, my way of connecting and communicating. I wasn't surprised.

After the massage, like in any massage, I was left to myself to gather myself back inward. I slowly awakened and then toweled off and got dressed.

Heading North? August 29, 2020

I checked out of my hotel room in Seal Beach for the drive north to San Francisco and then into the undiscovered country! So, of course, I went south. Beyond south. Tijuana!

A friend who I met through my orthodontic lab association lives in San Diego and goes to Tijuana almost every day. I had never been to Tijuana, never crossed the border by car, so he wanted to give me the experience. He even booked me a room in a five-star hotel for $60 so I packed a few things into an overnight bag, forgetting most of what I needed, and took the drive into the land down under.

I've heard stories and my posts on Facebook told me that many people heard stories as well or watched too many movies. Scary stuff is floating around in people's minds. A recurring theme in my website columns is: "it's not what you think."

Tijuana was the same. I got shortchanged here and there and my lack of Spanish didn't help, but I did not get kidnapped, robbed, hustled or anything else that people seem to associate with going south of the border. Who would want to kidnap me? I found a beautiful town with gracious and nice people.

Traveling anywhere in the world is the same. I've always said it all begins with attitude. You walk with a purpose. Even if you are completely lost and have no idea what to do or where to go, you continue to walk with a purpose.

Traveling is also about being smart. I've lived in Philadelphia most of my life. Even when I am there, certain changes occur. In the "green" areas, I'm normal. In the "yellow" areas, I take precautions like keeping my wallet and everything else in my front pockets and being more aware of my surroundings. If it's a touristy area, I also keep my phone in my pocket and don't do things that would mark me as a target for the petty criminals. The "red" areas? I stay the hell out because I know there is a chance I might not make it out. Tijuana was no different.

As I travel, the first thing I do is ask a local, usually the front desk person, where it is safe to walk and where it is not. In Tijuana, I had Federico.

Federico is a great guy who places a premium on friendship and being nice. He wanted to show me his world. He did drone on and on and on about the red areas and a lot of stuff I already knew, but I let him—it made him feel better. He knows Tijuana. It is 20 minutes away from his lab. Through him, I got to see the tourist area of Tijuana and the day-to-day areas.

Like most of the world, it was slow. The once bustling and crowded tourist street was slow. Caesar's restaurant was open, world famous as the inventor of the Caesar Salad. The main tourist street is about a mile long? It is more for the day tourists of average means where a dollar (20 pesos) goes a long way. The street is lined with clubs, bars, coffee houses, casinos, and everything you really need for a few days.

Unlike most of the world, Federico was not slow. I think I took the fastest walking tour ever of Tijuana.

"You walk too fast," I told him. "Slow down."

"I walk like a lab owner," he laughed, "there is always something to do yesterday."

"I'm not a lab owner. I'm temporarily retired."

He said something in Spanish or Portuguese (he's Brazilian) that I am sure was not very nice, but he did slow down and allowed me to catch my breath.

Federico took me to this one hole in the wall type of place for lunch. I love Mexican food. The best Mexican food I have ever had in the US, or even at the touristy areas on a trip I took to the

167

Yucatan, does not even come close to what I had there. There are no chips and salsa served with the meal. Instead, it's limes, salt, fresh fruit and pickled vegetables. To drink, they serve a kind of flavored water they make every day. Everything was fantastic, comfortable and relaxed.

I also saw the other side of Tijuana. At the end of the workday, bus taxis start lining the streets. The people who work downtown take these to get home. Business owners and locals start sweeping and cleaning the sidewalks and streets in front of them. Families start to gather at local restaurants to eat dinner.

A very interesting thing I saw about the place was they take Covid very seriously. Masks everywhere. Temperature checks upon entering every building—and I mean every building, including the local coffee shops and markets. Hand sanitizer everywhere and even these mats where you walk in a cleaning solution and then wipe your feet before proceeding. And they make sure you do. Nicely.

Federico took me to another popular part of Tijuana, filled with the ritzy malls and expensive restaurants. That meal was incredible as well. We went to a seafood place. The entire meal would have cost over $150 at home if not more. There, it cost $40. He told me you can rent huge, beautiful homes for $1,000 per month. An incredible apartment runs about $300. I can see the attraction of living there on an American salary. It's easy these days with the Internet and everybody working from home.

I wrote in my Facebook page that I walked the mean streets of Tijuana and the people populating them were very nice. At night, walking down a deserted boulevard, I was fine, taking in the clean streets and peaceful air. I was in a "yellow" zone. Federico had warned me where the "red" zones were, only a few blocks away. But as long as you stay out of there, you are fine. The police presence is noticeable–they keep their lights flashing continually. Even the locals beef up the security presence with guards. Aye, they want to keep the tourists coming. Federico also said something about the red zones, that the people there will stay out of the yellow zones for much the same reason. The fools will make their way to them.

I had another fitful night sleep in a beautiful room and then made my way back to the US with Federico the next day. He has a car pass so he dropped me off to walk through. There was a tense few moments there. Aye, you try answering questions at a tense checkpoint with a speech impediment.

We got back to Federico' lab. He wanted me to spend another night in San Diego but California was becoming like Texas and Florida: no exit in sight. I would have loved to spend more time with him and meet his family, but it was really time to move on. So, I jumped on some freeway or another, drove through LA once again, and got north of Santa Barbara before I stopped for the night and overpaid for a motel room.

Moving and Grooving, California Style; August 30, 2020

I woke up and it was 58 degrees. The Irish cap is back!

Instead of Route 5, the quickest way to San Francisco, I took the more scenic route, 101. My first stop was a place Federico told me about along the California coast, Pfeiffer Big Sur State Park. It was closed. California, like Colorado, is on fire. I regret not seeing the huge waterfall that crashes into the ocean, but I don't regret the 30-mile drive back and forth along the Pacific Coast Highway (PCH).

The PCH runs along the coast. The original thought was to drive it from LA to San Francisco, but friends warned me away. I saw why. A co-pilot is needed. As beautiful as it is, you can't really see anything unless you stop. With the mountains, passes and loops, you need to keep your eye on the road or else you will end up, well, dead.

The drive up from Santa Barbara along 101 was interesting. The views and temperature are both very fluid. I went from 60 degrees to 85 degrees throughout the entire day. It depends on so many factors like the fog, elevation, how close the highway takes you to the coast and a few other things. I passed through many manicured and neat agriculture farms, horse and cattle farms, a few oil fields, small towns, small cities, and just an amazing landscape as you twist and turn up and down mountains and in and out of valleys as you travel a sort of straight line.

Going back north from Big Sur, I went to Carmel by the Sea. A 17-mile loop starts there that takes you through what is considered the most scenic drive in America, through Pebble Beach Golf Course, along a hill of trees known for the American writers that enjoyed their time there (like Steinbeck) and then down along the coast. I think I made it through about halfway with a bunch of stops but my body and mind were telling me to get my butt to San Francisco, another two hours up along 101.

Highways into cities. It is interesting to me. I've flown into San Francisco and let Uber take me to my hotel. It's a different experience entirely driving there. Passing by Candle Stick Park along with so many other cities and sights that you only hear about on TV or in the movies. Coming up on what I thought was the final stretch, you see a huge sign on a mountain, "South San Francisco: The Industrial City." I didn't even know there was a South San Francisco, separate and distinct from SF.

I finally made it to a room and then called an old friend to meet him and his wife for dinner. I went to grade school with Dennis, and he had met Janice in college. I met them and we figured out that we had not seen each other in about 30 years.

I was exhausted though. It was great talking to them and learning more about the inside of San Francisco. Like every other place, it's not what you think. Dennis was so much the guy I first knew in 5th grade but also this wonderful man who had done a lot with his life since moving from Maryland to go to college at Berkley. He works in photography, design, 3D and worked on a lot of movies that everybody knows. He's traveled the world with production teams and the stories he has brought back can fill a book.

We grew up in interesting times if you think about it. The place where you spent it will reflect that. We entered the digital age, the wall coming down, the dot com boom and bust and resurgence and now the 3D age–he worked with the team that did the 3D image of President Obama's bust, the first president to have it done with technology.

Many people I know never left their zip code—or not too far from it. That's not a bad thing. I see it as where life takes us, or keeps us. Some of the most incredible people I know are like that and they have fantastic lives.

I started out in 19142, SW Philly. It sometimes feels like a few lifetimes ago, with each new life pushing further outward. It's been a hell of a run.

Nine Miles in San Francisco; August 31, 2020

9 miles. 18,880 steps. 60 flights. My circles on my activity app on my iWatch were spinning and I had absolutely no idea where I was. But Janice did. Dennis and I just followed along.

I really wasn't planning on writing another column about San Francisco. I was here about this time last year. I walked the city. With Janice leading the way, we walked a different part of the city, the Presidio. And then some. The plan today was just to take it easy before I head out tomorrow, rest up and relax before I head into the undiscovered country. With Janice and Dennis (and Zepp, their dog), it turned out to be one of the better days of my journey.

Today felt as close to normal as I have felt since the pandemic started. Just walking with friends and chatting. Dennis has traveled the world with film companies doing production and photography. Very unassuming, I don't think he realizes he is one of the more accomplished people I know.

Dennis and Janice moved out here to San Francisco I guess about the same time I moved to Miami, in 1991. They are about as San Franciscan as it gets.

Many people had warned me about this place. Both times I was here. Human excrement all over the place and tent city empires filled with homeless, illegals and other undesirables. I didn't see it. I could have, just like in any city, but I didn't feel like getting an armed escort to go into the Tenderloin.

This bastion of liberalism that accepts the dregs of society as actual people and wants to help them—and has them flown in by other cities and states—Hawai'i and Vegas were sued for giving homeless people tickets to come here—just has a different feel to it for me. It is as if the ideology that created America is real here. Give me your poor and tired and let's give them a hand up. It's what built America. People looking for a chance. But anyway, I digress.

In Janice, I think I found someone that MIGHT be able to out walk me. She would definitely get to anywhere we were going first, but she's had all of the training on the hills of San Francisco.

Everybody knows that the hills of San Francisco are notorious. It's just unfair. Every other place I have walked, you walk up and then you walk down. San Francisco is the only place where you really do walk uphill in both directions. And none of it really makes sense to me.

Just say you are walking up a block and come to an intersection and look left. Huge hill. The next block, it's level. The block after that might be going downhill. Dennis told me some people studied it and there is a path that goes along his street that follows the most level way in San Francisco for bikers. They built the city on the grid system, but I think they just placed the grid over top of everything that existed: mountains, hills, valleys, etc.

The day began walking to the Presidio, someplace I wasn't at the last time. Looking at the map now, I'm not sure how I missed it. It's a huge, wooded area. I think I walked the western edge the last time I was here as that's the way from the Golden Gate Bridge to the sea cliffs.

Dennis and Janice wanted me to see different things in the city, so we wandered there to something that I didn't even know existed. Dennis kept calling it ILM. As if I would know what that was? I finally did look it up on my iPhone: Industrial Light and Magic. It's in the Presidio, the campus that George Lucas built. There is even a famous Yoda Fountain.

And then just a lot of walking with some great views and interesting sights. We walked up one street where the sidewalk was steps: it was that steep, but I was informed not the steepest in SF.

173

Dennis was telling me that one street he lived on had steps and was even steeper but was also a big tourist place because of the view at the top. About 3-4 times a year, there would be runaway cars because people would forget to put the car in park at the top and they would roll back down, taking out a bunch of other cars along the way.

It was just a great day wandering around an awesome city with an old friend and a new one. About 30 years had passed since I'd last seen Dennis. I didn't feel like arguing with Janice over whether we met before or not. I think we did, at a campus party in Maryland, but she says no, and everybody knows what it is like arguing with somebody from Brooklyn.

I think one of the best parts of the day was hearing about Dennis' life. I don't know how he feels about it, but outside looking in, it seems incredible. I'm forgetting many of the details, but he did have an office right by the Yoda statue while working for ILM. He's been on photography shoots around the world, including the Arctic Circle. He seems happy and Janice (who I did meet long, long ago) is just as amazing. In this era of masks and social distancing, with a hush on the world and cities, and a distancing among friends and family as everybody tries to get their feel in the new normal, it felt great walking and chatting. The new barriers we have placed between ourselves and the rest of the world were as non-existent as the judgment here in San Francisco.

An Ancient Hush; September 2, 2020

After driving across a mist enshrouded Golden Gate Bridge, the plan was to head into the Redwood Forests of California's Northern coast and then find someplace to stop for the night. As

I was passing through the last of the scenic routes along 101, with the setting sun dappling the great trees, an almost full disc of silver caught my eye. Thoughts dissipated like the mists. There is just something about a long drive at night. Yes, you miss a lot of things, but it can be like driving into magic.

Into the undiscovered country, I wrote on Facebook. The Pacific Northwest--or PNW as it is called. What was beyond San Francisco and what kind of roads awaited me?

California, like Colorado, had had doubles doses of a very bad year. It was a very dry year, and all the forests are sitting there like dry kindling. In Colorado, some nitwits took illegal tracer rounds to a firing range. Tracer rounds are made to burn. They come out of the barrel on fire and can burn up to 1,400 degrees. They light up the night. Or set states on fire. The nitwits would eventually shut down the main east-west corridor as well as choking businesses struggling to reopen.

In California, it was Mother Nature. The people of San Francisco saw something unlike anything they had ever seen: a massive lighting storm. I believe there were well over 1,000 recorded strikes. California began to burn.

I had smelled it and saw it the entire time I was in southern California. There was a haze to the air. The fires were mostly around San Francisco. As I drove through wine country, the haze was still there. As I passed through and around each set of mountains, I kept hoping that this would be the last of it and I could get away from it.

It was a shame really. It's beautiful country. With all the signs to "wine tasting caves," it should be renamed The Drunk Coast in line with the Ivory Coast and the Gold Coast.

I am not sure when it happened, but I finally got beyond the smoke and the haze. Now it was time to go and see some trees. I had always heard of the Redwoods–who hasn't? But to experience them is unlike anything I could imagine. The entire highway is named Redwood Highway and they dominate the landscape. Huge trunks that a half dozen people couldn't grab hand to hand around sit alongside the highway. At various points as you drive north, you see "scenic alternatives" and they are the places to really experience the forests.

With multiple paths and pull off points, I was completely alone. I stepped out of my car into solace, a quiet that goes deeper than the roots of the massive trees. There is a uniqueness to the experience. There is no hush here like the Covid inspired hush in so many states. This hush has been here for centuries. Maybe even eons.

There are really some great spots along the PCH where the redwoods go down to the water. You are following the coast almost the entire way. It opens up into coves and beaches here and there. My goal was Eureka, but the real treasure to me was Crescent. I think it's the northernmost town in California along the PCH. But that was a far as I got and then I turned east.

With the silvery moon huge on the horizon, I started driving what I thought was northeast. It wasn't. The twisting roads weren't done with me yet. The moon was in front of me, then to my right, to my left and even behind me a few times as I twisted my way into Oregon.

As the sunlight disappeared, and the silvery light of the moon spread throughout the deep forests, the drive became magical. There was a little bit of regret as I passed the cutoff roads to Crater Lake and other things, and a little bit of fear as I saw a huge something or another eating plants along the side of the road, but the drive became the entirety of the evening.

It's always good to have a rabbit. The rabbit is the vehicle out in front of the pack. Not only will they be pulled over first for speeding, they also help guide you through the twists and turns. And they'll see the elk before you do. I was the lone car, though, on many stretches of the drive as people pulled off to their homes and I sped towards Bend, Oregon.

Sara McLaughlin kept me company for a while on my radio. It seemed appropriate. There is a column in that alone.

You spend all your life waiting for a second chance...

Then silence for long stretches. Then Robin Ford, a rocking bluesman, to take me home. Or the Hilton in this case, finally hitting a long, straight highway where I allowed a new rabbit to take the lead.

Around the Bend; September 4, 2020

What does a guy do when waiting for his car to be serviced? If you are in Bend, Oregon, and the guy is me, you climb a butte.

"I don't know if you want to, though," said the young woman taking my keys at the Subaru dealership. It was time again for an oil change and safety inspection. "It's really hot out there." I think it was about 95. I just kept my mouth shut about the 106-degree hikes I was used to.

"I'll be fine," I replied.

Pilot Butte is an old cylinder cone from an eruption years ago. A butte, according to Wikipedia, is an isolated hill with steep and often vertical sides and a small, relatively flat top. It juts up in the middle of Bend, and, unlike San Francisco, the city built roads around it instead of just plopping one down on top of it.

Yeah, yeah, yeah: I'm bent out of shape about San Francisco. Going up in both directions offends my sensibilities. As I don't have many sensibilities, you know it must be something. But doesn't it also offend the laws of physics? Anyway...

It was an easy hike, about a mile as I circled up and around the butte that gave me a spectacular view of the entire city with the Cascade Mountains as a backdrop. There is a road that goes up as well. Bend, I was told, was a dump about 30 years ago. Now, it is a vacation destination.

The idea of Bend as a "vacation destination" doesn't offend my sensibilities but it does put a tiny bit of pressure on them. Vacation destination? What do you mean? There's no beach. But that's the PNW mentality. I was starting to hear a lot about people doing PNW things. It's about camping, hiking, kayaking, white water rafting and things like that. That's vacation. Or just getting out of the city and escaping to a cabin where quiet reigns.

Bend was nice. After 13,000 miles, it was really the first place that felt "normal." I could actually see people smiling under their masks, there was midday traffic as there was supposed to be, businesses were open for the most part and people seemed to be moving forward instead of stuck in the Covid Hibernation. Precautions were in place of course: masks, physical distancing, Plexiglas, outdoor seating, etc. Much of what I had seen in other places. But in Bend, it felt normal instead of forced.

I found out Bend completely closed for the month of March but then slowly began to reopen.

That night, I went to an iconic bar, McMenamins. I was personally upset at Bill for never mentioning he had a pub and brewery. —that's an inside joke. It's just ironic that my neighbor from Springfield, PA, in St. Francis Parish, had the same name as a pub and brewery across the continent on the site of the old St. Francis School. Okay, okay: things like that tickle me.

One of the things Oregon is known for is craft breweries. McMenamins did not disappoint. I had a local favorite: a Ruby, a red ale. Two actually, with another local favorite: an elk burger. Great combination.

At the pub, I started talking to a couple. That was another thing: people willing to chat. Fantastic couple. They were from Portland and were out here to escape the city. It was another thing that pushed at my sensibilities. He was my age and was considering quitting his career. We talked about it. Money and security keep us in place. But should it? What really does lie beyond the next bend?

The entire thing also made me a bit sad to be honest. His wife (or partner?) was urging him to quit. I checked out their Instagram account. If he decided to make the move, he was going to have a cheering section, his best friend, and all her support. I wonder what is going to happen to me.

But then it was off down the road the next day, west along the scenic route to Sisters. I just find it fascinating how these towns spring out of nowhere. It's like someone chopped a bit of forest down, threw in a road, and decided to start a town. You come across a lot of them. Sisters was one of the nicest ones, small but orderly and scenic.

I've been through a few towns that I wasn't about to stop in. But you never really know. It's one of the interesting things about driving the scenic routes and smaller roads. On the big highways, you speed past everything. Sometimes, you must jump off for gas, or a bathroom break or something. Will the exit lead you immediately into a town to get what you need, or will you have to drive a few miles to a gas station with one or two pumps?

Along the byways, you are not assured of anything. Here in Oregon, when I first arrived from California, I went miles without seeing another car. I needed gas. A small town appeared that I really didn't want to stop at but I did. I filled up, headed north again, and then a few miles up the road was a nicer, shinier town.

Sisters was just about as nice as you could ask for. I had heard about it from someone when I had jokingly said I needed a haircut. They gave me a phone number. It was a salon sitting in a little strip mall. Great haircut and I think she wanted to refuse my tip, but then she gave me directions to the Sisters Coffee Shop.

Haircuts. Such a simple thing. Back east, when I first started out, a lot of people, men and women, were shaving their heads because they couldn't get a haircut. Salons were closed. My friend, Christina, had been cutting my hair for over 15 years. Her place was closed for 14 weeks. She was finally able to go back to work in late June, but only at 25% capacity.

I remember a meme on Facebook that was floating around. It is a picture of a hooker leaning against a car, talking to a guy.

"I'll do anything you want for $50," the woman says.

The guy replies, "Can you cut my hair?"

The drive from Sisters to Salem, where I picked up the speedway of Route 5 (the west coast version of 95, running from Canada to Mexico) was another lesson about the scenic byways. Sometimes you win and sometimes you get stuck. East Oregon is the high desert. Beautiful country, the roads twisting you down thousands of feet, that I had plenty of time to enjoy because there was no way to pass the cars and trucks in front of me.

Gorgeous day for a drive though. The windows down, the air conditioning off, and not cursing that much about the people in front of me. The thrill of finally getting ahead of the truck and having the road to myself for a dozen miles—only to catch up with the next pack. When I finally hit Route 5, I was ready for some speed.

Perception and Circles; September 5, 2020

Portland: it's not what you think!

There is rioting in Portland. Peaceful demonstrations began across the country in May over the murder of George Floyd by the police in Minneapolis, Minnesota. Things got ugly in Portland and continued regularly through October. There were numerous incidents of arson, looting, vandalism, and injuries during nighttime protests. There was one incident I recall where protesters tried to board up the police station and set fire to it, with people inside.

The news and social media would have you think the entire city was burning to the ground. It is like when I went to the Big Island of Hawai'i one year. There was a volcano erupting. Everybody was freaking out that I was going.

1) Volcanoes have been erupting in Hawai'i for millions of years.

2) I WANTED to see the volcano erupting and the lava flow. It took an easy three-mile hike and then a treacherous two-mile hike to get there so I could play with the lava.

I wasn't planning on playing with lava here in Portland.

There are a lot of similarities, though, between Portland and that time in Hawai'i. The Big Island lost big money in revenue from tourists that were afraid to go. I saw this interesting graphic that I passed around on Facebook.

What people perceive: the entire island was erupting and on fire.

What was really happening: a tiny little piece of the island was erupting and had lava flows running through it. Like I mentioned, I had to work hard to get to it.

I wasn't sure about the whole Portland thing, everybody writing to me was freaking me out, so I called a friend who lives in Portland to get the real situation. Lance explained it was only downtown, and only at night. As long as I stayed out of there, I would be fine. Like I said: I wasn't planning on playing with lava here, so I heeded his advice. It's a shame, though. I heard from a lot of people that downtown Portland was beautiful.

I'm an equal opportunity adventurer, hiker and explorer. As much as I love the hikes through mountains and national parks, I equally love driving and hiking through cities. Just the drive through Portland was exciting for me. I love the bridges and highways, the overpasses and rivers. How the engineers layer the highways on top of each other to create the ramps and underpasses. Portland's highways are more twisty than any other city I've been through. I like that.

Portland is small as far as cities go. I'm staying southwest, in Tigard, and I can make the drive to Northeast Portland in 20 minutes. Of course, it took me 40 minutes because I went at the wrong time and hit traffic. Encountering traffic was a rare event. My GPS did pull me off the highway and I am pretty sure I was driving in downtown.

Coffee first, coffee always. Extracto Coffee Roasters. Not too bad. Not too bad at all. Portland is known for, among other things, its coffee, craft beers, and there are more universities than I can count. I also heard--through conversations--that it also has the most strip clubs per area than any other US city (all closed).

Portland is also known as the human trafficking capital of the US, so women must be especially careful.

Portland is also where I had my new batch of Hawaiian Kona sent. Yes, I am having my coffee supply sent to various addresses around the country. Will ten pounds be enough to make it back to Philly or will I be bothering someone else along my route? Will I need the coffee to bribe my way into Canada? Eh, it's tough being me sometimes.

Tigard, where I am staying and where I had my coffee sent, is home to a friend of mine. Lance owns Excel Orthodontic Lab. He is also the person who was voted in to replace me as president of the professional association I founded. I felt I took the association as far as I could take it but it was time for me to step away. He'll be launching the AOLP v2.0, Orthodontic Resource Group, so I'm helping with that while I'm here.

I founded the association because it needed to be done. Technology swamped my industry causing it to change like no other time in its history, over 100 years. It created a new reality and small labs were struggling, dying. Predators began to circle. I didn't have the time or money to do it but then a friend and then an acquaintance killed themselves.

First, I established a Facebook group to begin to disseminate information. It now has over 1,000 members. Then, I began taking calls and spending hours on the phone with struggling labs. Then, I put a big, red "X" on my back for the predators to take the heat off the other labs. Aye, I'm Philly and Infantry and am always up for a fight. Then came the conferences where I really got into trouble: schmoozing, cajoling, bullying, threatening, being threatened, and just generally trying to make everybody play nice with each other and pay for memberships and sponsors.

It took off and I was now known around the world. Yeah, things might have been easier on me if I had just kept my mouth shut but that's always been a problem of mine.

I've been staying close to the city because of work and a young lady I met at Extracto Coffee Rosters, Joey, suggested I visit the Grotto. It's a place of sanctuary in northeast Portland, officially, "The Grotto, the National Sanctuary of Our Sorrowful Mother, a Roman Catholic Ministry of the Order of Friar Servants of Mary." It's an amazing, quiet place. Peaceful and serene. The city outside seems to disappear.

The ground level holds a huge open-air church. There are services regularly. Then, you take an elevator about 10 stories up to the grotto and sanctuary. One of the first places you go is the sanctuary house. You walk into reverie. It holds one of 12 official bronze statues, replicas, of Michelangelo's Pieta.

The original Pieta is housed in St. Peter's Basilica in Vatican City. It depicts Jesus on the lap of his mother, Mary, after the Crucifixion. Thoughts were tugging at me while I was read the description of Pieta. I could feel the undertow. Pieta is an Italian word for pity, sorrow or compassion. It can also signify an act of mercy. Mercy seems to crop up a lot wherever I go.

The Grotto is a beautiful place. Like the Temple grounds in Salt Lake City, there is just an unpressured welcoming. There is a walking path, with very few people on it due to the times, that takes you through an amazing landscape with plenty of benches to just sit and reflect. There are a few shrines donated by various parishes. One shrine I knew from growing up in SW Philly: St. Mary of Czestochowa, the patron saint of Poland.

I think the people who wrote about the Grotto put it best, so very apt at this time especially with what is going on in Portland and across the United States. It is from almost 100 years ago.

On May 29, 1924, three thousand people gathered for the first Mass and dedication of the Sanctuary of Our Sorrowful Mother. At the blessing, Archbishop Alexander Christie offered this prayer:

"Let this be a sanctuary of peace for all peoples of the earth and surely in this day a sanctuary is needed. Torn with differences, strife, and grief, the world needs sanctuary where the human spirit can seek peace and consolation."

Outside the Bubble; September 8, 2020

People holding hands. It's not easy being a solo traveler and especially so during Covid. When it hit, we not only retreated into Covid Hibernation but also into our Covid Bubbles. My stepfather has his neighbors and his Social Distancing Club. Friends cozied up with their families and couples expanded it to small groups of friends. My Pop was torn away from his daily routines and isolated himself inside of his house.

Elbow and fist bumps just don't cut it. I'm a natural hugger. I'm a talker and explorer. I enjoy striking up conversations with random people. I still do. I still try at least. But physical distancing makes it tough, as well as the ever-present threat of Covid. Strangers tend to remain strangers nowadays.

And that's why I almost got tased in Portland. How much of a wallop do those things pack? Is it any worse than what I did to myself trying to do electrical work? I almost found out.

When Justine texted me that her sister was doing an outdoor art show in Portland, I was excited to meet her. I didn't even know Justine had a sister. Portland has an open-air fair every Saturday and Sunday on the waterfront. They are slowly starting to open it back up. This was Erin's first time there since it closed for Covid.

I finally made it to the fair. I've always said that Dallas is the absolute worst for GPS. They lost their #1 spot to Portland. I swear my GPS stuttered! It did! (I stutter so I am allowed to say things like that.) There are just so many roads on top of roads and a dozen different ways to get anywhere. Streets look like on-ramps and on-ramps look like streets. I got rerouted a half dozen times. I finally made it to the waterfront, though, and nothing was burning down. There was a very nice open-air fair going on. Everybody had masks and were maintaining their distance. I masked up and found Erin.

Interesting art. Somebody to talk to! She quit all her jobs about a year and a half ago and started doing art, like her sister, full time. Erin, like everybody else I spoke to in Portland, was really surprised by everybody else's surprise that the entire city was not burning down.

I don't know anything about art, but I liked it. She has a huge range, from the fun and irreverent to some really unique stuff. Famous women sticking their tongues out seems to be a thing these days. Erin has a thing for buffaloes, "almost mystical creatures" she told me. She also shares a certain quality with her sister, Justine. There is just an adorableness and presence about her that as soon as I was near, I wanted to hug her. A great, big bear hug. Which may have gotten me tased—you just really don't know what women are packing these days.

But there is that whole Covid thing so I kept myself in check.

That evening, I got another treat. From a friend's sister I had no idea existed to a cousin I never knew existed. My Pop reached out to me to tell me about my cousin.

Yes, West Coast: there is another Gajewski out here. There was some debate on Facebook over what level of cousin he is, but he's my grandfather's brother's grandson. Charles is about my age and I liked him immediately. He was wearing a Led Zeppelin t-shirt. Then, another treat: he's also a gear head, has an awesome Challenger, and took me for a ride on those twisty Oregon roads the right way.

I had this big plate of Polish food for lunch at the waterfront and then some equally good German fare at a place Charles took me for dinner. And, of course, the flight of beers. Aye, I wasn't driving for once.

But it was nice to just talk. It's such a small world. We talked family, music (he's a metal head with far more knowledge that me) and he was telling me about his car driving group. His bubble I guess.

Portland is a bustling town. People doing what people do. The things everybody hears about is only happening at night in a certain area of downtown. Charles told me it's a shame because downtown was beautiful once. On the flip side of things, he also told me I was being spoiled. The minor traffic I was running into was nothing compared to what it usually is. That 30-minute drive I took to Northeast Portland could take hours.

But then I went back to my hotel room, back inside my personal bubble, to get some work done.

The PNW Way; September 8, 2020

I received some good advice from a fellow traveler, Joey, as I shared a cup of coffee with her. (Outdoor seating, great company, so-so coffee.) Each city, do a city thing, a suburb thing and an out and about thing. Joey had her travels stalled. She's a student. A bit of an overachiever in my mind: majoring in jazz and psychology with a minor in neuroscience. I personally think that could be considered masochism, but then I wrote my way through most of my college classes with the tunes and coffee going. I also ended up in an orthodontic lab with over $100,000 in college debt so maybe she has the right idea?

Talking to Joey brought me back to my college days. God was I stupid. As an expediter at Nick's Miami Beach, I was making a lot of money. In season, I could walk away with $1,000 per week. In the 90's. From Vegas, and a musician, Joey wasn't doing too bad for herself. Her weekend gigs were paying for everything. Then, Covid hit. No gigs and a ton of extra time struggling to make ends meet as a customer service rep at Home Depot.

Everybody had been telling me to make a trip to the Oregon Coast, so I did. An hour and a half drive winding my way back and across the Columbia River had me at a seaside town, Astoria. One thing I forgot, and everybody failed to remind me: holiday weekend. As I hit Astoria, I hit bumper-to-bumper traffic. So, I pulled in at the nearest place to grab some lunch and liquid fortitude.

From the pier I was having lunch on, I could hear the sea lions. I could also see this long expanse of bridge that crosses the mouth of the Columbia River, connecting Oregon with Washington. I guess I do have a thing for bridges. I had to drive it. I did, and then found a turnaround point at an overlook. I headed back across and south along the Oregon Coast.

My goal was Cannon Beach. Seeing the lines of cars and crowds, I kept heading south along 101. 101 is the west coast version of the east's Route 1.

Every view, every road, is just amazing. Pictures can't tell the entire story. With the slowdown in the traffic, I did have a chance to look left and right safely. It was all amazing. I didn't want to do just a driving tour though. I wanted to do some hiking. I pulled into a half dozen parking lots. Full. So, I kept going south. Hope was dwindling. The coffee was gone. Then…

Kismet? I finally found a parking spot as someone else was pulling out. I had no idea where I was but I stopped. It didn't matter how long the trail was, I was going. I traded my driving shoes for the fancy hiking shoes I picked up in Moab, loaded the backpack with some water, and set off into the woods along the Cape Falcon Trail on Rockaway Beach. It's a 4-mile one way trail that brings you to an overlook on the cliffs.

I lost my favorite mask somewhere on the trail! Then, I lost my damn hat! My "Infantry" cap I bought special for this trip, along with an "Infantry" bumper sticker for my car. It's the state of the country. A Subaru Outback screams, "liberal." I tried to offset it a bit with the Infantry cap and bumper sticker.

But there was my Infantry cap. The winds are strong at the cliffs. It was ripped off my head and went floating down. I offered some kid $50 to get it for me, saying it was the patriotic thing to do. A very angry mother hugged her six-year-old to her and said that was not a very nice thing to say.

The view from the cliffs overlooking the Pacific Ocean was amazing. The clouds were moving fast and seemed so close I felt like I could reach out and grab them, that if I could only reach a few inches higher, I could play with them like a wet, white cotton candy.

There was also something I needed to do. I didn't want to do it, but it was time.

The emptying of my home had been a purge of my past. I was still holding on to a piece of it, though: my wedding ring. I was still officially married. I wore the ring long after I asked my wife for a divorce and then I always kept it in my pocket after I finally did take it off. It was the only piece of jewelry I had ever worn in my life. I still remember the day I put the ring on. "Forever" seemed like such an easy thing. For months, and every once in a while after for over ten years, my thumb would find it and rub across the smooth, titanium surface with the three grooves. Now, at the oddest times, my thumb finds the emptiness, skin and a callus from work.

It was an amicable separation with my wife, never any ugliness. There was no cheating or fighting or abuse. We would still talk from time to time while I was on the road. Our last conversation had been a few days before when I was making my way to the butte in Bend.

A thought had been on my mind for a couple thousand miles. I had asked both my business partner and my wife for a divorce after thinking about it for a long time. Over a year. I hadn't felt I had a partner at work or at home. I thought, maybe, that it was all wrapped up together: the exhaustion, depression, working too much and that my wife and I just hadn't tried hard enough.

I slipped the ring on my finger one last time on the cliff, rubbing the smooth titanium with my thumb like I had done for so many years, finding the grooves.

"No," she had said. "The way my friend talks about her husband is the way it should be, and it is not that way between us."

I had started to cry in a tunnel in Bend, Oregon, sitting on the side of a bike path with joggers and bikers passing me. It was ironic because it was still the way spoke about her. Such an incredible woman, so beautiful. There had been so much hope, so much promise. But the world had moved on and we had as well.

The long, lonely miles can make you think too much. Doubts can begin to transform into almost certainties. Rights can begin to shimmer into wrongs and wrongs into rights.

I slipped the ring from my finger. It followed my Infantry cap down the cliffs. I watched it bounce on rock a few times and then it disappeared into the Pacific Ocean. The largest ocean in the world. It could swallow my ring easily. But could it swallow the regrets?

I thought about endings. Being alone can be hard. I also thought of the quote attributed to Robin Williams, about how he always thought that being alone was the worst thing but then he found that being made to feel alone, while surrounded by people, was worse.

I stared out into that expanse for a while longer and then continued my journey. I had to make my way back, first by finding my way back to my car.

I'm not very good at one-way paths. I don't like them. I like loops. I had passed one slope on the way to the cliffs and had given it a look. It had to be an old runoff or rockslide. On my way back, I gave it another look. It looked promising. Four miles back the way I came or this. It was kind of a path down? --if it was covered in snow and you were a downhill skier. Black diamond. I think I was only four to five hundred yards up. And I did have those new fancy hiking shoes.

Then, a common theme of my life popped into my head. "What's the worst that could happen?"

Aye, I made it and that's the important thing. I think I scared the living hell out of a couple that thought they hiked all the way to the end of Rockaway Beach for some "alone" time.

"Beware falling rocks," I called down as I slid and then climbed the last 100 yards. Slowly. Very slowly. To allow them time to gather themselves. And put some clothes on.

It was worth it, the fall/slide/hike down to the beach. It gave me a unique perspective of where I had been and the views from the beach were spectacular, something I would have missed had I just made the return trip along Cape Falcon Trail.

I put the cliffs behind me, the ocean to my right, a forest to my left, and trudged back along the edge of the surf to the exit for Rockaway beach and go looking for my car. I kept driving south, trying to avoid the easy routes back to Portland. I think a lot of people had the same idea as I was stuck in bumper-to-bumper traffic for an hour.

Oregon is beautiful. It's a state that defines the PNW way. Hiking, camping, kayaking, biking, or just long drives through amazing scenery. The greens jump out at you with each mountain looking like it had been manicured. It's a place to get lost in and find yourself in—if that's your thing. Or just enjoy nature.

I did the city. I did the suburb. I did the out and about. I also did some work. But it was time to start heading north, go fully into Washington. Now knowing it was a holiday, I planned my trip a little bit to avoid traffic. The ride to Seattle is about three hours. I was planning on an eight-hour drive to avoid traffic.

Not that I was able to avoid traffic, but I did try.

A Woman's Temper; September 9, 2020

There was a slight pang as I left Oregon. Actually, there were many pangs as I have no idea when I left Oregon and entered Washington. Sometimes, there will be a big sign saying, "Welcome to This State." On the back roads and byways, you see a cow or something.

There was a lot more in Oregon I wanted to see. They were all just short drives from Portland. Of course, with close to 14,000 miles now, anything less than five hours is a short drive for me. I was warned that some of the hikes were closed due to Covid, others due to fires. I didn't want to bother with holiday traffic so it was time to head north and finish the west coast.

My first stop was Mt. St. Helens. There was a lot more driving in what I now consider the "Pacific style." That's one of the things that struck me about California and Oregon: their coastline. On the east coast, coastline means flat. In Florida alone, you have close to 66,000 square miles just above sea level. The west coast isn't like that at all. The hills and mountains jut right up against the ocean.

I do love the driving out here. The winding roads, passes and regular signs telling you the elevation. After I left Route 5, firmly and without doubt in Washington, I gradually made my way up to Mt. St. Helens.

To jog your memory--or for those who might not know--it blew in 1980. Scientists predicted in 1978 that it would blow before 2000. On my birthday in 1980, March 20th, there was a slight earthquake heralding what would be a massive eruption on May 18th. At the time, it was the worst natural disaster to ever hit the United States. Logging interests were at odds with geologists and nobody was evacuated. 57 people died when it blew with the entire southern face crumbling and 540 million tons of ash exploded into the air.

On the drive up to Mt. St. Helens, you can see what the area probably looked like. Through the mountains and passes, all the trees look like they have been manicured on the mountains. Broad stretches of logged lands form straight lines along the tree lines. That was a bit more than 40 years ago.

The viewing area has spectacular views of the mountain and surrounding lands. It's interesting to me because it is as if I got to see the land naked. In other viewing areas and scenic overlooks, trees typically cover everything so I only got brief glimpses of rivers and streams and the layers of the land itself. In the area below Mt. St. Helens, that covering is stripped away. New growth has begun but the land is just scantily clad.

Off in the distance, I could see two lakes: Spirit Lake and Cold Water Lake. Hiking trails go to both, but I wanted to get back on the road. The left knee is fully recovered but now the right leg was starting to bother me.

My GPS told me the direct drive into Seattle was bogged down in holiday traffic so I took a more indirect route. A few hours out of my way? I really hate traffic. But I passed by the entrance to Mt. Rainer State Park and swung along its western side. I was supposed to be on the eastern side but my GPS couldn't tell the difference between a road and a dirt path with bars across it.

And then I hit the holiday traffic anyway. I made it to Bellevue, Washington, just to the east of Seattle.

Now to see what Washington holds for me. I see lots of lakes, bridges, rivers, ferries and islands in my future.

Clearless in Seattle; September 12, 2020

Clearless in Seattle? Or clueless in Seattle? And sleepless. I haven't been sleeping well. Can you get jet lag while driving?

But I finally jumped off the highways and bridges and went downtown. I don't think Mother Nature enjoyed my joke about women and Mt. St. Helens. As soon as I started across the bridge, I knew it was a bad day for sightseeing. A blanket of smoke had been thrown over the city. Oregon is on fire and parts of eastern Washington, some arson and some Mother Nature. Walking outside now is almost as bad as when I was in Colorado, worse than stepping into a backyard bonfire.

It was weird. I was talking about it with some friends that had me over for dinner a couple nights before. The smoke came in between one moment and the next. When I first arrived at my hotel, it was clear. I took a long walk down to a restaurant. I walked back and everything was still fine. I went to my room, traded my shoes for my slippers, and went out into the courtyard. There was a hazy smoke. I thought the hotel had the fire pit on and went in and asked them to turn it off. They told me it wasn't on.

It happened that quick. And it has gotten worse since.

My body told me to slow down and rest and now the universe was telling me to get back on the road. I'm skipping my last night here and heading north in the morning.

But Seattle. It really is a shame. It is such a beautiful and interesting city. The closest I can come to describing it is a mixture between Philadelphia and Venice. It has the older city feel and organization, and then with all the waterfronts there are just so many walking and biking paths, footbridges, and art.

There are tiny little neighborhoods tucked away and hidden places. I was at a coffee house in what seemed to be a rundown neighborhood under a highway. I watched as many expensive cars came from around the back of this huge, old red brick warehouse type building next to the highway. I walked around and found a row of shops, an underground parking garage and spoke to a local. There were open studios inside: the warehouse had been converted.

If I had walked the waterfront on any other day, I was told I would have seen houses all along the other bank. I just saw smoke on the other shore, and, by the end of my walk, I couldn't even see halfway across the water. Of course, I went to the Space Needle, but I didn't bother going up. With all the smoke, the wait seemed pointless. But I did find a great sushi restaurant, again, in what seemed to be a rundown neighborhood.

The noise from the city and highways was interesting to me. In some cities I am in, the noise disappears in certain places. In others, it's just annoying. Here in Seattle, whether I was near the buildings or walking along the waterfront, it just kind of blended into a white noise background if that makes any sense?

I liked Seattle. I had seen a lot of it from my drives and more when I was visiting friends. And Seattle seems to be doing Covid right. Most states suck at Covid and the outdoors. Washington doesn't. Along the waterfront, there was a sign and others like it. "A crowded park means a closed park so keep it moving." It's like "it's up to you; play nice and you can have nice things."

Covid testing was spot on as well. I did a drive through and had that nasal swab shoved up my nose and tickling my frontal lobe again. I was emailed a questionnaire, a satisfaction survey. What can you really write about a procedure that makes you look forward to any other uncomfortable procedure? I gave them five stars. I dealt with four people driving up and through a converted firehouse with three lanes. Every single person made me laugh and smile, even the one jabbing the thing up my nose. They made me feel comfortable in a way the other testing center had not.

It did make me wonder about something that I really need to talk to a doctor about. My friends who had me over for dinner said a friend of theirs went to a drive through where they did a self-test. There was no discomfort, my friends were told. Easy peasey. My test, done by somebody else, was just as uncomfortable as the first one. It makes me wonder about the self-tests.

I know, for a fact, that the test done on me went way past the point that I could have done on my own. How far do you have to go? What do the swabs capture? Were my testers sadists? Am I just a sissy? Or are the self-tests pointless?

Aye, I've shoved things up my nose before. I was a little boy once. The depth of the swab went well past the point that I could have tolerated doing it on my own. It begs the question.

[Question later answered. Short answer: The self-tests are okay but not ideal; they will not catch the virus as quickly.]

I'll be back to Seattle. The waterways and Olympic Peninsula are on my bucket list. But it's time to be in motion again. The car is repacked along with the additions of a full sized spare and a 5-gallon gas jug that I'll fill up before I hit the Canadian border on Sunday or Monday. I think I need another Covid test as well as I don't think the one I got will be valid when I get to Alaska–it needs to be within three days.

I have some hard driving in front of me. After tomorrow. After, hopefully, seeing something I have always wanted to see: orcas in their natural environment.

I saw a meme once that said one thing is common to every household in America and possibly the world: a junk drawer. We don't know what is inside of it but can't seem to clean it out. Well, repacking my car for my drive to Alaska, I realized I have a junk bag. I'm with you America. From the road.

Orcas in the Mist; September 13, 2020

Okay, okay: it was "orcas in the smoke," but "mist" sounds better. A friend of mine from the east coast, Mary, sent me a graphic showing that the west coast now has the worst air quality in the world due to all the fires. I was hoping that driving a little north would get me beyond them. Nope. I went to this tiny town called Anacortes, about an hour north of Seattle. I was hoping the "fog" I saw during the early morning drive would burn off as the sun climbed higher. No such luck.

Anacortes was smokey but it did hold a few things in store for me. One thing on my bucket list was seeing orcas in the wild. I jumped on a whale watching boat that was recommended to me. I wasn't disappointed. About an hour into the trip, we found a small pod of orcas. It was beautiful. I have been fascinated with orcas for as long as I can remember. A "killer whale," or apex predator, they have never been known to kill or harm humans, except in captivity. Seeing them slicing through the water outside of a theme park or in a movie? It woke the little kid in me.

Island Adventures offers a guarantee, and they came through. In between really bad jokes, the naturalist was full of information and he knew the pod well. This was their territory.

These inland pods are small hunting groups, led by the oldest female. The males stay with mom for the rest of their lives, except to mingle with other pods and try to catch the attention of a mate. The bond between mother and son is so strong that the sons have a 60% chance of dying when the mother dies.

198

The male was the biggest. There was also another female besides mom, not yet at the age to start reproducing and forming her own pod, and a baby who was not even hunting yet.

The smoke forced another surprise on me. I haven't run into too many other solo travelers. But there was Abby. She was behind me in line boarding the boat. The captain was asking everybody where they were from. When she said "Baltimore," I tripped going up the steps. She was out here to do some camping and hiking but the smoke forced her to go whale watching instead. I found out that there are some incredible hikes close by. For her sake, I hope the weather report is right and it clears up by Monday.

It was nice just talking to someone. It can be odd. Talking to a solo traveler is different than talking to a couple or a group. She does a lot of traveling for her photography. We chatted about different places we had been and shared pictures. We even took off our masks but kept a few feet apart. Abby was traveling alone by choice. Her husband and kids were back east.

Something else that was nice? I was back in my comfort zone with my jacket and Irish cap in chillier weather. I always feel like I look like an ass wearing warm weather clothes, shorts and such. I think I can carry the cap and jacket look fairly well. All I needed was something I left behind in storage of course: my boots. How chilly will it get before I head back east? I think I'll be buying a pair in Alaska. I like my own boots but buying a new pair will be cheaper than flying home.

The harbor itself was nice as well. I got there early after yet another night of little sleep. I wandered around first before going to find a cup of coffee. In a rare event, I took a picture I enjoyed. The Lady of the Sea, a monument in the harbor. It is a life-sized bronze statue of a woman and her child awaiting the return of her seafaring husband. The smoke created an eerie backdrop to everything. Interesting views of the harbor and islands, both walking and from the boat.

After the tour, I went and grabbed another cup of coffee and made my way a little bit further north into Bellingham, about 20 miles from the Canadian border.

The entire time I was driving south, west, then east, then west again, then north, etc., I was thinking that Seattle was the gateway to Canada. Seattle even calls itself that. It's a crock. Seattle is a couple hours away from Canada. The Peace Arch is in Blaine and I'll be trying to cross in Sumas. They are the true gateways to Canada from Washington.

Gateway or locked door? I'm still wondering if Canada will let me in. There was the Alaskan Travel Loophole, where Americans were permitted into Canada to travel to Alaska but with restrictions. Canada cracked down on it after finding Americans not playing by the rules. Go figure. I wrote and called the Canadian border agency numerous times, but all I received back were articles that said different things. I figure the only way I'll know is by going and trying tomorrow morning with my car packed for the long drive.

If I do get in, according to the articles, I'll be restricted to a certain road and can only stop for gas, sleeping in my car, and drive through food. It's about a 30-hour drive to Alcan Border. Going by air or ferry just don't seem right to me—though Bellingham is the port for the ferry, a 3-4 day trip up the coast with numerous stops in Alaskan communities that you cannot get to any other way.

I'll find out soon enough. I'll see about getting another Covid test tomorrow as the one I got in Seattle doesn't meet the three-day requirement for Alaska. Tomorrow's might. Or else they might not let me in. Or I'll have to get tested and isolate until I get the results back.

After all the awful jokes by the naturalist on the whale watching tour, I went up to him. One of the things he told us about the orcas is that they are very indecisive. The pod can be going along in a certain direction and then, for no reason that anybody can figure out, they'll start going in a different direction.

"I know why they are so indecisive," I said to him after making sure nobody was around to hear me.

"Really," he asked in that tone of an expert talking to an upstart wannabe.

"Yes," I replied. "You not only mentioned that they are very indecisive, but they are also always led by the oldest female. There ya go."

He looked around quickly, smothered a laugh, and then said, "I'm never saying that out loud."

But I'm getting some rest. I'm nervous for the first time on this trip. Will Canada let me in? I've been trying not to put too much thought into it but? We'll see.

Sulking in Idaho; September 14, 2020

…and then the fire alarm in the hotel went off in the middle of the night.

It was just one of those days. But I'll take it. I wish things had turned out differently, but there was good mixed in with the bad. Like the very nice Washington State LEO who pulled me over for speeding. Yes, he was giving me a ticket–that I deserved--but he was so nice about it. Then, after taking care of business, he was kind enough to answer a few questions about the area I had been driving through.

But let's rewind.

I was up bright and early for the moment of truth. Would Canada let me in? It had been bothering me for 14,000 miles. It's even why I made the trip the way I did, going through the hot south in the middle of the summer and then working my way up north, in the hope that the fluid Covid situation would change. It just got worse.

Idealistically, I gave myself a 50/50 chance to qualify for the "essential traveler" the Canadians needed to allow me in. Writer? Working on my book? Realistically, it was 10%. I drove up, was in Canada, asked to wait, and then asked to pull my car over and step inside. I waited in a nice office for about 15 minutes as the border patrol discussed me.

Denied!

I was also informed I was put on "a list" in case I tried to make it through again.

So, I went back through US Customs, found a parking lot in Washington, and sulked. I had no idea what to do. I had bought a full-sized spare, a couple extra cases of water for the trip, food, and was just so in the moment that they would let me pass that I was now completely lost. It was like that feeling of stepping down onto another step--only the step is not there. So, I sulked. I didn't get angry, kick anything, or anything else like that. I just slumped against the hood of my Outback and had myself a nice little sulk.

At that point, I just wanted to get the hell out of Washington and off the West Coast. Covid is unlike anything we have seen before. The fires out west are also unlike anything that has been seen. The air quality on the west coast is now the worst in the world with a thick layer of smoke covering everything. I wanted to go somewhere, anywhere, to get away from the smoke.

I knew from talking to other travelers that an incredible park was on my route, so I made my way to the Cascade Mountains and Diablo Lake. There was a loop that went through the mountains and I took it. There were also some great hikes but I passed on them. I was still sulking and I could smell, taste, and feel the smoke, see the misty haze lying across the land at every elevation.

My GPS took me to the lookout point. Being there bothered me. I found the lookout point by using Instagram and saw pictures of a gorgeous lake. I could see the possibilities shown in the pictures but my reality was a hazy, obscured view. I spent a few minutes there and then got back on the road.

The road eventually poured me into a nice little town where I was able to grab lunch and sit for a while, with GPS, and figure out my next step. The route I chose would take me along northeastern Washington towards Spokane and then into Idaho, where a friend has a dental lab. After all these years of people thinking I make teeth, I would finally have the opportunity to see how teeth were made.

It was an eerie drive. Really nice towns kept popping up and then I got further east and started to run into something that was familiar to me but also very different: desolation. I began driving through the area where fires had swept through.

It was familiar to me because I've seen it in Hawai'i on the Big Island, where lava flows lave a darkened wasteland. In Washington, it was the same, but blackened trees dotted the landscape. The earth was black with spots of light brown that was the dirt underneath pushing its way through. Green popped out at you here and there and trees along with houses that had been spared. I even spotted a herd of cows running through a blackened pasture. But there was still the ever-present blanket of smoke.

When the LEO pulled me over, I asked about it all. He told me the fires had swept through the way that I came but I was heading towards a new one. In a few miles, I passed a fire camp.

My day ended passing through Spokane, crossing into Idaho, and finding a hotel for the night. It's just your average tourist hotel sitting on the river. The smoke I was hoping to escape was as thick as ever with the Spokane weather reports saying it was going to be here for a while.

My evening ended with a truly great meal–and good company. The new chef at the Red Lion Hotel is doing amazing things. I ordered my favorite because, well, it had been one of those days: Shepherd's Pie. What I got was not Shepherd's Pie, but the chef's take on it. It was incredible. And then a little buddy, a puppy, came up to join me–he got a piece of the flank steak.

But the question still bounced in my head: what do I do? I'm tired of smoke. It looks like the smoke is drifting far to the east and Yellowstone National Park is affected. Not seeing a clear Washington state bothered me. There were a few hikes I missed. Do I go back to Seattle and fly to Alaska? Do I continue east and fly there from another point?

At a loss, I finally went to bed.

And then the fire alarm went off in the middle of the night.

All About the Smoke; September 15, 2020

Smoke is all that you see. When I woke up this morning, there was ash falling on my car. Unless you are here, experiencing it, you just can't imagine it. People are jumping on the numbers. Air quality is based upon a 0-500 system, with 0 being the best. Some parts of Oregon were 500+, off the charts. Portland is around 490.

Seattle is a bit better at 425. Post Falls, Idaho, where I was and right next to Spokane, was in the high 400's.

People were gathered around the television watching the weather channel for smoke concentrations like they do in Colorado for fires and Florida for hurricanes. It wasn't expected to get any better. After my sulk in Sumas, the drive to Idaho was really to get away from the smoke. Maybe that's what has been affecting my sleep since I arrived on the west coast? It is just depressing, that ever-constant blanket of smoke on everything, the constant smell of being close to a bonfire, everybody coughing and it just being generally miserable staying outside, especially as outside is where everybody is supposed to be.

It wasn't looking any better for me. The smoke is being pushed east by high- and low-pressure systems. I don't think I would have been able to get ahead of it. I just heard from someone that they are talking about smoke in the air on the east coast. And I WAS NOT going to Vegas—the only place in the country that seems not to be affected. Go figure.

The title for yesterday's post was my second choice. The first choice struck me as being too negative. "Where is the Reset Button?" It was an awful day as days go, but there were some positives to balance it a bit.

Then, I started thinking of whales. Orcas, but whales in general, are very indecisive. The pod I watched in Anacortes was going along in a certain direction for quite some time. After a deep dive, they came up in a completely unexpected place going in a different direction.

Mentally, standing outside of the hotel, watching ash fall on my car, I was stuck. Confused. Pushed underneath layer upon layer of smoke. A deep dive. Too deep. The Canadian border thing bothered me. The smoke-filled pictures I had taken bothered me.

Not being able to go on even one hike bothered me. The fact that I was driving into what seemed like an unknowable number of days in smoke bothered me. It all made my teeth itch.

Then it hit me: why couldn't I hit the reset button?

Most times in life, you can't. There are thousands of times I wanted to. I had resigned myself to the fact of driving through smoke, eventually making my way to a major airport like Chicago, and then flying to Alaska. Why not just drive back the four hours to Seattle? And that's exactly what I did.

I had lunch with a guy I met at a conference, an owner of a huge dental lab. I had met him and his wife at the conference in January, right before the shutdown. They were sort of expecting me, like many people. I learned early on not to give exact dates. Among other discussions, they told me about their trips to Alaska. Everybody was telling me about their trips to Alaska. He also mentioned that it was only a four-hour drive back to Seattle.

I hit "reset."

In a few hundred miles along smoke filled 90, and 4 1/2 hours, I was back at the hotel I had stayed in Bellevue. They remembered me. I checked in, stashed my stuff in the room, and got to work. I made the appointment to get my Alaskan mandated Covid test tomorrow and booked a flight on Wednesday. I reserved hotel just north of Anchorage for four nights and will wing it for Fairbanks. All I needed was a car.

The hope is that the weather will change in the next 10 days by the time I return. And something is calling me to Alaska.

But, then, something is also nudging me.

"A solo, outward journey," I wrote for my website, "necessitates an inward, intimate odyssey."

Layers upon layers. Why am I out here? There is the upper layer, the surface layer I share with everybody through social media.

It is based upon what Steinbeck wrote about in "Travels with Charley," about needing a destination, a purpose. I want to see the other states I haven't seen yet, even if it is just brief glimpses of some like Arkansas, or just along the highway like Mississippi. I wanted to share that with everybody while I took my notes chronicling this most unprecedented year in America. It gives me destinations. It gives me a purpose.

But then I dive deeper. The inward journey always had a destination and a purpose, needing no artificial construct like Steinbeck's book. I went to find teachers. And see if I could find some things in myself that I desperately needed. I wrote that staying in motion helped. Staying in motion was necessary. I have found things, pieces, in that motion that I might be able to bring back with me to be at rest.

There are paths to travel in both the worlds that I have always known. I found myself too much in this one, the world of an orthodontic lab owner. I needed to step into the other world, to at least know it still existed. Or find a way to close the door on that other world and only exist and be happy in this one. Or make the choice to pass beyond both worlds.

I lost balance decades ago. I lost clarity. I was able to make myself not think about it for a long time, dive deep into work, chores, routines and live the co-dependent's dream. Then I awoke. Everybody was so happy for me. Owning a business, married to a beautiful woman, a gorgeous home. I hadn't even realized they were so happy that I was so miserable. My three-year plan for the lab had stretched into fifteen years and I was no closer to my personal goals while I had helped others thrive and attain their goals.

I wasn't bitter at all. I was happy for them. But I had awoken to the winter of my discontent.

I found myself still shivering underneath the layers of my co-dependency. I was so damn exhausted. Years of arguing with my business partner had gotten me nowhere. Years of a growing distance between me and my wife until we were completely disconnected. I had started thinking about divorcing both of them a couple years ago. But could I give up everything I had built?

Then came the end of 2018. The lab hit a rough spot. I first went to my business partner.

"We need to do this and you need to do this to make things work." He ignored me. And stopped talking to me. I stopped paying the both of us and arranged to sell my share of the business to an employee.

I went to my wife, my life partner.

"I need help. It's going to be a rough year, but I'll be able to sell the lab at the end. Cash is going to be tight."

"Why should I help a failing business," she replied.

Then, she went on vacation. Two of them. I wiped out my 401K. When she returned from the second one, I asked her for a divorce.

He sees things differently. She sees things differently. I was going to Alaska.

I don't know if I'll find more pieces in Alaska, but I think I will. The Last Frontier. And in Wyoming, Montana, South Dakota, Wisconsin and all of the other states still yet to visit.

But on to state number 32 for the current journey. With the Covid test, airline ticket and hotel reservation, all I had to do was camp in a nice hotel by the airport until my flight. I could even park my car there for free if I stayed one night on my return.

Into the Last Frontier; September 17 – September 23, 2020

Well, that didn't go as planned. Damn Canadians. But it's not their fault and I can't blame them. I had a plan! It was a good one. As much as my car is a chaotic mess, it's home and my base of operations. It got left in a parking lot in Seattle.

When Canada first shut down their borders, they was an Alaskan Travel Loophole. I thought the Canadians were being nice about things. Americans, of course, couldn't play by the rules and screwed it up. One story that I read named Texans in particular. Not Americans, not Pennsylvanians, not Floridians. Texans. They were found all over Canada, hundreds of miles off the route and throughout the state and national parks. Canada cracked down.

As much as I like you, Texans, y'all owe me a drive to Alaska.

But that's why I found myself in the airport in Anchorage, instead of arriving by car at Alcan Border, being "tsk'ed" by a very friendly woman, Whitney, from Alaskan Airlines, who was helping me find my suitcase.

It was purple! I swore it was purple. That's the one I had in the back of my car and would carry into every hotel. I had two purple suitcases: one had my clothes and the other had my kitchen. Only, the purple one was still in my car in Seattle. My blue one made the trip, the one she had pointed to a dozen times asking, "are you absolutely sure that's not yours?"

I was unsettled as I made my way through the airport. On the verge of being pissed off. I had very bad words in my mind as I listened to the whine of other passengers. "Nitwits" was the nicest one.

Alaska had made it very easy for people to fly in. On the Alaskan travel site, I had uploaded the required trusted partner negative Covid test and my hotel information. Upon arrival, I showed them my ID, the bar code from my phone and was able to proceed right away. Even my Covid test in Seattle had been free.

"What do you mean I need a Covid test," I heard a lot of people saying as they were stopped at the security checkpoint. "It's going to cost $250 to be tested?" "I don't have my hotel's information!" "I need to isolate until I get the test results back?"

It was all on the travel site. Pack of rabble.

I didn't see my rental car, an SUV, as a shiny new toy to play with like I did the Mustang I had rented in Florida the year before. All I saw was something that was not my car, my home. It didn't have the ordered chaos, the buttons I knew, the plugs I knew, the junk bag and the dozen things I had gotten used to and needed. And I knew it was not going to drive as well as my Subaru Outback.

My journey to Alaska was not starting off very well.

It's the Texans' fault.

I needed a cup of coffee.

Elephants −coughing— in the room

Toto, we're not in Kansas anymore.

The line from "The Wizard of Oz" planted itself into my head and grew roots. Alaska's nickname is The Last Frontier and everything about the state reinforces it. There is nothing to prepare you for it. Not even the maps we've seen all our lives are accurate.

Alaska is the biggest state by far. Texas, the second biggest state, would rattle around in it. The maps we tend to see are the inset maps in a map of the continental United States. The inset map distorts perception, making Alaska seem smaller and manageable. Nothing can be further from the truth.

210

I looked it up. Alaska is about 1/5 the size of the lower 48 states. If you combined Texas, California, and Montana, it would still be smaller than Alaska. There are maps online that show Alaska superimposed on a map of the continental United States. The bulk of Alaska covers the entire heartland of America. The western islands that almost form a land bridge to Russia and the sliver that extends south along the Canadian coast, with many towns accessible only by boat or plane, make Alaska extend from Florida to Los Angeles.

Alaska makes you feel small.

Just grabbing a cup of coffee and standing outside a sporting good's store (to buy a number of things I left in Seattle) slaps you in the face. In the middle of Anchorage, Alaska's largest city, doing the ordinary and mundane, you look up and majestic mountains are there. I would write that they stare back at you but they don't. They don't care you exist. They just are and you have to get over that fact.

Nope, I'm not in Kansas anymore. – I haven't even been to Kansas yet.

Humbled, I was also free.

Sitting there on a bench, sipping some really good coffee, an elephant came up and sat in my lap. "It's okay, Chris," it said. "We can talk about it now."

Ever present in my planning for my odyssey, as I packed and made plans, as I drove and went to hotel rooms, as I hiked and explored cities and parks, as I stopped at gas station after gas station, there was an elephant in the room. There was the memory of a 25-year-old madness, an insanity. There was my greatest sin, my ultimate crime. My arrogance.

The simple diagnosis for my mother was bi-polar disorder. Even a description I once heard did not even scratch the surface:

"bi-polar disorder with schizophrenic and paranoid tendencies." In an apartment outside of Philadelphia, 25 years ago, I had watched my mother's madness evolve into a terrifying insanity.

The short story, that I can now tell as she has passed, is she contracted herpes. Only, she didn't contract herpes. Her mania demanded that she have herpes so she could punish herself and so, despite multiple doctors and multiple tests proving that she didn't have herpes, having herpes became her reality.

Her madness induced herpes evolved. I had a front row seat as I tried to save her. It was fascinating—though terrifying. Mom was a mental monster, with an IQ close to or even surpassing Einstein. Her madness smothered her intelligence and herpes became something that covered her body. Then, it evolved into something she could spread by simply touching someone or even being in the same room. At the end, she was an instrument of Satan sent to spread disease.

Within my memories, the long elephant trunk wrapped around my shoulder. Was I spreading disease everywhere I went? Was I a super spreader? Had I killed people? Not enough was known about Covid, but I knew I could be asymptomatic while being contagious.

With the negative Covid test, and with Alaska's handling of the pandemic, the elephant and questions could become smaller things. They could be the baby elephant in the video I saw, climbing into a person's lap to play with them.

I read something somewhere that said elephants like people. They think we are cute.

Ends of the Road

Anchorage is a grid like Philadelphia, with numbered streets and lettered streets, but it is massive. Anchorage makes me think of a ranch style house as opposed to a multi-level house of other cities: both share the same square footage, but the rancher has a bigger footprint.

There are no raised roadways in Anchorage or in Alaska. There can't be. I later found out that Alaska replaces all the roads every three years, so if you arrive in warmer months, there will be road construction. It has something to do with permafrost. It raises parts of the roads so they can feel like a roller coaster driving down them. The bumps can get bad. I was told that if you hit the right one at the right speed, you'll snap an axel.

I had no idea what I was doing, so I made reservations at a small hotel about an hour north of Anchorage in Wasilla, straight up Alaskan Route 1. I was just trying to ease myself into the trip, find coffee, and get the feel of the loaner car...

...and I'm struggling. The quick hits on Facebook and Instagram were easy to write. But I didn't have time to write columns. Even going back through my website, I'm still overwhelmed by the experience. Alaska is overwhelming. Is it home? What's back east for me besides the end of this journey? But Alaska. In the moment...

But which way do I go? Late September means winter is coming and the weather starts getting trickier. No snow yet, but cold rain. Alaskans, I was told, ignore the weather. I don't. Another woman I met at the motel suggested I go south. The weather reports for Anchorage, Fairbanks and Homer agreed with her, so I made the drive down to Anchorage, stopping again at Cabela's for the warmer gear I needed, and then I grabbed another great cup of coffee from these drive up stands that I was told popped up all over the place in the 90's, and headed south—but I didn't get far.

Byron Glacier awaited me, one of the last remnants of the last ice age. Just a bit south of Anchorage, I got to the trailhead and it was pouring rain, cold. I got about a minute into the trail before I realized jeans would not work and another trip to Cabela's was in order. So, instead, I went up to the end of the road. One of many "ends of the roads" I encountered in The Last Frontier.

Whittier sits on Prince William Sound at the head of the Passage Canal. Population 272, mostly all who live in one building, the Begich Towers. There is a single lane tunnel to get to the old Cold War Army Base. It's unlike any tunnel I've driven through. It shares it with train tracks and goes up about 3 1/2 miles. There's no finesse to it, just a hole punched through solid rock.

Whittier is a small town with a few inns, places to just get away. It is a great little place with a good wharf. I drove around a little bit and then had dinner and a beer while waiting for my turn to head back down the tunnel. The tunnel is "down" every hour on the hour and "up" on the half hour.

It is all beautiful. Alaska is the most prolific landscape artist of all time. Sun and rain, clouds and sky, snow and mists, the rising and falling of the tides, the changing of the seasons and even the rising and falling of the sun, on a canvas that can only be called majestic, makes each moment different. Each drive along a road. Even as you just sit and wait, the canvas morphs into something else that is beautiful.

I found myself in Anchorage. Again. In some hotel for the night. Then, I was at Cabela's. Again. But I was set this time! I bought the perfect waterproof pants for hiking in the rain! That I never had to use. But now off south...again...to that last remnant of the Ice Age, Byron Glacier.

It turned out to be a beautiful day with every turn in the road providing new views. The road up to the glacier is off an incredible drive along Route 1 (Seward Highway) following Turnagain Arm where there are plenty of places to stop to watch for Beluga Whales.

Back up, again, onto the road to the glacier. This time it was sunny with clouds. A one-mile hike brings you to the glacier. There are plenty of paths to keep on going higher up, but I just wandered around. I seem to be using the words "amazing and majestic" a lot, but what else can you call it?

But then I got moving. Back down to Route 1 and winding my way down to Homer on the southern tip of the Kenai Peninsula. It's a 220-mile drive from Anchorage to another "end of the road" that takes you through mountains and glaciers and then along the coast of the Cook Inlet. It was yet another one of those unplanned adventures with me having no real idea what I was doing or where I would stay. And there were plenty of stops of course.

I was told to go to this little working farm outside of Homer to find a cabin for the night. It's home to a youth hostel and a bunch of little cabins. It would be home for the night. No electricity and an outhouse, but a nice wood stove, plenty of firewood, and a chair on the front porch overlooking the beach. It was peaceful, so I made a run into town for a few snacks and then settled in for the evening.

The next morning, in dire need of coffee, I went into Homer where I found another end of the road. Route 1 ends and the ferry system begins. Along my way back north, I found something that

I had to stop and take a picture of: the westernmost point of highway in the continental United States.

But then it was time to drive north, through Anchorage again (but not Cabela's) on a 580-mile trek that would bring me to Denali State Park. It was over a 10-hour drive. As I covered the road back up to Anchorage, I passed by something I had seen before and was curious enough to stop.

Many things are like this in Alaska. You don't know what lies beyond the trees. You'll come across small communities out of nowhere, mailboxes and power lines that seem to be sitting in the middle of nowhere. About a half hour south of Anchorage is the Alaska Wildlife Conservation Center, where they take in orphans or injured animals. I thought it would be a good place to check out Alaskan wildlife without the danger of, well, death.

The big kid appeared again, with the childlike wonder and awe. There was a pack of wolves, a herd of reindeer and a black bear cub. Caribou, elk, eagles and a hawk also made the sanctuary their temporary home. My favorite was the porcupine.

I had never seen a porcupine in the wild. I think Alaskan porcupine are very different from the ones I may have encountered elsewhere. This one was huge, and she moved fast in her enclosure. When climbing on the fence, as if she was standing on her hind legs, she must have been three to four feet tall. The picture in my mind of her standing next to what I had imagined was like a pro football lineman standing next to a normal sized person. She was adorable.

Up back by Wasilla, I jumped onto Alaskan Highway Route 3 for the ride to Fairbanks. I had been warned about the drive. Boring. Lots and lots and lots of trees. I was also told that almost nobody ever goes to Denali. I drove through it.

There were more than a few people who thought Denali would be my final stop. Much like my responses to my post about Tijuana, they had read too many books and seen too many movies. I had a copy of "Into the Wild" in my car in Seattle, a book by Jon Krakauer. I shared more than just a name with Christopher Candless, aka Alexander Supertramp, the main character of an article Krakauer wrote, "Death of an Innocent," that he then expanded into a book. I was at Denali at a good time to hike my way out to the school bus where Candless had made his final camp. I had wanted to go. Someone had even given me coordinates of where she had buried something. I wanted to explore the area like people explore a pain in their mouth with their tongue.

I didn't even stop. The pull of the undertow was too strong. Maybe if I had my own car. Maybe if my father had not just sent me an article saying Alaska had just flown the bus out because too many people had died trying to get to it (it's now in Fairbanks). Maybe if the trees had seemed more welcoming.

RIP Christopher.

Courageous or foolish, I do not know. I do tend to agree, however, with his sister's interpretation, that he was a broken thing, unable to fit the pieces back together.

With the extra stops I made, it was full dark (about 9:30) three hours south of Fairbanks. I pushed through. I could have stopped at one of the many places they have for it to sleep in the car, but the Canadians didn't allow me to have my car with all my car camping gear and something a friend said in Colorado stuck in my mind.

Ben had said, "you can leave cash and anything else in your car and nobody is going to bother it. But don't leave chocolate or food. The bears know how to open doors."

I was traveling with chocolate and snacks, so I pushed on for a very rough ride through mountains in the darkness. I eventually made it to Fairbanks. With no idea what time it was.

It was another one of those things that I find interesting that others might not. Alaska is in the next time zone over from the west coast, so four hours in front of the east coast. Hawai'i is five hours. The gap I always assumed was there had always bothered me. Finding it was continuous from the east coast to Hawai'i made me feel better in a geeky kind of way.

Misadventures in the Wild

After the long road trip to Fairbanks, I decided to take another long road trip north of Fairbanks, another end of the road. I had heard about natural hot springs about 3-4 hours away. I arrived at the trailhead for a six-mile hike but decided to push on to Manley first to get gas. A sign I read a while back mentioned there was gas there, at the end of the road, but I was afraid of arriving after they closed on Sunday so drove the additional 25 miles.

It's the last frontier of the Last Frontier State, off the grid. What I think of a "gas station" was not what I found. It was a gas pump. An old one. A person in the general store had to turn it on and she wasn't there. Some extremely nice locals told me where I might find her. I did not find her, but I did find a sign saying, "back at 5." I was almost out of gas. So, I waited.

I'm glad I did. I had passed the path for the springs but it was not what I thought. Paths aren't much of anything this far north. The locals told me I was given bad information. The springs are wonderful–after the freeze. Right now, it's about a six-mile hike through swamps.

Manley truly is the end of the road. Hunters come there with their boats to go out on the river and hunt moose. Or elk? It's a tiny town, with a general store, an airstrip, and no cell phone coverage for miles. It's really the place to get away from everything. People were nice, as they all seemed to be in Alaska. One couple told me they keep a house up here and a house down by Homer.

I was waiting at the bar when a guy drove up and said the woman was at the general store so I better go find her immediately. I went.

"You're lucky you caught me," she said, "or else you'd be waiting till the morning to fill up with the hunters."

I got my gas and then proceeded back to Fairbanks, catching some great shots as I navigated the almost passable roads that I was told were much improved. I had wanted to avoid the "touristy" Chena Hot Springs, just an hour northeast of Fairbanks, but after encountering all I did in Alaska, I thought it might be my best bet after all.

One very interesting thing to me that seemed to encapsulate this part of Alaska. On the way to and from Manly, there was a huge parking area on the side of the highway. A lot of cars were parked there. I stopped, wondering if there was an attraction or something to see. It turned out everybody was there for the same thing: cell phone coverage. It's the only place to get it within a hundred miles.

The Last Frontier State is truly the last frontier and is treated as such. You need to come prepared with the right equipment and thick skin. A lot of people enjoy living off the grid and this is the place to do it, with small communities all around.

On the way back, there was a turnoff that I thought, "maybe?" Route 2 turns into Route 11. 11 will bring you to the end of another road, Prudhoe Bay, within the Arctic Circle and the beginning of the Trans Alaskan Pipeline.

The Arctic Circle is just a couple hours north. Next time. Exhaustion and the constant driving were telling me I needed to slow down and get some rest.

I also wanted my damn car.

Lessons from a Pipeline

Fall in Fairbanks.

A question was nagging me about Alaska and it was finally answered when I went to meet a friend and her son at a nearby park. I arrived early and chatted with a guy who had lived here for decades. A Brit, his father had worked on the pipeline and then he moved here when things went in a different direction in South Africa.

"Alaska is the perfect balance between humans and nature," he told me.

It nailed it. Before going to the park to meet my friend, I went just a few minutes north to see a Trans Alaskan Pipeline Viewing station. It sits right by the highway among the trees. I had seen the pipeline the day before zigzagging down mountains in the distance and would see it more on my drive back to Anchorage the following day.

The pipeline runs from Prudhoe Bay in the north, up in the Arctic Circle, down to Valdez, the northernmost ice-free port in Alaska. The pipeline, beyond being an engineering feet of its time, had to balance both nature and humans because nature is unforgiving. It sits above ground at points because the ground underneath is tested to see if the oil running through it will defrost the ground and make the pipeline unstable.

My friend, Lily, arrived with her young son, Billy. I connected with Lily years ago on a Facebook group, a stuttering support network. I'm freezing and Billy showed up in shorts! The freezing temperatures we hear about in the continental US that will kill us if we stay out in it for more than a few minutes? Yeah, the kids here wear shorts all winter long. The parents just always keep extra clothes in the car in case they hit a moose (it happens frequently) and there is winter hiking to be done.

They showed me some of their favorite places around Fairbanks. Hiking, I found (and had been coming around to the idea) is not all about paths marked with stones. Sometimes, it's just wandering into the woods.

Even wandering into the woods was interesting. Lily pointed something out to me that I thought but wasn't sure about: I wasn't walking on dirt; I was walking on a leaf covered bed of moss. Much more comfortable with that soft springiness under your feet. She goes berry picking here often. Then, Billy took me up to the top of a hill to get some great shots. It was steep! He slid down on his butt. It was epic! I went down the old-fashioned way, being reminded that going up might be physically more difficult but going down a steep grade like that is murder on the knees.

But then it was time to rest up. I was denied hot springs in two places so decided to do Chena, the touristy thing. I made the drive as the sun was setting. I was running around a lot and wanted to be there at night in case the northern lights were out. $15 entrance fee. You can't beat that. The resort had an 80's-ish style, but I wasn't complaining as soon as I entered the springs.

It was an incredible way to end my day. I entered a changing room and then walked into the cold evening to wade into the springs. The spring area in much bigger than anything I had encountered before. It was lit up with multi colored lights and had fountains at various places.

My last adventure in Alaska came the following morning. I passed through North Pole, Alaska as I took the easterly, longer route back to Anchorage. You miss Denali, and lots of trees, but the majestic landscape artist is at it again the entire trip down along route 4. Another couple of hours would have taken me to Valdez, but I was too exhausted by this point and feeling the weight of traveling so much and so fast. So, I just kept going to Anchorage, got a hotel by the airport, and then jumped on an earlier flight home.

I want to make it back. In the summer, in my own car. In the spring, maybe, to set up my lab? Maybe do it right this time.

"The perfect balance between humans and nature." I just like the sound of that, and the feel of it, the balance.

Part Six: The Rubber Band Effect

Directional Decisions; September 27, 2020

There and back again: a coffee addict's story? A story of Covid Hibernation boredom gone horribly wrong? A story of a well-deserved midlife crisis? Or maybe just a journey of miles, memories, and thoughts as 50 approaches as inexorably as the consequences to the changes I set in motion. In any case, I hit the 20,000-mile mark yesterday, though I didn't do too much driving. I think I was still wiped out from Alaska.

The early morning found me driving down from Yakima, Washington through south central Washington and then eastern Oregon into Idaho. East. It gnaws at me a little bit. I spent a long time on the west coast. Between California, Oregon, Washington, and Alaska, it was over a month. Back in Seattle, I felt the pull. As well as the uncertainty. But east I went.

I enjoy the drives. Especially when I am refreshed–or at least somewhat refreshed. The changing landscape is different in each state. I like driving towards what looks like a solid cliff face and then you round a bend and there is an opening. You drive up to the pass and over, with a new vista before you. I was in Idaho before, but northern Idaho, before hitting the "reset" button. Now, I was in the south at the first exit, a welcome center along the Snake River on my way to Boise.

Boise was the original crossing point on the Oregon Trail. I stopped in Boise, much like any other major city, for some supplies (coffee creamer and food) and then pushed on the next two hours to my planned destination for the night: Twin Falls.

I didn't really stop there for any other reason than it was a point on a map that looked interesting. I arrived and realized I was in a "place." Oh. Did you know that "here," Twin Falls, was "a thing"? A "place?" I didn't.

For the first time in 20,000 miles and 74 days, all the hotels were booked. I had to go looking. Weekends aren't always the best times to get a hotel, but with Covid it has been simple. In many hotels, I was one of only a handful of guests. Here, I went to four hotels before I finally found one and the only reason I did is because I happened to be standing at the front desk when someone called and cancelled their reservation.

Driving into Twin Falls, I crossed a bridge that had a lookout point. Next to a shopping center is the visitor's center and this incredible view of the valley below. That gave me a hint and I looked it up. Yep, Twin Falls is definitely a "place," a "thing." I have some sight-seeing to do tomorrow before continuing.

I felt the pull east. About three hours southeast, just north of Salt Lake City, I can jump on 80, the fast way back to Philly.

But I missed an entire state! Arizona. Doesn't surprise anybody, huh? How can I not go to Winslow and sing an old Eagles song? And then on the way back up north, I can stop by Vail. I missed it the first time because the state was on fire. From there, I can strike north into Wyoming and Montana. Then east to North Dakota. Then south…

I don't HAVE to hit ALL 50 states. Scratch that. Yes, I do.

It was 32 degrees one morning when I woke up in Fairbanks. The leaves are starting to change. Fall will be arriving in the north soon. The temperatures are already starting to dip at night. Layers are required to follow the movement of the sun.

Really, I am just tired, now both mentally and physically. I want to soak in the heat of the desert one last time. I know the cold is something that awaits me back east. It is the only thing I am sure of.

Roulette; September 28, 2020

The day did not start off well. My first stop, Shoshone Falls, was easy to find. It was a ten-minute drive from where I was. It was a beautiful park with an overlook to the falls and a lake. The falls, though you cannot tell at this time of the year, are called the Niagara Falls of the West. It's bigger than Niagara Falls. In the spring, with the winter runoff, it's thunderous. By September, it is just a trickle.

I was impressed by the area. Like so many other places I've been, it's nothing like I imagined. The Snake River creates canyons, valleys, and a fertile crescent along the Oregon Trail where you can imagine why early settlers found the place so appealing. About an hour north is the City of Rocks, which I skipped to find Blue Heart

Springs. I was only a couple miles away. How hard could it be to find?

I was a mile away from the spring a half dozen times, driving about 40 miles in circles with my GPS bringing me back to private roads. Do people in Idaho shoot trespassers? I wasn't sure so I kept driving. Finally, I stopped (at the same private road I had been to a couple times) and finally Googled it. It turned out I was never going to get to Blue Heart Springs. It is accessible only by water. Go figure.

It was fun just driving through the area, though, somewhere to put a pin in a map to return to in the spring or summer. I found myself parking my car and walking across and under bridges just to take pictures. I decided to head south, though, but not before passing a big sign that said, "Box Canyon." A two-minute drive down a dirt road had me at yet another incredible view of hot springs. I need a kayak. And more time.

But then it was all about the drive.

I don't like entering Nevada. Have I mentioned that? I love driving through it, but the first place you hit in Nevada, driving south from Twin Falls, is Jackpot. It's like that everywhere and all roads seem to rush you to Las Vegas.

I have a deal with Mike that I will not stop in Vegas—even though I am only 150 miles from it now. My first drive through Nevada, I made it a point to take the long way around, bypassing Las Vegas by hundreds of miles—with every sign I passed urging me there. A joke, that might get my ass kicked eventually, is that I would put everything on black at the roulette wheel. Double or nothing.

But that is really part of what this trip is about. My money is on black. Or red. Or maybe even green (35-1). I put it there the day I started out on July 9th and the sound of the ball rolling around the

226

wheel has been in my head ever since. It was a titanic spin, but I know that once I truly start heading back east the ball will begin to slow. Will I hit? Or will I lose everything? Any editors, publishers or agents reading these columns?

Either or doesn't really matter. It's also like I explained to Mike and others. I'm the guy who got the huge bonus check from work. I put that down. If I hit, I retire. If I don't, I go back to work on Monday. No harm, no foul.

But the drive is epic. I bypassed the fast way, the highway, Route 5 that would have taken me down through Salt Lake City, and instead took scenic route 9, a double lane highway running through the desert and over mountains. I had to do some high-speed passing to get beyond the trucks, but then I went for miles without seeing another car in any direction. Small towns pop up here and there with signs saying, "no service for 100+ miles."

My destination, after changing my mind a couple times, was Cedar Springs in Utah. I began making the final push just as the sun began to set. The moon was rising in the east and the mountains in front of me under the moon were turning purple.

I like Utah. I've been moving hard and fast since leaving Seattle. Even though the decision to head south instead of east felt right, I feel a pull of time and direction. Shoshone Falls is a good example of what I am experiencing. The thunderous waterfall is a trickle of what it typically is in the spring. America has been the same way, with all the desolate towns and cities due to Covid.

"Next" awaits me back east. Whether I hit or not on the roulette wheel, I need the tools to face it. I need to put the pieces together to figure out what "next" is instead of allowing the depression to force me down the path of least resistance, the clogged major highway as opposed to the scenic route that is my love and passion.

I'm on a few journeys here, and the long drives help with all of them.

Lost in America the Beautiful; September 30, 2020

Well, I didn't mean to drive through two national parks but there you have it. It got confusing. Utah, Arizona and I am pretty sure I was briefly in California? —that's what my GPS said. That's three time zones (Arizona passes on daylights savings time). I also think I entered Utah four times.

My goal was a little-known national park: Vermilion Cliffs National Monument. Coming from Cedar Springs, you pass right by Zion National Park. I entered from the south. Zion sits high and the drive up through Springdale is like driving up the ramparts, over the drawbridge, to a castle.

I drove from the south entrance to the east entrance along a well-paved road and through a couple tunnels. Every view is amazing. People say you can spend days and weeks at the park hiking. The real gems of the park are along a different route, a roundabout, for buses only. It's season and the buses were packed. I like crowds as much as I like Starbucks coffee, I was only passing though, so you'll have to look up the gems for yourself—but I've heard they are stunning.

At the end of the road, I parked. I was going to hike the rim trail. My luck being what it is, the trail was blocked, before you could get to the good stuff, by a rockslide.

I had a close encounter with a big horned sheep. That sucker came running right at me—with me filming it the entire time. I wasn't too worried. There was a woman standing in front of me and she would have been taken out first. At the last second, though, the big horned sheep turned and completely disappeared into the brush.

I had two other close encounters after leaving Zion. One was at the coffee shop.

"We're out of beans," I was told by the young woman. It happens I gather.

I bet this was the first time she heard, "if I bring in the beans, will you brew them?" I got my coffee.

A little further down the road were buffalo (American Bison to be specific.) They were curious about the people standing on the side of the road watching them and they nonchalantly approached and started slurping from a pond between us. There were some young ones and a big one. You never know about the young so I kept my distance and then rode south along scenic route 89 to 89A–because that's what the GPS told me to do. My goal came from a picture that Kate Denin (Mom2) sent me.

Kate…wait, that doesn't sound right or feel right. Mom.

Mom has been following my travels through Facebook and my website, though she had been following my adventures and misadventures since I was a sophomore in high school when I met her daughter, Maureen. I think I make Mom cringe a lot. Maureen had never been shy about saying exactly what she felt. I wonder what she would think of this odyssey? She had a certain way of rolling her eyes with a half-smile that spoke volumes. She could call me an "ass" twelve different ways just with different inflections.

Maureen was one of the people I lost a few years back. After a 14-year battle with cancer, I sat with her in a hospital room every night after work for a month. There hadn't been enough hours in the day, but I made them anyway. Mom and the rest of her family was there as I read to Maureen from my journals.

I love Maureen, but I'm glad she isn't here for me to read to her or get her looks. It was a long, tough battle she fought with the final month torturous. As I read to her in that final month, hoping the massive amount of pain meds were doing their thing, a poem was reverberating inside my head.

"Rage, rage against the dying of the light."

It didn't make sense to me. "Do not go gentle into that good night," a poem by Dylan Thomas, was written for an old man at the end of his days, not my dear sweet girl. She had raged, turning a six-month death sentence into a 14-year celebration of life.

After a couple weeks of the poem tap, tap, tapping in my mind, it hit me. It wasn't for her to rage anymore. It was time for her to let go and slip peacefully into a gentler and kinder existence.

I had never heard of Vermillion Cliffs National Monument. When Mom had sent me the picture and asked me to go, how could I say anything but, "On my way."

The main attraction at Vermilion Cliffs National Monument is "The Wave," deep inside the park. Instead of just winging it, I did some research—but obviously not enough. There was very little chance of me making it in to see The Wave. It's very small and the sandstone has been taking such a beating that you need a permit to enter that part of the park. Only 20 permits are offered each day, 10 online and 10 in-person. I was told, though, that you can see something like The Wave as you drive through the park. That's where things started to go wrong.

Both 89 and 89A take you down into Arizona. I took the cutoff for 89A, the Vermilion Cliffs Scenic Byway. Wouldn't you? It kind of makes sense, especially as GPS was telling me to do it as well.

The change from Utah to Arizona is dramatic. Instead of just more cliffs and mountains, it's cliffs and mountains with forests. Dark trees and canyons. I stopped at a lookout point. You can see the ages of the earth in the cliffs behind you as you wander through a forest.

Vermilion Cliffs National Monument is in both Arizona and Utah. 89A takes you to the western entrance, 89 to the eastern one. There are no nicely paved paths here. It's rocks, gravel and lots of red dust. I pulled in and just started driving. I remembered reading something about how you come to the Condor Reintroduction Center after a very long drive. That's the first thing that told me I might have gone the wrong way as I came across it first. Massive cliffs rise in the distance where the conservatory is reintroducing the condors.

More red dust. Lots more. I lost my phone signal. I did, finally, come across a park ranger with absolutely no sense of humor.

"Mom sent me here."

"I don't know what you mean by that," he replied.

I played it straight. People going to The Wave without a permit can get a $10,000 fine and a year in prison. "Where can I go hiking without getting into trouble?"

"Just keep going up this road until you get close to the east entrance. There's a big parking area and lots of trails you don't need a permit for."

So, I kept driving. Just me and the dust. I found something, though, that most park visitors don't see. On this side of the park, at the base of some cliffs, you see hints of the vermilion inside. While taking pictures, I was "huffed" at by a cow. I had no idea it was laying inside bushes a couple steps away from me. Its calf was not too far away.

I kept driving.

Yep, there was a parking lot on the other side of the park. It is about two to three miles in from the eastern entrance. I think I drove about 30 miles, back into Utah, to get there.

The hike was gorgeous with narrow openings and the layers of rock, but all browns. I was told by an older gentleman that the vermilion is under what we were looking at. In a few more hundred thousand years of erosion, it will all look like The Wave, a formation with multi-colored layers.

I met a young woman who asked me what time it was. I mentioned it was about 5:00 but, about a mile south, it was 4:00—time zones.

I made it out of the park, into Utah, on Route 89, where I went south into Arizona. Again. Different route but incredible view. The first place I came across is a lake with a dam. The lake is not like other lakes. The water fills up the canyon that seems to be cut so it looks more like a man-made pool than the lakes I am used to seeing, with the gentle rise and beach. There is no beach, just a place to fall from.

But then it got dark and I was driving through the Arizona night. Route 89 gets you to Flagstaff and then a combination of Route 17 and then, again, 89A, brings you into Sedona. That last part is tricky, even worse at night and exhausted. There is a section that is only hairpin turns, one after another, on a narrow road with no sides.

Sedona, Alaska; September 30, 2020

Through my travels, I'm finding the oddest similarities between places that should not be. Sedona is appropriately beautiful as expected. Just driving through the town, you can stop every 50 yards for a photo opportunity. I found it interesting in that it is much like Alaska, just cozier. In Fairbanks, you have an imposing majesty rising all around you with an endless array of opportunities for fishing, camping, hiking, four wheeling, etc. Sedona is much the same, but with the more cozy and comfortable red cliffs and forests all around you.

The feel is much the same as well. Peaceful. Easy to get away from the noise and into the quiet. And it is spiritually powerful. It was really odd because I was talking to this woman on a hike and she was telling me that she just moved back here from Poland to open up a belly dancing studio dedicated to helping women find the feminine divine. She did not have a business card on her so told me the name of the studio. I looked it up—and found one with the exact same name in Alaska.

I need to come back and explore more. Sedona is popular for a lot of reasons but one of them is the artist community. It is also known for "elemental power vortexes" that empathic people can tap into to. My hike took me to one of four. It was a bit off the trail but easily found, even marked with a pile of stones. I sat and contemplated, breathing in the air and the peace in the shadow of the mountain. It is what brings artists, seekers, and teachers: those looking to get more in touch with themselves. Aye, I've seen enough in my 49 years not to knock anything.

I ran into the female hiker –the belly dancer— and started to discuss it as she was coming from it as well. She wanted to know what I felt. I felt peace, calmness and an ethereal quiet. It was different for her. She had been uneasy. She said she thought the power vortex was male/female so didn't know why it made her feel uneasy. With my reaction, she felt it must have been more male.

My take was a little different. The search for the feminine divine can create an imbalance, with the emphasis on feminine? For me, I've gotten in touch with my feminine side so feel more balanced? Like I said: I'm not knocking it.

I also ran into another pair of hikers, a mother and daughter who were setting out at night. That surprised me so I asked. The answer I got was simple enough: heat and tourists. Makes sense. No talk of power vortexes or the feminine divine, only to be on the lookout for wild pigs: they are small but can be aggressive.

The daughter had lived in Philadelphia and the son was still there. Philadelphia can be overpowering. The young woman said she lived there for three years before she realized she lived close to Valley Forge National Park.

I think we forget. But I also think with Covid we must remember. The Danes even came up with a word for it, that I cannot pronounce let alone spell. But it has to do with getting out and about and getting in touch with nature to get away from the negativity that is pressing in on us from all sides. It is easy in a park or a place like this to get away from that pressure. Getting more in touch with it helps build a barrier between us and the negativity.

I got my three-mile hike in. I found my power vortex. I found interesting similarities from places so different from one another.

If a journey like this ever happens again, I'll have a hard decision to make. I like running quiet in my Outback, but I'd really like to have a roof rack with a bike and kayak.

But this was veg day. A day to relax, catch up on my sleep, and I received a reminder that a simple three mile hike each day and a good night's sleep can do wonders for my spirit. I'm learning lessons. I need to remember them, actualize them. I enjoyed my last couple days of summer, driving with the windows down and walking in shorts, feeling the heat seep into me. But now it's time to finish what I began and head north.

Navajo Nation; October 2, 2020

"I feel like a kid," the older man pouted, while his wife was positioning him for just the right picture in front of the flatbed ford in Winslow, Arizona. His wife just gave him a look. I know that look. I tried being helpful while waiting for my turn. "We're all kids here," I called out.

And we are. If you are in Arizona, you can't not stop by the little town made famous by the Eagles' song. And if you don't know the song, you are either too young or grew up listening to the wrong music. It was under two hours from Sedona and just a nice little town right off Route 40. Thriving but quiet, with people lining up to have their pictures taken on a street corner.

Well, I'm standing on a corner in Winslow, Arizona
And such a fine sight to see
It's a girl, my Lord, in a flatbed Ford
Slowin' down to take a look at me

A store on the opposite corner is the trinket and gift shop. It plays Eagles songs all day along with songs from the band members from their solo efforts. I had just taken my turn having my picture taken by the flatbed Ford, sat down on a bench to enjoy a cigarette and cup of coffee, and then THE Don Henley started to play, the one that I have written about so many times, used to explain what I am doing, and has been on my mind since I first heard it.

Graduating high school, eventually making my way to college, I knew Henley was talking about my future and there was not much I could do about it. I just didn't have the tools. I had always hoped to find the tools, fit the pieces together to exist in both worlds, but the world moved on and I did as well.

I sat there in Winslow, sipping my coffee, smoking a cigarette, and listened to the song.

Rest in peace, Harry. I'm far too much in this world but I'm trying to finally change that. The hope is my clothes will be found scattered on some beach with a foo foo drink with a tiny umbrella waiting for me, a respite before unfolding my wings and launching back into the other world.

The original plan when I was in Moab a couple months ago, before I got sidetracked by Salt Lake City, was this. I was just doing it in reverse. From Winslow, you take the scenic route up through the Navajo Nation to Moab. The only way I can describe the drive through the Navajo Nation is a full emptiness.

All states I have driven through have their empty lands, dozens of miles of nothing except scrub brush, fencing, and the occasional cow. It's desolate. The Nation was like that as well, but it had a presence to it. I just had the feeling that if I stopped, someone would appear from nowhere to greet me and welcome me.

Behind the fences were horses instead of cows and they were beautiful. Here and there, nice and neat houses and farms would appear along with schools. Driving through, I felt something akin to the "Aloha" I feel in Hawai'i. A gentle spirit, that if you are open to it, you can be a guest.

I have heard nothing but wonderful things about the Navajo people and hope to go back one day and meet them.

I didn't stop too much except for lunch. The windows were down and the heat felt good. I eventually found myself back in Moab. It is at the top of my list of favorite places. It was very different than from the two months ago I was last here. The 107-degree heat had dropped to the high 80's. Season was in, and the hotel I had before cost me almost three times the amount from the last time.

The hotel clerk recognized me. I tried the "but I was here helping out when you first reopened!" It got me a little discount. With the crowds and prices, I knew I was only going to stay the one night. I also knew I'd be back when the temperatures were high again to chase away the people and drive down the prices.

North Through the Rockies; October 3, 2020

Just simply gorgeous. Moab and the vicinity are one of my favorites of the trip.

I returned to Grand Junction by the scenic route along the Colorado River and past Cisco. I made a quick stop for coffee (putting money in the meter so I wouldn't get another parking ticket) and then headed north.

My destination: Wyoming. Of course, the scenic route took me back into Utah. A few different times. The scenic route meanders across Utah and Colorado. I think I have now entered Utah about 10 times? I was on this wonderful road, cruising through northern Colorado, when I hit the Rocky Mountains.

The torturous (but enjoyable) drive I took down into Sedona with the hairpin turns? This road was its big brother. In Sedona, it was red buttes and hills. This was the Rockies and there was no playing around. 1,000-foot drops, roads that seem to cling to the face of the mountain, 20mph posted speed limit signs that might be too fast for some of the turns, and, just to make things even more interesting, cows. But not the good kind of cows, the obedient kind, the kind I usually saw along my journey. These cows don't stay on their side of the fence. They are right there on the sides of the road and sometimes in the middle of the road. Sometimes they are in the middle of the road at a hairpin turn.

Could I have fit one in the back of my Subaru? One was cute enough to make me think about it as it stood staring at me right in front of my car. I couldn't remember the weight capacity and I was thinking of where I might be able to find wood to make a ramp. Everybody said to travel with a dog. A cow? But she finally shuffled out of the way and I continued along.

I was racing daylight when I finally came out of the last valley, passing through a small town, not really having any idea what state I was in. The guy at the convenience store said when he moved here, it was the first time he knew what quiet was. He said he was afraid his neighbors could hear everything he said inside of his home. It was also the first time he saw the Milky Way, thinking it was clouds until he looked it up on the Internet.

I had some fun with the drive, but also a regret. I really wanted to stop. I made a left hand turn at one point onto Brontosaurus Drive in Dinosaur, Colorado, gateway to Dinosaur National Monument. As night descended, I started a long drive through another National Forest, Ashley.

Ashley National Forest is alongside another place I'd like to go back and see: Flaming Gorge National Recreation Area. I was told the Flaming Gorge is a beautiful three-hour scenic loop drive and Dinosaur National Monument can have you looking thousands of feet down–someone even said it is better than the Grand Canyon.

When I was almost at the end of my drive, a bird swooped down in front of my car and raced the headlights for a few seconds before veering off. I'd swear it was an owl.

But then I made it. Green River, Wyoming. State #35 along the journey.

A Very Big Backyard; October 3, 2020

I was having one of those days. Confusing. Where do I go from here? A bunch of things, I think, are starting to catch up to me. Almost 90 days of hotel rooms. One and two day stops. My trip picked up speed in Alaska and I can't seem to slow it down enough to just enjoy the moment. Enjoy the beauty unfolding before me. I didn't even break out the coffee maker today—that's how bad it was. But let's see how tomorrow goes.

I was on Google maps a lot today. It is a 28-hour drive between here and the place I used to call home. There is a pull eastward to finish things up, finalize things, before I begin "next." We'll see what tomorrow holds.

But today. I caught glimpses of the extraordinary. I drove to Green River because I did some planning. I had a general idea for many of the other states I have been in, but in Wyoming and Montana, I'm lost. So, I looked it up. "Things to do." Something caught my attention: The Wild Horse Loop.

It was about a two-hour loop of dirt and gravel roads in a sanctuary for a herd of wild horses. I had misgivings when I mentioned it to the woman at the front desk of the hotel and she said, "You will see a lot of birds."

On the loop, it was anti climatic. I did see horses. Three. I also saw lots and lots and lots of horse poop. It is how the stallions mark their territory and they like to do it on the road so it is noticeable. They'll keep returning to the same spot and sometimes the pile can get three feet high.

The herd here is controlled. They like to keep the population to 250 and it can grow by 20% per year, so they round them up and put the extras up for adoption. Adoption fees start at $185.

It was an interesting drive. I found it ironic that the hotel I picked wound up being on the start of the loop, The Hampton Inn & Suites Green River. Another point of interest on the loop is the second highest point in the area: Pilot Butte. It rises above the surrounding lands and is unmistakable. But I had no idea how to get to it? Smaller dirt roads crisscross everywhere and there are no clearly defined paths or signs. The roads twist and turn and double back. Which one do I take? I finally just went down one and hoped for the best.

It was tough driving. You can drive the main road, dirt, and gravel, with any car. The minor roads, you need something raised higher with all-wheel drive. It's really pick-up truck kind of driving, though my Outback handled it fine by being very careful. The ruts in some of the roads would have easily taken out my axle. It was slow going to Pilot Butte. Now the question was: how do I get up there?

It was a harsh climb up to the base of the butte, closer to "vertical" than "sloped." People coming down told me they couldn't find a way up. I just thought to myself they didn't look hard enough. With the lack of horses, the rough, slow road, I was going to make it up to the top.

Things got tricky. There is a lot of slate so I had to be careful of foot and hand placement. I saw one promising place, climbed up, and then realized I had a three-foot jump to make it to the butte. That was not going to happen. So, I climbed back down and moved further along. I finally did find another place that looked promising, a crevice with handholds and footholds without any slate. I was determined. I made it up.

Do you know what you can see from the top of Pilot Butte when you first make it up? You see the top of Pilot Butte. That's all.

All the way across was a higher ridge, so I trekked some more along a multicolored ground and through scrub brush. It was an amazing view and a fun adventure, but then I started wondering: how do I get down? I sort of got a little lost. All the edges of the butte look the same.

Personally, I thought I was screwed. It was not exactly easy to make it up or even find my way to the spot to climb up. I finally got some help. Some kids climbed up and it turned out the way I took up was the way up. I made it down and back to the car safely. Then there was another very slow drive to the main road. I eventually hit the paved road.

There was one more stop along the Wild Horse Loop in Rock Springs: The wild horse corals. Seeing all those horses made the day a bit more worth it.

The drive back to my hotel was much easier, 75 mph along 80. The sight of all those horses and a fresh cup of coffee had me feeling better. Then, I got back to my hotel and realized what was in the backyard of the hotel. I was tired, but how can you not hike into your own backyard? So, I did. The cliffs, rock formations (called Tea Pot and Sugar Bowl), and small buttes were amazing. A spectacular view awaited me after I climbed the hundred yards or so up to Tea Pot.

But now it's time to pack up and see how tomorrow goes. It will be a shorter drive, another scenic route and some hot springs. I'm making it a point to buy some more of my coffee creamer and break out the coffee maker tomorrow. The coffee has been okay, but mine is still better.

I'm just hoping for a good night's sleep. Eventually, in a couple days, I make my way to Buffalo, Wyoming. That's where the decision must be made. I can go north into Montana or just head east. East lies the last thing that was really on my "bucket list" for this trip: The Badlands, South Dakota.

I'll see how I feel after a dip in the hot springs tomorrow.

Tilting East; October 4, 2020

Everybody knows about western Wyoming. Yellowstone National Park and the Grand Tetons are heavyweights, so they tilt the state west. I never had any intention of stopping there. Maybe another trip when they are not in season. And then there is the whole fire thing. I've had enough smoke to last me a while. I decided to go east instead, from Green River in the SW to Sheridan in the NE, about 25 miles south of the Montana border. There's a lot to be said about the lighter side of the state.

The people are nice. More cowboyish? I saw plenty of horses and cattle on my trip, along with a bunch of other stuff that I'll be getting to. I saw a sign that said, "Wyoming beef is delicious!" I thought to myself: "and pretty damn cute too."

My first destination for the day was the hot springs of Thermopolis in Hot Springs State Park. Beautiful place with two main attractions. One is the hot springs of course. All hot springs get diverted. This is the biggest hot spring in the world (so says the sign). There is a public bathhouse and then two commercial businesses with outside pools and water slides. Open year round— and this is heavy winter country. The other attraction is the buffalo herd–though there aren't any buffalo left in the US. They are American Bison. You can go on a loop drive through their territory. You can get as close as you want as there are not any fences but they highly recommend not getting too close.

The ride there was amazing. I passed through the Wind River Indian Reservation and one pass said it was the continental divide–I looked at a map and realized I crossed the continental divide quite a few times. I also passed through Shoshone National Forest.

Looking at the continental divide on the map makes sense. It passes through Moab, Utah as well. The ride was similar but different. Mountains, passes, valleys and rivers. The final ride up to Thermopolis included something very much like the ride away from Moab. I followed a river with mountains on either side of me, down through valleys and up through passes. The colors are different, more like pastel earth tones instead of reds, and the mountains are higher with the gorges deeper.

Another scenic route took me across the Bighorn Mountains. I passed a lot more cattle and a bunch of goats that were chomping away on the side of the road. It's all just so incredible. Pictures, videos and writing about it doesn't do it justice.

As I was standing outside of the hotel waiting (it's laundry day), I heard the old Rod Stewart song. "I wish I knew then what I know now, when I was younger. I wish I knew then what I know now, when I was stronger."

In the next few days is the time for the big decision. I'll pass through Montana tomorrow on my way to North Dakota. It is much later in the year than I expected. Today saw a high of 70 and the land was bathed in sunshine with a cloudless sky. But how long do I have? Colder weather and snow come earlier this far north. All my good cold weather clothing is in storage.

In my road atlas, the main highways are shown in purple and the scenic routes in dotted reds. 94 can take me to Chicago and then something or another in the purple range back to the east coast. The last "place" I want to visit is just a little out of the way in South Dakota. Friends I want to visit are along that northern route. But it leaves a patchwork of red roads throughout the center.

Someone just mentioned to me that it is getting sidetracked that keeps things interesting.

Well, hopefully, my laundry is dry.

Driving Through an Ocean; October 4, 2020

It was just a beautiful day for a long drive, and nothing like what I expected this far north in October. 80 degrees and the day like a bathtub full of sunlight. It was something that I needed, refreshing and revitalizing. I finally made it to Montana and then turned east along Route 94.

There was something about the drive I thought about in all my rides west and north: the setting sun. It really is about the small things. Throughout so many miles, I typically found myself driving with the sun glaring into my eyes, trying to position the visor just right in front of me or to my left, swinging it over so I am not blinded. The drive to Bismarck had the sun at my back and I watched the shadow of my car speeding in front of me.

The mileage is interesting to me as well. The country can be so big and so small at the same time. If you drive across the entire state of Montana, even starting from the first major city west, Missoula, to the first major city in North Dakota, Bismarck, it is 756 miles, or about 10 ½ hours of driving. That is more than the trip through the entire Northeast. Bangor, Maine to Washington DC is 670 miles through 8 states — and most of that is Maine.

I'm still winging it. I really did try to plan things out a few times and it tends to just overwhelm me. There are definite disadvantages to winging it, as I have shown in the "misadventures" category. But

I think the surprises make up for it. Just wandering and rambling has its advantages. I had one on my way to Bismarck.

The other day, I was on the phone with Papa Bear, who has been keeping tabs on me. He asked where I was. I told him the truth: "I have absolutely no idea." I was somewhere in Wyoming with very sketchy cell phone coverage.

I later posted on Facebook that, for once, I knew exactly where I was. I was about to blow past it on the highway but slammed on my breaks and swerved right to take the exit: The Battle of Little Bighorn National Monument, Custer's Last Stand.

As far as National Monuments go, this one was excellent and very well done. We all hear and learn about the battle, one of the last major conflicts of the era, and Custer's blunder over splitting his forces and underestimating his enemy. You can read about it, see pictures, and even watch videos but nothing comes close to what the monument has to offer.

Through signs, markers, and monuments, with paths and roads, you see exactly how the battle played out, almost reliving it. Markers are placed where fallen soldiers on both sides were found, and then their remains removed for proper burial. There is a cemetery there for both sides and civilians killed in the battle. Until the cemetery reached capacity in 1978, veterans could request their remains be interred here so there are also graves for soldiers up through the Vietnam War.

Special note for one thing that annoyed me: uncover in the cemetery! You can wear hats all over the place, except in the cemetery. Show some respect.

The monument was not what I was expecting. Though it shows how the battle played out, it also shows the evolution of peace. In the present, The Battle of Little Bighorn National Monument hosts the annual prayer for world peace.

Two of the higher ranking survivors met at this place and shook hands and "buried the hatchet" years after the battle. There is a memorial for the Indians killed. In 1991, the name was changed by an act of congress and signed by President Bush. The experience of being there took me by surprise.

The northern states are taking me by surprise. It makes me wonder a lot about our nation's history. I speed through in my car. People, trailblazers, and settlers walked here or traveled by horse. If I just simply walked back along the way I came, on the nice, even, paved highway, it would take me four days walking nonstop. I try to imagine what it was like for the original people out here. Through wilderness.

Montana changed to North Dakota and the change was subtle at first. Montana is true cowboy country, with long straight flat highways and vast herds of cattle. North Dakota was an ocean of grass. I don't know what I was expecting. Reindeer? I guess I read too many fantasy books. I always remembered a line I read about how cold it was somewhere because the only thing between the Arctic Circle and the place was the occasional reindeer. But I entered North Dakota on this gorgeous, sunny, 80-degree day with the ocean of grass before me.

An ocean of grass. I had read the phrase many times and used it many times, but I never understood it until I arrived in North Dakota. It is not just an endless expanse of water. An ocean has swells, waves, chop and rocky outcroppings jutting up from deep beneath the surface. That's North Dakota. The road winds through all of this with the grass rippling and rising, falling, and broken here and there by outcroppings. It was beautiful, mostly brown with the turn of the season.

And then there was the time zone. Time zones have been screwing me up since day one. Who made these things? I realize that science dictates a certain uniformity, that the movement of the sun has a defined path, but still? East and west coast states have it easy–aside from the Florida panhandle. Mountain and Central Time Zones? It's a mess. I entered the central time zone from mountain time about an hour into North Dakota. I'll be going back into Mountain Time tomorrow when I drive southwest to Rapid City.

On the other side, and during the first part of my journey, I hit the same thing. Indiana, Kentucky and Tennessee are split between Eastern and Central Time Zones. I don't know, but if I were a citizen of these states, I'd rise in revolt and demand they pick one time zone or the other.

But now for a down day in Bismarck. I'm going to go for a walk in a city I know nothing about but have always been oddly curious.

Down Day in Bismarck; October 6, 2020

Bismarck is a nice little city, only three exits along the highway. The only thing I really knew about North Dakota was from the movie, Fargo, and from a television show, The West Wing. In the television show, someone attends a meeting of the state leaders talking about wanting to change the name of the state to "Dakota," feeling that "north" gives it a bad reputation. I have to agree.

Traveling, for me, can be like going to an art museum. I need help. Going to an art museum is so much more enjoyable with someone who understands art. I can look at something by a famous painter and be like, "that's art?" Or see something that I do like but do not understand, why it is valued as high as it is. I'm pretty much lost, looking at the pretty pictures. If I go with someone who understands art, though, it is like being in a different place. They can explain everything, the history and evolution and reasons behind it all.

I'm just a guy on the road. If I had my way, to truly appreciate everything, I'd have company in the car: a geologist, a meteorologist, and a historian. They could help me put everything into context.

There is a beautiful river walk here that goes for miles. Bismarck is nestled against the Missouri River. I think the town leaders would do well to discuss the river walk with other town leaders like in Austin or Memphis. There is so much possibility here in this break from the ocean of grass along Interstate 94.

But I just took a down day. Bismarck was always someplace I wanted to visit but it is not on any of the well-traveled routes. I had a long walk along the river and then made my way back to my hotel through cape cod housing developments and along a golf course. I had a couple of great meals. The culinary experience is not quite up to par of other cities but, at this point, anything beyond a gas station packaged sandwich is a great meal.

I was talking to one guy along the river. Nice enough young guy. How bad can a guy be that is wearing a Pink Floyd t-shirt? I first had to assure him I was not going to kill him but then we chatted. I asked him about the Bismarck experience.

The guy referred to the city as "BisNarc" as everybody knows everybody else's business and shares it. I imagine it comes with the small town like atmosphere with long winters and nothing better to do. He explained it's a great place to live if you can deal with the winters. He likes it as it forces him outside of his bubble. And then he went skateboarding along, smoking a cigarette before he had to go into work.

I did break out the coffee maker again and the beans. And the case of water. I'm sure the water is fine here, but I got some advice last year from a guy who traveled for business a lot. We were in LA at the bar and I asked him if it was safe to drink the water–I didn't want to have to walk down to the store and buy bottled. He replied it is never safe to drink the water. He explained that the water could be perfectly fine–for the people there who are used to it. But he learned through his travels that you just never know, there could be something in the water that is fine, but something our bodies are not used to.

The ride here felt good. The walk yesterday did wonders. The nap helped.

The Destination; October 7, 2020

23,500 miles and 93 days later, I finally made it to one of the top places on my list. Rapid City, South Dakota. It's the "hub," or gateway, to southwest SD. There is so much to experience here. I got a taste of it in eastern Wyoming–I'm actually just a few hours away from where I stayed there a week before. The terrain and scenic drives are what has driven most of this trip, though I do enjoy wandering in cities.

The ride down from Bismarck was confusing. The time zones really screw me up. I started in Central and somehow, somewhere, went back to Mountain. I've never really known what day it was but now I don't know what time it is.

I'm just hoping this weather holds. It was another gorgeous day, 80+, but it was also a nerve-wracking start. I ALWAYS pass a small town to grab a coffee refill. I wasn't allowed to. I barely made it into an Indian Reservation. They had a Covid check point and were about to turn me around, but, UNLIKE THE CANADIANS, they decided that "writer" was an essential traveler and allowed me to pass—but I was told I couldn't stop at the one general store I saw.

I was out of coffee! A hundred miles of undulating hills, where I could see a rise in the far distance and thought, "there has to be a place after that." Nope, just another rise in the far distance. It was just me and lots and lots of cows again. Eh, that's the chance you take when you avoid the major highways and take the scenic route.

I did finally find a cup of coffee and made it to my first geeky stop: the geographical center of the US. It was once down in Kansas, but then, when they added Alaska and Hawai'i, it moved north to South Dakota. It is just north of Belle Fourche.

I had planned on going right to my hotel but it was still early in the day, (12 or 1?). Rapid City was my destination, but so many things I had planned on seeing were along my route, or just a little off of it. So, I drove on down through the outskirts of the Black Hills, away from the straight roads and back into the twisty ones with passes to a remnant of the Wild West: Deadwood.

Deadwood was disappointing but I guess I should have expected it. It has burned down a few times and built back up. Now, the entire area is like a theme park, complete with adventure parks for the kids and casinos for the adults. I did get to see the bar and chair where Wild Bill Hitchcock was assassinated.

Because of his reputation, Wild Bill always sat with his back to the wall to play cards. One night, he was talked into taking the empty chair with his back to the door. He was shot in the back and now aces and eights are called the Dead Man's Hand.

I got out of there quick. I grabbed another cup of coffee and headed south through South Dakota's version of Disneyland.

Mount Rushmore National Monument was my next destination and it was still early. It was epic! In my head, it was much smaller. A lot of people asked me if I thought it was smaller than depicted. The reality? It is carved into a mountain! It IS the mountain! I could fit up inside one of the president's nostrils! Is it smaller than depicted? I couldn't tell you. Maybe? But it is a sculpture that covers the face of a mountain!

I could write a lot more but right now I'm excited, like a kid on Christmas Eve. For as long as I can remember, The Badlands have captured my imagination. It is about an hour east of Rapid City. It was one of the few true destinations I had in mind when I began this odyssey over 90 days ago. With the weather still beautiful, I'm going for the scenic drive along the Badlands Loop.

A Little Boy's Smile; October 8, 2020

In the words of the great philosophers, Bill and Ted, "That was most excellent!"

This part of the journey really began about 40 years ago. As a young boy, I heard, read or watched something about the Badlands and it excited my imagination. Outside of Grandmom's and Coci's houses in North Cape May, it was the only place I ever wanted to go.

I don't know? It sparked something in me? That little boy's dream never faded. Today, it was satisfied. Oh, the man wants to go much deeper into the park, explore and hike when the sun is like a hammer with the Badlands an anvil. I want to travel the paths and wander through the hills. But I'll do that another time. Today? It was bison, prairie dogs, big horn sheep, jagged hills, ravines and canyons cutting through the plains. It was?

It's the perfect way to end this next to last segment of the journey, the drive along scenic route 240 with a few short hikes. The east end is about an hour's drive along Interstate 90; the west end about 30 minutes. Both entrances are about eight miles south of the interstate. I took the western entrance on a sunny, cloudless day. The road wraps around the northern edge of the park, 244,000 acres, once home to ancient horses and rhinos. It was the land of the Lakota Tribe and later the Great Sioux Nation which included the Oglala Lakota.

Even before I arrived at the park, I saw the bison (I should start calling them by their correct name. There is no such thing as buffalo in the US anymore. Bison are what we refer to as buffalo.) You can get as close to them as you want. I highly recommend not getting too close.

Inside of the park, on a side road, is a "prairie dog village." Cute little things. They won't get close or allow you to get close to them, but they appreciated the grapes some women brought. The prairie dogs make some fantastic sounds. I have no idea what they are saying but it seemed important. The women told me the night before, when they went out to wander around the prairie dog village, they looked back and there was a bison standing next to their car. They slowly backed away. Far away.

I even caught a picture of the big horned sheep as they made their way through the grass. The southern side of the park is the largest mixed grass plain in the nation.

Tomorrow begins the final portion. I can't call it the journey home and too many things await the 49-year-old and the 49-year-old's choices and consequences and...

But that's tomorrow. It was an hour-long drive back to the hotel. It was a quiet ride with the radio off. I smiled a little boy's smile. And I even bought myself the only thing on the trip. A baseball cap of course: Badlands SD, 1978

Into the Heartland; October 9, 2020

I drove down from South Dakota into Nebraska. I didn't even have a "destination" in mind so just picked a random city that has the same name as a friend from high school. So here I am, between point A and point B, in Kearney, Nebraska.

The drive into Nebraska was like, in most states, uneventful. You would not even know you are entering a different state if there wasn't a sign saying, "Welcome to X." –and some of the roads I've taken did not even have that, or cell phone coverage, so it got confusing. I wonder how they created some of these borders? Longitude and latitude I'm thinking. But after you get down through the hills, the changes are subtle at first and then it becomes "Nebraska." The cows become fewer and fewer, with horses in with the cow herds, and then the great train tracks, checkerboards of fields, silos, and farming equipment along with the rumbling of trucks and machinery getting the last of the stuff done before winter hits.

Even the road atlas in the "heartland" is different. Nebraska, Kansas, Iowa and Missouri have a checkerboard map, with all of the roads true east and west, north and south. All the states around it, the roads seem to go everywhere. I took a slow turn south by southeast to jump on Interstate 80—that runs from San Francisco to New York.

You see a lot more trees in Nebraska along the side of the road and highways. I saw new trees being planted. I think it has something to do with protecting the fields? But the interstate is different as well. Road kill. It is what I consider "normal" here, with a skunk and other small animals. On interstate 94, the main route through North Dakota, it looked like something out of a slaughterhouse or horror movie. 18-wheelers doing 80 mph vs a deer isn't pretty. You DO NOT want to drive that road at dawn or dusk I was told.

In the morning in South Dakota, you could feel that fall might not seem like it is here, but it's just waiting, giving us a little bit more time. The wind was blowing as if there weren't any reindeer blocking it from the Arctic Circle. Chilly, in the low 40's, but it warmed up fast as I got down into Nebraska, topping out at 86 with clear blue skies.

I'm hoping the weather holds. I still have that one last pass through the far north of the US. I remember going to a friend's house in Minnesota last October, about this time, and I woke up to an inch of snow. There is nothing really to rush me along. Cold and heat don't bother me. I don't mind driving in the snow either. I just don't want that cold rain. I feel like I'm in a race.

And I also feel like that quote I mentioned all the way back when I first started writing these columns, from the movie "For Love of the Game," about pushing the sun back into the sky for one more day of summer. Mother Nature seems to be cooperating with me, with a lingering summer.

There were a lot of pictures I missed. It would have been nice traveling with a photographer, or even someone to yell at me, "pull the hell over!" I get caught up in the driving sometimes. The trees were different here, with more fall and more of the gradual change with oranges and light reds. In South Dakota it was either yellow or green. The fields were brown and green—I'm guessing the green ones were the fields that went unplanted this year? Fields are switched up over the years—I read that somewhere—so the nutrients can be replenished.

Kearney is a nice enough city that could be plopped anywhere in America. When I arrived, I had to run to Target to pick up a few things.

That's the thing about winging it—I had no idea there was going to be a Target. Or anything for that matter. Pulling off the highway or byway can reveal an entire city or nothing, not even a gas pump. But the main road, 2nd street, was like any main road in any city, filled with your Targets and restaurants, etc. It reminded me a lot of Baltimore Pike back home, running through Delaware County. The big difference is that Baltimore Pike curves here and there with some hills. 2nd Avenue in Kearney was straight as an arrow and as flat as the plains.

Still in Nebraska; October 10, 2020

Thankfully, very few people have witnessed the epic arguments I've had with myself. It's not a multiple personality thing; it is one personality trying to make a decision.

It is tough being me sometimes.

I'm not sleeping well. Not sleeping well and long drives don't go well together, especially along straight roads that shimmer in the distance. That shimmering has a hypnotic effect.

"Start driving," I was telling myself.

"Go back to sleep," I was telling myself.

"You have to be somewhere," I was telling myself.

"You don't have to be anywhere anytime soon and you don't even know where you are going, so stop it and get some rest."

That went on for about an hour or so. Google maps took over. Distances and destinations. Routes and highways and byways. The weather app came into play. What's the forecast for Duluth? Any snow forecasted in Minnesota, Wisconsin or Michigan?

"You should have started this trip in May or June."

"I couldn't: the house hadn't sold yet."

"And you were sitting around twiddling your thumbs instead of learning how to use the GoPro, Website and you can't even figure out how to update your phone with the laptop. You STILL don't know how to use the laptop. You're treating a $2,000 computer like a $200 word processor."

"Now don't go there."

"I wonder how the Phillies are doing?"

"Oh, shut up."

I got an extra night at the hotel. Seven more nights till gold status with Hilton. I think it was in CA that I stopped screwing with the hotel apps and just stuck with one hotel chain, Hilton. The points add up for something or another and I liked the idea of knowing what I would get when I got there. Whether it is a Hampton Inn, Hilton Garden Inn or Home2 Suites, they are all similar and standard across the US. Free breakfast is nice, though Covid has it shut down in some places or just a platter of wrapped breakfast sandwiches in others.

And now I am up at 4 am. Sipping coffee. Not arguing with myself. The plan is to get ready, shower, pack, and then go back to sleep. I might make it to Tulsa today. I might not. I tend to not make hotel reservations until I am a couple hours out now.

I do think I am finally getting the hang of this packing and unpacking thing. It's going quickly. In a couple thousand more miles, I'm going to have to completely empty out my car for a good detailing, inside and out. That is when I'll probably find out that the packing and unpacking is going so much easier because I have left stuff all through America.

I do think I've developed tennis elbow from cleaning my windshield when I stop for gas. I'm scrubbing. Lots of bugs have lost their lives in my pursuit of the 50 and they take effort to scrape off.

Did I mention it's 5 am? –Central Time Zone. I think. I have absolutely no idea what day it is. I know it is October but beyond that?

After each drive, I've been tracing my path in the road atlas. Roads I've driven are highlighted in red and states I have visited are outlined in blue.

That was an argument as well. The "judges" ruled that my walk to Arkansas did not count. When I was in Memphis, I walked across the largest walking bridge across the Mississippi River and spent 10-15 minutes in Arkansas before walking back. So, now I'll be driving through a couple states I already have outlined in blue before striking north to finish the 50.

In Philly, I know, another argument awaits.

"And now?"

I took to the road for a lot of reasons. A big thing is I was looking for tools, teachers, and inspiration to get on with my life. Do it right this time. I think I found them. Now, I have to put the pieces together.

"Where?"

"Let's save that argument for another time?"

"Sounds good. Get some rest. Tulsa is a long drive with shimmering highways. Do the trick and see if you can get more sleep."

The trick? It's an old one. I lie in bed fully clothed and pull half the comforter over top of me. It works.

"Sounds like a good plan."

The Great War Machine; October 11, 2020

That's what I was thinking of! It just had to percolate in my mind a bit more with some more clues.

Nebraska was tugging at me. When I was sitting outside at the hotel, sipping coffee, I noticed my iPhone was quickly covered in a weird kind of dust. It didn't remind me of the ash I found with states on fire, and it wasn't normal dust. It had a texture to it that I couldn't place. Kansas was much the same as Nebraska, with every railroad crossing surrounded by silos and great machines.

I was driving past farm after farm. They were slowing down after the harvest and most of the machines were silent. Here and there was a huge tractor or other implement sitting in the field like a sentry. The great irrigation sprayers were at a standstill and the farmhouses nestled behind a fence of trees.

The dust that covered my phone that I had to wipe off a few times? It was like cornmeal. I finally put the pieces together and realized that Nebraska and Kansas (and probably the other heartland states) are like Great War Machines, battling the elements in the spring, summer and fall to feed the nation. What I was seeing was oddly reminiscent of the trench warfare in WWI, where the soldiers would hunker down in winter, waiting for the spring.

Kansas was a bit different after the northern part. I still want to find out about the trees and new plantings. I saw a sign somewhere up north about planting trees to protect against…and then I flew past at 80mph. Getting to my destination was sort of funny. After months of hearing from my GPS "merge onto this highway" or "bear right or left," it was "turn right," "turn left." Everything was so straight!

But a left turn, right turn, left turn and another right turn, all with dozens of miles between them, brought me to my first stop in Kansas: the geographical center of the continental United States. It is just north of Lebanon, about 550 miles southeast of the center of the nation after the introduction of Alaska and Hawai'i. There was a sign, a little chapel, the American flag, and a covered table to have a picnic.

All the reviews on Google said the same thing. "You must stop by if you are in the area. Nice little place." 5 stars. Except one. There is always just the one. One star. I could hear the whine as the person typed the review: "This is NOT the center! What about Hawai'i and Alaska? The real center is…"

There really is always just the one.

But let's be honest here. How many people really know that Alaska and Hawai'i are part of the US? I know people that think they need a passport to go to Hawai'i, and Alaska is like that mystical place far to the north that you cannot even drive to right now.

But I did enjoy stopping there. Someone pointed something out to me on the post I did for Instagram. One of the pictures I took is of the sign marking the exact geographical center. You can see my reflection in it. How fitting.

Leaving there was a bit confusing. GPS had me on track for Tulsa, Oklahoma, but I was passing signs for cities called Minneapolis, Lincoln, Augusta, Cleveland, Peru, and Billings. It had me thinking a few times that I was really off track. The lack of originality in naming places bothers me. And can confuse me.

I did pass a scenic road that I wished I could have taken, the Prairie Road, but I wanted to make it down to Tulsa.

I'm back in Oklahoma now, about 110 miles east of Oklahoma City, where I made my turn west coming up from Dallas a couple months ago. The more I travel, the more I am starting to see how close I was to someplace I was at not that long ago. A tiny, weird thing for me with Kansas is I finally filled in the left part of the atlas. All the states are outlined in my blue marker with my red "current" travels running through them. It is getting closer to being filled.

Except Hawai'i. But that will, hopefully, be the last place. I am still waiting for them to open. As I wrote to someone, my final post will be me with my feet in the sand, the view of the Pacific Ocean, and a link to the short book I already wrote about Hawai'i. Everybody is telling me I have to check out Kauai, but I'll be sticking to the Big Island, still one of my favorite places on earth.

Today? I'm just a little bit southeast of Tulsa. The name brought me here. Broken Arrow. I've passed through many Native American Reservations along my travels. Reckackv is "Broken Arrow" in the native Creek Indian language, the name they brought with them along The Trail of Tears from Alabama.

Arkansas Surprise; October 13, 2020

Well, I'm still a little miffed that my very, very, long walk (did I mention it was a long walk?) into Arkansas across the Mississippi River from Memphis was ruled incomplete by the judges. I threw my challenge flag, but the ruling was upheld.

I'm glad it was.

The drive from Tulsa to Little Rock was interesting, as I found my way back onto Old Route 66 somehow—at another coffee shop. I met these incredible young ladies that were retrofitting a school bus to start traveling across the US. I had no idea that retrofitting school buses was a "thing," but there are communities on social media, Schoolies. I saw the pictures of what they had accomplished and they invited me back to see it when it was finished. They are hoping for a May departure.

As many people as I have met and spoken with that wish they were doing what I was doing, there are just as many doing it. All along my journey, I've met other people who, for one reason or another, were traveling the US. I really think that Covid woke people up to things, gave people a different perspective on their lives. I'm seeing changes in people and attitudes and the value they place on things.

But down into Little Rock I went, first along a toll road in the Cherokee Nation and then back onto route 40, reminding me why to never drive Route 40. I ran into the exact same thing driving from Nashville to Memphis: trucks. Lots and lots of trucks. Some nitwit almost put me into a ditch, swerving into my lane. The difference between Nashville to Memphis and Tulsa to Little Rock is Nashville to Memphis is straighter. Arkansas has turns and hills.

Downtown Little Rock was a nice surprise. It's a beautiful city. It is very clean with a waterfront that reminds me of Philadelphia where they converted old warehouses and factories into shops, restaurants, and condos. I was able to take a short tour of the surrounding area before grabbing a great meal at an outdoor restaurant up on the second floor of a building.

There were definite changes between "east" and "west." I guess Tulsa is more "west" but the highway driving through the city reminded me more of "east" and Little Rock is the same. I had to switch gears. Fast. I got so used to moseying along, I was caught by surprise by the NASCAR circuit in Tulsa. But eh, I'm from

Philly and lived in DC and Miami. I was up for the challenge. And my Outback was surprisingly up for it as well.

In Steinbeck's "Travels with Charley," back in 1961, he ponders why all the states can't get together on a speed limit. Well, John, they still haven't gotten their act together. It's always somewhere between 55 and 85.

About an hour southwest of Little Rock is Hot Springs. I thought of going but a local told me it is not what it sounds like. I enjoy the natural hot springs. The one south of Salt Lake City was ideal, natural pools that you must hike to and then you just get naked and jump in. Many aren't like that. Here in Arkansas, like in South Dakota and Alaska, the springs have been diverted into bathhouses, commercialized. I'm still thinking about it though. A warm soak and a massage would be nice.

I really have to go back to something I have been saying for the entire trip: I'm really not giving any state enough time. Even the samplings now are becoming shorter and smaller. I feel an increasing pull back east to settle a few things and be somewhere for a while, nest for a little bit. It is the feel of a rubber band stretched as far as it can go before snapping. It's my brain. It would feel better to release it than keep it stretched. There is not a sense of urgency, but there is a sense of tomorrow.

On my drive south from the Dakotas, I noticed the winds are picking up. It is unseasonably warm but the winds bring the hint of winter. Here in Little Rock, as I wandered down to the riverfront walk, I crunched through dry, fallen leaves for the first time.

Beautiful Arkansas; October 14, 2020

I'm a big enough man to admit it: everybody was wrong.

A big reason why I didn't come to Arkansas on my way west was I was told by a lot of people not to bother. There was nothing here. Well, there is a lot here. The cities, countryside and the people are amazing. The history is terrific as well.

I started off my day with a nice stroll along Riverwalk. Like in Philly, they transformed it from an industrial zone into a beautiful place with sculptures, natural architecture, and bridges. I do have a thing for bridges so walked over to the other side of the Arkansas River, strolled up along it and then crossed another bridge to get back. I got my two plus miles in and felt great for it–it's something I have gotten away from and something that I need to get back into. A morning stroll. After coffee of course.

I drove down to Hot Springs, about an hour southwest. That was a pretty little city as well, even beyond the bathhouse row. It's just such an inviting place.

The people. I had to backtrack a lot. They were so damn nice. One older guy started a conversation with me when he came out of the store at a gas station and saw my out of state tags. He's lived here all his life and said he'll die here as well but loved the idea behind my journey.

Friendly people, and direct. I said, "not what I was expecting" too much and it was always answered by, "what were you expecting?"

Let's be honest. You know what I was expecting. Big city, east coast guy. Arkansas. Deep south. Supposedly one of the poorer states in the South. The race relations as they are today. I wonder what these people think of what is going on around the country?

Every place I go to is confounding expectations. I'm trying not to have any expectations, but at 49 it is hard, especially me at 49. I'd love more time to wander the cities and country roads and talk to people some more. Little Rock was also a point along the Trail of Tears and I would love the opportunity to explore that more.

The Trail of Tears is a little-known part of the darker side of American history. I think I first learned about it as a footnote or inset in a high school history class textbook. It occurred between 1830 and 1850. It was the forced displacement of the so called "Five Civilized Tribes," about 60,000 American Indians, from their ancestral homes in the Southeastern US to designated Indian territory west of the Mississippi. The Cherokee, Muscogee (Creek), Seminole, Chickasaw and Choctaw Nations were forced to march thousands of miles. One of the trails they took passes through Little Rock.

But I need to get going. I got such a wonderful night's sleep last night I am getting a late, late start. I'll only make it to Springfield, Missouri today instead of all the way to St. Louis as I planned.

Crazy in St. Louis; October 16, 2020

(This is modified from a Prince song if you don't know.)

Dearly beloved, we are gathered here today to get through this thing called journey. Electric word journey. It means getting lost for a very long time. But I'm here to tell you there's something else: GPS. A word of never-ending happiness, you can always find the route, day or night…

No, Mighty Purple One. St. Louis beats out Dallas and Portland for the uselessness of GPS. A local called St. Louis "the biggest small city," but I think it has more highways, freeways, expressways, access roads and ramps than any four large cities combined. I ended up across the river in Illinois on multiple occasions. Prince was playing on the radio, "Let's Go Crazy."

I had fun. Being back in that kind of driving environment with that song playing? I was lost, with the GPS not being able to reroute me fast enough through the twists, turns and forks. Speed limit? I had no idea. It changed so many times I ignored it. Everybody else was too. I did finally make my way back over the Mississippi River into St. Louis and found my hotel.

I found St. Louis interesting. I made the mistake of staying downtown by the Arch. It made other ghost towns in America look lively. I was talking to the people that worked in the hotel and they explained this area feeds off the convention center and sports arena. I was one of six guests in the massive 20-floor property.

With the backdrop of the ghost town, it is easier to see the difference between the haves and the have nots. I just read an article that said eight million more Americans have fallen into poverty. I feel bad for the have nots, but I haven't been accosted like this in any other place I went. And the homeless population is much different than it once was: younger, much more diverse, male and female.

Hotel workers, bartenders, waitresses, and all the easy college jobs went away. I was told this massive property has only a handful of employees. One former employee tried to guide me to the stores I needed. I saw it coming but let it happen as he talked about how he was trying to get a new job at a close by hotel. The plea. I haven't eaten all day. I gave him $20. Covid has clamped down on this area harder than others I think.

The unemployment ran out but there was never any unemployment for many.

The Gateway Arch, a gateway to the west but I see it as a gateway back to the east, a reflection of the east. Coming up through Missouri was still "west" or "central." St. Louis has the feel of "east."

The mighty Mississippi River that was the original north-south highway, splitting the country. Just as I did 280 miles south in Memphis, I walked across it—I really do have a thing for walking across bridges. The bridge next to Arch Park gives you the perspective of passing it as you walk the bridge, turning the Arch east, west, and even north and south.

The walk was much colder than the one I took in Memphis. Two months ago? It was over 100 degrees that day. I had my jacket liner on today, getting ready to head north into early winter. I think I'm going to have to put my liner back into my jacket. My northern route weather report is showing snow showers, with highs in the 40's and 50's and lows in the sub-freezing range.

I think it really is time to pick up some more speed now. It's a shame. One of the people I went to see here was an old work acquaintance. We knew of each other by me fighting with his boss. He's from Minnesota. He called St. Louis a cultural wasteland. He loves his Minnesota though, telling me about the great things to do in the other months. I just missed the best time, September.

The paradigm shift in my industry was a lot like the changes we are seeing. It's odd. My industry didn't change since the mid 70's and now people are scrambling to change, or their companies dying. It was a foreshadowing of what was to come with the pandemic. People don't like change.

I think it is going to be a very cold winter for many. Eight million more than usual.

Civilization; October 18, 2020

Something that has been on my mind as I traveled the country was a computer game I used to play far too much: Civilization. You start off and build one city. It is essential you build it in the right place. Your goal at the beginning of the game is to build three cities and then expand from there. The capital city is never the biggest or strongest as the game progresses and your empire expands into dozens of cities.

I played the game for endless hours. You start at 4,000 BC. I took many civilizations to the end—which I believe, ironically, was 2020. Traveling America, I can see the placement of cities. By rivers, by fertile land, by mountains. You can even break it down state by state. Look at PA. You have three main cities, with Harrisburg, the capital, being the smallest behind Philadelphia and Pittsburgh, both by rivers and heavy into manufacturing.

America is like that grid at the end of the game of Civilization. The game ends by either conquering all the other civilizations or winning the space race. But all the cities are there, with the populations and manufacturing outputs maxed out.

The Mississippi was America's second superhighway. The Atlantic Ocean was the first. Cities sprang up along it. Its tributaries created cities as well, like Peoria along the Illinois River. Maybe that is my thing about rivers and bridges?

Peoria, Illinois? Well, it's not like I was going to Chicago. The drive to Peoria reminded me why. I don't know how the police know if a person is swerving because they are drunk or just getting their butts kicked by the wind.

I do love Chicago in the summertime, though. Months ago, I had to break out a hoodie when I woke up in Colorado. It was chilly. Now, it is getting cold. About a month back, I took the liner out of my jacket and have had to use it more and more, but only in the mornings. It was just 85 degrees! –A thousand miles south ago. Today was the first day I put the liner and jacket back together and wore it for the drive. I don't see things getting warmer. Looking ahead at the forecast, I'm seeing wind, rain, and snow showers.

I was hoping the nice weather held out a bit longer but there will always be the southern states for that I guess. "Cold" in Tulsa is 50 degrees. Tulsa is nice. So is Austin. Maybe Sedona?

Yeah, it's getting to be "that time." The drives aren't as fun anymore and "next" is weighing on me. I figured out what "next" is, but I need to be somewhere to put it together. Or maybe the weather just has me down? A couple shitty nights in consecutive hotels? Leaden clouds add to the oppressiveness with crinkly cornhusks blowing across the highway.

But then who knows what is around the next bend or over the next hill?

I'm in Coralville, next to Iowa City. For those keeping track, Iowa is state number 43. The next six states will be tumbling like dominoes. Then. Finally.

I dreamed of something after I sold my lab. A small thing. After working as much as I did for as long as I did, all I wanted was to sit in the warm sand with one of those foo foo drinks with an umbrella in it and do nothing. My cousin, Dawn, bought me the umbrellas. I'm saving them to sip coffee for my final column in this series.

State 44 is tomorrow. I was going to stay here another night but I just found out the thirty or so young girls screaming through the hallways are staying another night and then kids are coming in for college stuff–Iowa City is home to Iowa University.

It's also supposed to rain, a cold rain.

Convergence and Divergence; October 19, 2020

Cheers as I start my way to state #44! Is it Wednesday? Sunday? I'm in the Central Time Zone, right? Where the hell am I? –Chris' World gets pretty confusing when I start paying attention.

But I think I have grown as a person. With over 26,000 miles on the road, I haven't had to hit Starbucks a single time. Craft coffee shops are springing up as quickly as craft beer breweries. I've come to the decision, though, that we are all coffee lovers/addicts and I no longer think of Starbucks' fans as Philistines. Aye, any way we choose to satisfy our passion or addiction, we're all in the same boat. Each to their own!

My morning started out with a nice little blend from Central Illinois. Not too bad.

I finally found fall as I traveled north, and a brief touch of winter. It was 34 degrees as I pulled into my hotel for the night, just south of the Twin Cities. I had a fantastic day meeting up with an old friend as I continue my one-man University of Miami reunion tour.

It was kind of kismet? Am I using that word right?

The last time I saw Francis was when I was returning home from my first major adventure. She was living north of Boston by then and I changed my flight to visit her on my way back from my semester abroad in Scotland. I still have the red Marlboro backpack I've been meaning to throw away for decades but just can't seem to get rid of it.

I was in a house again! –It's the small things I guess. I can count on one hand the number of houses I have been in since I started this journey over 100 days ago. Dinner was fantastic. Francis and her husband, Chris, have a propensity for taking in strays and feeding them—their backyard deck could be considered a refuge for feral cats and the opossum or two that seem to get along with the cats perfectly fine. The conversation was natural and flowing, covering a dozen different topics. It was just as if we were back at UM. Frances had left me at UM, though, to head to Boston to become a doctor or some such.

After we finished dinner, we were chatting in the living room when her daughter came home. We did the math. Aubrey, 19, is the same age as Francis was when we first met.

Francis and Chris told me the best choices to stay to venture up into the Twin Cities and the best route to take away towards my next destination. It looks like I'll be taking a beautiful scenic drive along the Mississippi River before heading east into Wisconsin.

The day was just…comfortable. And seeing Francis again sublime. A shy young lady grown into a woman, doctor, wife and mother.

But what is it about women? I have an issue with all of you— as I am sure it is returned. No, ladies: beautiful is beautiful, changed with age but not diminished. I had a conversation a few days ago about the philosopher Descartes and the nature of reality. No, I'm not blind or stupid. Age affects all of us. I see it every time I look in the mirror. But there is something about beauty. I don't know what you see in the mirror, but I see a smile and a warmth when I look at you. The spirit of our younger years gets superimposed on the images of today. Reality is perception, something we create.

When I first started on this journey, I let Frances know I would be there. Eventually. She said she would explain why she was in such a small town. After traveling through all these major and minor cities, through small towns and places that make towns look like cities, she didn't have to explain. I can see the attraction.

"It's beautiful here," she said at dinner, "as long as you can ignore November through April."

Her husband interjected, "Which is like asking Mrs. Lincoln: besides that one incident, how did you enjoy the play?" —I liked his sense of humor.

Minneapolis and St. Paul look like one big metro area, but Francis and Chris explained they are two distinct cities, each with their own downtown.

The columns have been pulling at me as I get closer to finishing this journey. And beginning the next journey. I've been trying to keep them light and easy for people at home, a "see what I see and experience" type of column. But like the Twin Cities, the thoughts that go into them each have their own downtown. I won't pick on one of the twin cities. Downtown "Travels with Coffee" has a few trips into a deeper topic that will be one of the books. Travels with Coffee, though, is just a construct on The Coffee Chronicles website. Soon, very soon, "Travels" will be pushed back into a sub section of the website all to itself and the Chronicles will take center stage again. Soon, very soon, it will be time to dive deep.

The metaphors call to me. Rivers and bridges. My first real short story that seemed like a foreshadowing of my future. It's hard keeping it all straight as I pick up speed and the drives get shorter. Soon, very soon, after a trip through Wisconsin and a northern route through Michigan, I'll be on 70, the fast lane to Baltimore. With a side trip down into West Virginia.

Roads that crisscross the nation. No meandering on them. Just a speed limit.

But. For now. For tonight. A very nice day indeed.

Sleepy Friday; October 23, 2020

I arrived in Gaylord, Michigan about 4 pm yesterday, after passing through Green Bay and taking the northern route around Lake Michigan. Before starting my trip, I hadn't even known there was a northern route along Lake Michigan. I had always thought Wisconsin shared a border with Canada. It doesn't. A piece of Michigan juts out above it and Route 2 wraps around the northern shore—that I was told was a gorgeous drive in nicer weather. There is even this awesome bridge connecting St. Ignace on the northern shore with Mackinaw City on the southern shore along 75.

I thought about doing the things I had done a hundred times: unpacking, setting up the coffee maker, etc. But then I thought I'd lay down for an hour or so before I unpacked and went to get something to eat. That didn't happen. My body had been telling me something. I had been ignoring it. So, my body stopped screwing around with me and took control.

I laid down on the bed and never even got undressed or even under the blankets. I think I looked at the clock a few times, pulled half of the blankets over me at 8 or so, and the next thing I knew, it was 8 am.

It had been a long, rainy drive around Lake Michigan. My body had had enough.

The final leg of my journey is officially on pause for the day. I looked at the weather report and it just doesn't make sense. There is a cold front moving into the area. Cold fronts bring rain. Today is supposed to be rainy with some flooding all along my route south. Tomorrow is supposed to be colder but without rain. I'm well rested but I know a long day of driving would wipe me out again.

Driving in the rain is different than driving in the sunshine. The movement and sunshine along empty roads revives me. I guess my body is more tense during the rain. I could feel it when I finally woke up this morning: I hurt everywhere

A small lifetime milestone yesterday: I finished the 50 when I crossed over into Michigan. I never really intended it, but there you have it. With the blue marker, I outline the states I have been to. The red highlights my routes. For this journey, I still have four more states to do but I've already been to them. With Michigan, I have now been to all 50 states.

The final run, I'll be loosely following a previous trip I took a long time ago, not too long after I graduated college. I helped somebody move back to Maryland from Kansas City. I drove the car while he and another friend drove the truck. I'll meander my way through Indiana, Ohio and West Virginia. Starting tomorrow.

Before Michigan, I had stayed the night in Baraboo, Wisconsin which turned out to be a fantastic little town, filled with crafters and great little shops and places. An old friend, Rachael, moved from DC to Madison in 2000 to get away from the hustle and bustle. At one point, she told me, she had to excuse herself from a friend's wedding in DC because she knew if she went back it would be permanent. She was used to the hustle and bustle. Madison is not Washington DC.

She eventually found her way into an even smaller town that has its own culture and opened an art studio, Cornerstone Gallery. She said you lose anonymity, but then you gain so much intimacy. When you pull over, as she did, to chat with the mailman in the middle of town, there's definitely a lack of anonymity there.

Like in everything else, it is easy to give "definitions," but places to live in America are on a spectrum, a sliding scale with as much variety as the cities in America. You have the major metropolis, squeezed against another major metropolis, like DC, on one side of the spectrum. Baraboo is more towards the other end of the spectrum. It's a small town, about 50 miles from a small city. Francis' small town, Canon Falls, is a tiny bit higher on the spectrum with a major metropolis 30 minutes away.

Lifestyles drive people to and from the various types of cities and the various types of climates. Jobs weigh heavily in the equation, but it all depends on what you are willing to give up and put up with to live someplace. Nothing is ever really far away. Or it is as far away as you want it to be. Even that is changing now.

The weight of jobs is getting lighter as Covid has forced us into what I see as a natural evolution. Telecommuting for work became possible when I was in college in the 90's, with the introduction of email and the Internet. Now, with things like Zoom and lighting fast connections built to handle the new technology, why not live wherever the hell you want?

Of course, there is the useless tug of regret, about the trip I wanted to take when I left college in 1997. I ended up spending my entire life on the East Coast, traveling between major metro centers. What is in our backyard? What's in our next-door neighbor's backyard? It's something to explore. If you want to. I can also completely appreciate the comfortableness of being "home" and the lure of faraway international destinations.

That was my original plan after college. I was in Miami. I was going to make it back to Philadelphia, by going east. Instead, I settled into the comfortableness and safety of the DC metro area and then the Philadelphia metro area.

I will be making it to Hawai'i. I'm not sure when. It's open now with a recent negative Covid test, but the reopening has people upset. The state went months with zero cases. They chose tourism over their people and the people are not happy. The island of Lanai is facing an outbreak of Covid and they don't even have a hospital. The people who live in Hawai'i are not allowed to travel between islands and their children, excited to be going back to school to see their friends and teachers, will now continue distance learning.

When I get there, though, I'll be bringing my backpack along. Just in case. "West" can be a very ambiguous word.

I'm taking another nap.

Damsels in Distress; October 25, 2020

The day started out in northern Michigan before the sunrise. That's been something interesting about the trip: latitude and altitude. It's just something that you don't think about much, but it's important as you zig zag across America over a few months. When is the sun going to rise and set? It's important when hoping for an early start with the temperatures hovering around freezing.

My day started out in darkness and I was sliding all over the road. Until I realized I wasn't sliding all over the road. Somehow or another, I pushed a button I had never pushed on my car before. It keeps you in the lane. So, when I attempted to switch lanes, thinking, "damn, those lane markers must be icy," it was actually just my car trying to pull me back into the lane. I wonder what the other buttons do?

I wasn't touching them as I drove south and watched the sun rise over Michigan.

The weather held me back for an extra day in Michigan, but it was interesting to see it change. My ride into Michigan was the first drive during my entire trip when it rained all day. I had passed through a few storms here and there along my journey, but all I had needed the weather app for was smoke. Until now. The cold front pushing in brought rain (and snow) so I just waited it out. As I drove south, the temperature increased into the 50's and the clouds parted until the sun was shining as I made my way to Fort Wayne.

But there were side trips to be made. I went a little west one last time to go to Notre Dame in South Bend. I'm not a fan. I never have been. But I know a lot of people who are. I think every Irish Catholic American? And I know a lot of Irish Catholics. My stepfather is still upset that I bypassed Penn State and Notre Dame for the University of Miami–it's a football rivalry thing (though I was at UM for a national championship). So, for him and others:

I was going to tour the campus, but as I was taking the pictures, a couple young ladies approached me. The road ends where you can take pictures of the iconic golden dome. It's a circle, where the pick-ups and drop-offs are made. I saw parents unloading cars.

"Sir," I was asked by one young lady, "are you here to pick somebody up?"

"No," I replied, thinking the question odd. I took my pictures and was about to head back to the parking lot to park and walk around.

"Sir," the young lady asked again, "can we pay you to take us to the airport? Our Uber just canceled–again–and we already missed the first train. We can't miss the second one."

I looked up from my picture taking and thought, "why not?"

I quickly emptied out as much of the back seat as I possibly could, explaining that the shorter of the two friends had to sit there. My car is a packed, jumbled, dirty mess and I didn't have time to clear the floor. I swiped a bunch of stuff off the front passenger seat and then I was off to South Bend Airport/Train Station. It's not much of one. In Philadelphia, it would be something like a large trolley stop.

I'm thinking that the ladies were either really desperate or I don't look as disreputable as I think? Maybe it's the Irish cap?

I didn't take their money. One lady was a student at Notre Dame; her friend a student at the University of Florida. Both of them were from West African countries. I remember the Notre Dame student said Senegal. The UF student Sierra Leone? Or Mauritania? And both had fathers who would probably be angry if they heard about this. For payment, I demanded two things: 1) A picture. 2) They NEVER do this again, asking a complete stranger for a ride.

We chatted about a few things as we made the drive. Notre Dame, Gainesville, Miami. When talking about where they were from, they said it must have been obvious they were foreign because of their accents. Their accents had not even occured to me. I've met other people from their countries during other travels, but I've met a lot of people with accents. I've been the one with the accent for most of my journey. Nobody can really place my accent except for a few words.

Whenever I call one friend in Austin, he always insists I say, "I need water for my coffee." He gets a kick out of it. Jason is as easily entertained as I am.

I dropped off the ladies and they ran as soon as we took our picture. And then the trip to Fort Wayne. An hour and a half of the most boring and annoying drive of my journey. I wish it had been more boring than annoying. 60 mph, for the most part, with towns every so often and speed traps. But at least the sun was shining. I did get the history of Fort Wayne from my stepfather,

277

though, as I talked to him from my car phone. You can get the history of anything and everything from him.

There is a very strong connection between Fort Wayne and where I lived outside of Philadelphia. Wayne, PA is named after the same person: Alexander Wayne, who, after the Revolutionary War, would be named the first general with a command in the US Army. Another interesting fact is he is buried both in Wayne, PA and Erie, PA. It's a macabre story so I'll allow you to look it up if you'd like.

But Fort Wayne, Indiana. I'm just a day's drive now from "home." It would normally be a ten-hour trip. I'll be breaking it up into two days to hit the final two states: Ohio and West Virginia. A couple hours east of Morgantown, WV, I'll be on old roads again, ones I've driven hundreds of times. The journey is just about over. Close to four months and 27,000 miles.

An EPIC final column did occur to me tonight. Back to the music, a song I love but had forgotten. A connection with the University of Miami.

But there is still about 360 miles to Morgantown and then another 300 after that to a pharmacy for a Covid test.

"Show me the way to go home, I'm tired and want to go to bed…"

The Beginning; October 27, 2020

This odyssey has come to an end. Or maybe it is just the end of this segment? The final tally was 108 days, 49 states and 28,000 miles. I found a hotel room a few hundred yards from where I started. Well, where I started the second or third time. Now, I'm just waiting for my Covid test results so I can stay at my stepfather's place while I figure out how to go about "next."

I did figure out "next" while I was on the road. But is this the end? I think I left my passport in Memphis? I know I left a suitcase in Austin. I'm pretty sure I left my favorite something or another in Nebraska?

What is it about Kearney, Nebraska that makes me want to go back?

I don't know how long I'll be here. I need to wrap up some things but then I need to start working on the things that I learned as I traveled those 28,000 miles.

It was a long drive back here, down through Ohio and into West Virginia.

I was talking with a friend of mine who is from West Virginia and he was saying, "where are you at? What road are you on?" He had no idea so he kept me on the phone until I hit the major interstate and that made him feel better. The plan was to stop in Morgantown, someplace I had been a few decades ago, but the weather reports were telling me the weather was going to be crappy no matter where I went or how long I stayed.

Route 79 brought me to Route 68. East. I knew that Route 68 would eventually bring me to 70, a road I had driven on hundreds of times. Through Maryland, around Baltimore and then that short stretch of 95 north that would bring me back to the beginning. So, I pushed through.

I still hate Baltimore, the loop and that final stretch of 95. Back when I first started driving it 30 years ago, it was a comfortable stretch of road, one where I would leave at night to enjoy the empty road. It hasn't been empty in decades, no matter what time of the day or night.

There is something about West Virginia I have always loved and been fascinated by. I got to see it from the other direction this time. I came down through the flatness that is Ohio and then began the climb up into the Appalachian Mountains. The borders of West Virginia are odd. If you draw a straight line on the northern edge of WV, it passes through PA, MD and WV multiple times. It is as if PA, Maryland and West Virginia couldn't agree on the border so they brought in a two-year-old to scribble something on a map and went with that.

I wish I could have seen more, but the weather wasn't cooperating. Fall was in all its splendor on the mountains, a sea of rising and falling reds, oranges, yellows and greens with breaks of rivers and mountain passes. That is a trip I would gladly do again through nicer weather: west from Philly, through WV, up through Ohio into Indiana, up into Michigan and then north around Lake Michigan into Wisconsin.

Everybody had something negative to say about their home state. I saw beauty in every state. The hidden gems that each state offered amazed me. The gems are free for the taking. All that you have to do is ask…and maybe get lost a time or two. Or three.

People are asking me about my favorite state. The answer is difficult. It is like asking what your favorite thing on the Cheesecake Factory menu is.

[For those of you who might not know, the Cheesecake Factory menu is the largest restaurant menu that exists. It's a book. Something for everybody. What do you feel like having? It's there. What do you feel like trying? It's there. What have you never heard of? It's there.]

In no particular order: Utah, Oregon and Alaska. But that's just me.

I wrote in Alaska that it was an ever-changing landscape, depending on the sun, clouds, and direction you were looking. America is much the same, but slower. The change of seasons will change each state. One of the favorite places I visited was Moab, Utah. But I was there mid-summer with the temps hovering around 106. It will start icing over soon, with many residents fleeing to Southern California to escape the cold. The hot springs that I attempted to get to in Alaska? It was a six-mile hike through a swamp. Now, with the freeze and snow, the hike there would be ideal.

But I need to wrap this up somehow or another. It's difficult.

I ended my drive playing one of my favorite songs on repeat. I was going to make a video of me singing it, and I still might, but it's a simple song. "Show Me the Way to Go Home." My favorite version is by Emerson, Lake and Palmer. For an acting class I took at the University of Miami, for the necessary fine art credits, I lip-synced the song for my final project. I got a B.

I sang the song with gusto as I pulled into the hotel parking lot. I thought it was an "A" effort.

Part Seven: The Road to Papakolea

Unfinished in Philadelphia; November 14, 2020

"I'm not finished!" –Al Pacino in "Scent of a Woman," slamming his walking cane down on the table and rising to deliver a blistering tirade.

How apt. In the movie, he's blind. I was blind to a lot of things. My vision is still blurry, but, after four months, some things are beginning to come into focus. Also, if you watch the movie and know the movie, you can catch a glimpse of why I did what I did. The movie has been on my mind the entire trip.

Something I see clearly is Philly is not home. It hasn't been for a long time. It gave me enough of the illusion, though, that I felt comfortable enough to settle into it, forcing myself into the illusions to keep my mind occupied, to give myself the illusion of sight. For 18 years? As I mentioned, I lived the co-dependent's dream.

No, no blistering tirade–though that is my favorite scene in the movie. Just a soft commentary to myself as I drove in, stayed at a hotel while I got tested for Covid, and then went to my stepfather's apartment to organize things. I knew Philadelphia was no longer home after the first day. The illusions had been stripped away and the realities confronted a blind man.

Four months out on the road felt good. I thought it would feel good to settle somewhere, at least for a while. Organize things. Put some of the lessons I learned into motion. But I couldn't. In Sedona, the mystical blends perfectly with the mundane, power vortexes shimmy up to capitalism. Nowadays, the power vortexes in Sedona are easy enough to find–they are marked on GPS. I read an article on the vortexes that said if you can't find one, close your eyes and feel your way towards it.

Aye, I'm not discounting anything anymore. I was shown that particular lesson a long time ago. A cocky, intelligent, creative young man went to Miami and a person I had a lot of respect for started talking to me about chakras. Yeah, right. That was just a bit too much of a stretch for me: I was still too Philly and chakras were just nonsense. Me being me, even that long ago, I told her so.

Sara, one of my journalism professors wasn't having it. "Come over to my place and I'll adjust your chakras."

Cocky: yes. Stupid: no. When the person who helped you published your first article tells you to stop by so she can align your chakras, you go. So, I went. Remember: this was the 90's, long before eastern thought started to even brush up against mainstream western thinking.

She greeted me at the door and had me sit and get comfortable on her sofa. The room was dark. We chatted for a little while. My cockiness was being smoothed away. Her credibility was putting pressure on my total lack of belief. Then, without touching me, she started to align my chakras. I remember starting to feel weird. Not an uncomfortable weird, just a different kind of weird. Over 25 years later, I still remember feeling a "snap" inside of me. Something broke, and I passed out.

I came to. It was about 20 minutes later. Sara just looked at me. "Well?"

I wasn't cocky anymore, or so intelligent.

So, I closed my eyes in Philly and stretched out my senses. Power vortexes were thousands of miles away. Something did greet my attempt. Chaos. Imbalance. Unsettled. A riot of hot and warm colors. No, Philly wasn't home anymore. But where? Back to the softer temperatures and the welcoming of Texas? The power vortexes of Sedona? Or some other place? Salt Lake City pulls at me for some reason. So does Rapid City. Neither of which offers softer temps. Seattle and its rain? Colorado when it's not on fire? I don't know.

I've been joking a lot about midlife crises, both mine and the world in general. How do you define a midlife crisis? Fast cars and young women didn't do it for me. I had always felt that was a guy trying to relive his youth. Personally, I had had enough of my youth. It had been a fun time the first time around but I wasn't looking to relive it.

I did still think about my Lexus 350 F Sport I had traded in, but the Subaru Outback fit my lifestyle and pace much better.

The world's pace had ground to a halt and people were struggling for normalcy. They had had to trade in all their cars for scooters and mopeds. The world had become a whole lot smaller for most, trying to live within their bubbles and mitigate the dangers of a pandemic.

"I just want my chips and salsa," one friend wrote to me.

The desire for chips and salsa to define a way of life. With restaurants closed and even outdoor seating being closed for the winter.

Every state had been different in both scenery and restrictions. The softer temperatures of Texas and New Mexico reflected the softening of restrictions. Philadelphia and the Northeast were colder in both ways. Many people were still shaving their heads and looking for a place to grab chips and salsa. The weather and atmosphere were both chillier.

Home is where you can get a hug and a haircut? And chips and salsa?

As Steinbeck wrote in "Travels with Charley," a man needs a destination, even if he doesn't get there, or else he is just a rootless vagabond. You can be completely lost without being rudderless as long as you have a destination.

How can I really stop at Pennsylvania? In no way did I do a circle to make my way back to Philly. It was more like a snake on acid. But it brought me back with only 49 states under my belt. Yes, I had been to Hawai'i before, but not on this particular journey. And there are still so many stories out there, waiting to be found or follow up on. Maybe another 6,000 miles is what the ending of this odyssey really needs? There are direct flights to the Big Island from Seattle. Or Phoenix. Or Dallas.

And there are things I can still share.

I'm seeing a paradigm shift in the world. Covid is bringing wave after wave of change. People don't like change. They rebel against it even when they don't realize they are. "I just want my life back," I heard from a lot of people. There is, of course, the smart-ass answer on the tip of my tongue learned from the famed Dr.

Dennis Leary in the stand-up routine, "No Cure for Cancer." But I bite my tongue.

A paradigm shift is nothing new to me. My industry got swamped with one like a tsunami. Orthodontic labs had not changed since the mid 70's. Owners had been ready to just ride the course untill retirement. I had been ready. When a tsunami hits, however, your choices are much more limited. I saw people drown or starting to drown. I made my small, tiny lab –I think– the first one in the US to be 100% digital. Then, I went out and taught others, founding a national association to do so. You not only have to adapt or drown, but you must adapt well.

I'm seeing people drowning and adapting. Creating bubbles. I'm seeing people ignoring it and states nearing shutdowns again as cases and hospitalizations spike. I'm seeing people trying to find balance between life and safety. I'm seeing states balancing their shattered economies against reopening. I'm still seeing a lot of stupid people out here that won't wear a damn mask, pay attention to the experts, and that is why we can't have nice things.

An expert said on NPR that economies couldn't begin to recover until the virus is brought under control. I'm seeing an unprecedented and vile power struggle in Washington DC–not that I wasn't expecting it.

And I'm looking inward, seeing a man that still has things to learn, with the pieces to build a better foundation, but without a place to do it. I'm seeing a red backpack that I tried to throw away for decades that never made it into the trash–the backpack that took me through Europe and still seems to have some life in it.

I'll miss my cat. At the beginning of my odyssey, I had left her at my stepfather's. Both the cat and my stepfather made it known that they belonged to each other now, and I was out of the picture.

I was out of quite a few pictures.

As the infantry say: "Follow me."

As a romantic has been saying for decades: "Come, take my hand. Shall we dance?"

The Road to Austin; November 16, 2020

With a packed car, half of the stuff from my storage locker, I headed out, just stopping for a night here and there as I made my way back down to Austin. What a huge difference. The major highways. The purple routes on the map. 24 hours straight through along 81, 40 and then 35.

Friends, hugs, a winery and a Bloody Mary were awaiting me. And a place to finally unpack my car and get it scrubbed inside and out. A home? Maybe. I like the place, like the weather and the people are incredible. Crystal and Jason and their children where they instantly make you feel at home, like a part of the family.

I vowed to finally see the bats so got a hotel in Austin. Unlike the Northeast, Austin was opening up and getting livelier. I had to stop at lights this time to walk across streets.

When I was having dinner at an outdoor restaurant, I heard a guy having a heated argument with a pole. Apparently, the pole judged him on his choice of clothing, and nobody had the right to judge him. I'm glad it didn't come to blows. Man vs pole never goes well.

But even the homeless are nicer in Austin. They don't seem as angry. Bummed a smoke here and there, had no problem with me saying no, and were just generally nicer than in other parts of the country where an encounter with homeless people would put me on edge.

I did start talking to one homeless guy. I was sitting outside of my hotel having a cigarette and he came up and asked for a cigarette. He offered me a quarter, but I turned him down and gave him a cigarette. Then, we started chatting.

He loved his animals, God and the Great Water Bringer. "They" were building great tunnels under the cities to steal the water, but the Great Water Bringer would eventually stop them. Interestingly, he put the three in order of who he loved most. The Great Water Bringer was #3. God #2. His animals #1.

I had always wondered about that. I thought it cruel, or at least limited survivability, if a homeless person owned an animal. It became two mouths to feed, two bellies to fill. But it makes sense now. Unconditional love. Yeah, I'd beg twice as hard for that. I gave the guy a couple more cigarettes and $20. He gave me a glass bead that he said he prayed into every day. With the lesson, I thought it was a very fair exchange.

The drive to Austin had had a different feel to it, beyond only staying on major highways. It was a lot of places I had already been with little variation to Austin. One night in each stay after an 8-hour drive. I didn't like it. It was rushed and hurried. There was not even a place for me to stop to take pictures when I crossed the Mississippi River again in Memphis. There is a pressure when you are trying to get somewhere. The last hour of the drive is the hardest because I know I am almost "there" and just want to get "there" and be done with it. It's very different from taking my time and meandering.

I guess it is also difficult because I know the end is coming. My sabbatical year was not quite what I intended, but awesome all the same. I'll eventually make my way out to Seattle, fly to the Big Island, return to Seattle, and then write, "The End."

What's "NEXT"? The question I have been very adept at ignoring with the motion of the road are now starting to pull at me.

There are still so many stories out there, stories I'd like to delve into more. I've been tossing out "Hail Mary Passes" as I have traveled. The Associated Press, The Philadelphia Inquirer, The New York Times, and a half dozen other newspapers. I even stopped in at the Austin and St. Louis newspapers. Like many places I went along my journey, it's not the same. Covid. Everybody is working from home; there is nobody to talk to. I went to Subaru as well with my story. Nothing. Not a word. –Nothing I was not expecting.

It is like I told people at the beginning of the journey. It was like being in Vegas and putting everything down on one number at the roulette wheel. The ball has been spinning now for five months. Just allow the element of pure chance to take its course, hoping to hit, but not depending on it. The wheel is slowing and it doesn't look like my number is going to hit. Unlike many people I see gambling, I won't be doubling down. It will be time to start making money the old-fashioned way.

It is time to find a place to settle down and start building and processing everything I have seen and learned. But where? Austin? I'm still on the fence about it but I don't know. Like I said: such an incredible place, an incredible city. Everybody that knows me chimed in that it would be the perfect place for me.

A word has resurfaced throughout social media and the public and has become as common as it once was in the 60's: vibe. Austin has an incredible vibe, but it is too "noisy" for me. I don't know how else to describe it, but I feel like I have to go with my gut on this. I found over the decades that when I ignore my gut, bad things happen. Very bad things.

I'll know it when I find it? You would think after 30,000 miles I would have found it by now. I had really been hoping I'd find it by now. There are still some warm places to visit, some places I haven't been to yet, opportunities to explore. As much as I don't want to go back to California, there is a CEO that wants to talk to me. And it would be nice to see some states when they are not on fire.

"Next" awaits.

After Hawai'i.

A Friluftsliv Interlude; November 17, 2020

Friluftsliv is what we all need to embrace right now. I wrote to the editor of National Geographic saying I was living it as I read the article in the magazine. Like many Danish words, I can't spell it without looking at it let alone pronounce it. It roughly translates to "open-air living" and is deeply ingrained in the Nordic heritage.

Jen Rose Smith, a writer for National Geographic, wrote, "From the remote Arctic to urban Oslo, friluftsliv [pronounced free-loofts-liv] means a commitment to celebrating time outdoors, no matter the weather forecast."

Friluftsliv found me at yet another park: White Sands National Monument, the largest area of white gypsum sand dunes in the world. The park encompasses about half of it, protecting it. It's majestic. It has the look of snow, as well as the way people react to snow. There are sleds to buy to slide down the dunes and plow marks where the park rangers keep the spaces and roads open. Many of the roads through the loop are covered in a white dusting, just like you would find in a light snow dusting up north before the sunshine washed it away.

On my Facebook industry page, I posted that by the powers not vested in me, I hereby rededicated the park "The Orthodontic Lab National Monument." No, I did not make teeth, but we always used gypsum, plaster, to make models of mouths to create our appliances. Before the change.

The world is going through a paradigm shift. We are in the age of masks. Lives and businesses have changed, possibly forever. I'm an old hand at this. I'm pretty damn good at it.

About nine years ago, my industry went through a paradigm shift. Technology hit us like a tsunami. 3D printing, intraoral scanners and tens of thousands of dollars needing to be invested in software, hardware and machines that all lab owners never thought they must have, that was beyond anything they had even conceptualized. It was just a matter of time before the doctors would start opening their pockets for the intraoral scanners, so I did what I had to do, becoming one of the first small labs in the country that went 100% digital. Then, I created a national association and taught others how to adapt.

A friend couldn't adapt and took his life. An acquaintance did the same. I did what I had to do because it needed to be done.

There was a gypsum 3D printer on the market but everybody went with the resin printers. Plastics. Everybody hates the resin models for various reasons. And they are now printing millions of them, probably enough by now to completely cover the 275 square miles of White Sands National Monument. Sticky, smelly, non-biodegradable plastics. When there was a perfectly fine gypsum printer available, using the same material we had used for a century.

And there are people taking advantage of it. I got into a bit of legal trouble by calling people patent whores. I explained to my lawyer that I thought "patent whore" was the same thing as "patent troll." He explained they were not and to play nicer or else it was going to cost me more. But everything was already costing everybody more than they ever expected.

Everybody took the path of least resistance, the easiest way that was offered them.

The lessons I learned in that paradigm shift in my industry I am seeing in daily life. Some people are not adapting, like the labs who are no more. Some are adapting, but not well, like the labs still in chaos. Some labs are adapting well and flourishing.

Friluftsliv is, what I see, the healthiest way to adapt to this new reality we live in. No, not everybody can do what I did and travel cross-country and live it. I really couldn't, but that is a longer story. But you can get outside, no matter the weather. Live. Create your "pods" that I heard about, the people creating groups where they continue to interact with each other, trusting that everybody in the pod stays safe.

White Sands National Monument. How beautiful. I'm glad someone pointed it out to me. The only thing you must be aware of is missiles. Seriously. About 20 miles south is the birthplace of American missile testing and there is still an active range. About 60 miles north is the first place they tested an atomic bomb.

Me? I'm going to go hiking, the pure white swallowing my steps, erased with the next breeze.

The Road to Escondido; November 19, 2020

Every time I have started to write a "road to" column, I've wanted to title it "The Road to Escondido." I didn't even know where Escondido was. It pops into my head because it is one of my favorite albums, a collaboration between Eric Clapton and J.J. Cale.

Escondido? I just passed it. I knew I saw a sign a couple months ago! It is northeast of San Diego.

But this "road to" column is not a normal one. First, I am still trying to catch up. Out of Austin, I headed due west. "To" is LA, to meet with a CEO about starting to adult again. As I was telling my cousin today, driving isn't as much fun anymore. It has to do with the timing, the destination and the "to." Moving fast on interstates is much different than taking the scenic routes. It's more white-knuckle driving. Those big highways are crowded with a lot of trucks. You can tell the full trucks from the empty trucks. Having a few sway into you with wind gusts teaches you to get past them as soon as you can. If you can. On a lot of interstates, the truck speed limit is lower than the car speed limit. Some trucks go really slow, especially going uphill. Other trucks pass them in the left lane also going under the speed limit.

I just like my roads open with little traffic. It was something I saw a lot of at the beginning of my journey but not so much as I am coming to the end. Is it the interstates? Did traffic pick up as people started driving more? Or is it just me, getting closer to the end of the journey? –That last hour of driving is always the hardest. Maybe this last couple of weeks of the journey is like that last hour of the day? There is a push to just finish and be done with it, causing me to grip the steering wheel a little tighter.

The days are shorter as well which doesn't help, and there is more rain. I'm driving into colder climes, winter, to see states at their worst instead of at their best. I still need to find home. But there is that need in me still to break out the red marker at the end of the day and continue tracing the routes in the road atlas, though it is a lot more like connecting the dots now.

It was all interstates, except for a brief blissful drive north of Phoenix. West from Austin to El Paso, north to Las Cruces, then west again to Phoenix. Just a night stopped here and there as I was on the move with a date in LA. Fighting with my GPS in Cottonwood to NOT take 17 back to Phoenix to pick up 10 to LA. It could wait that extra hour as I meandered my way west into the mountains of Arizona, around Prescott Valley and then zig zag down a mountainside to race across the Arizona desert.

Is this home?

Softer weather, softer restrictions. A budding technology hub in Phoenix with Sedona not too far away. As I traveled, I grew more and more fascinated with the Southwest, with the landscapes and the stillness.

But back to Interstate 10, west towards LA. Driving in Southern California is unlike any other place I have driven, especially on the interstates. I knew what was waiting for me. You don't just "enter" Southern California. Especially at night, tired, and knowing that the promise you made to yourself to stop after two hours may be impossible. It is like taking a boat over a waterfall into rapids. You just hold onto that steering wheel for dear life. Smart cars? With lane departure warnings, change lane warnings and intelligent cruise control? Useless. You need a co-pilot and the radar system like in an F-16.

Bogey at 6 o'clock!

50mph truck in front with 110mph car coming up fast at 8 o'clock!

Right lane open for a half-mile and window closing fast!

Screw them: I got J.J. and Eric serenading me with the window down and my arm hanging out in the soft evening. Let them flash their high beams all they want: there's no place to go in front of me anyway. Until you hit the three and four lane highways through the cities and then it is time to wake up your inner Tom Cruise with no Goose.

Pushing hard to get to another Covid shutdown town. Yeah, the meatballs and penne are going to be awful, but from the choices on the menu, it's the best chance at having a somewhat decent meal. It wasn't. But it filled me up.

A brief interlude at adulting. It felt good. Sitting down and talking shop with a CEO. Unlike all the editors I have contacted, who have ignored me, he knows my worth and what I can bring to the table. "Email me your resume just so HR can have something on file."

How do you write a resume? I haven't written one in 25 years. I haven't needed one. "Sure, I'll get it to you by end of day tomorrow." It's end of day tomorrow. Guess what I'll be doing after I finish this column? I wonder what the offer is going to look like? I think I confused him while negotiating. "This is what I made, this is what I am worth, but I'll take less if you offer me something without soul crushing hours."

A desperate need for a lessening of the exhaustion pulls at me more than any other thing or place.

Then, back up route 101 to San Francisco. That's not where I need the red line! Just 20 minutes out of my way and I can catch 5! But the reviews all said the same: stick with 101, especially if it is faster. It was, so I did, not having to break out the red marker at the end of the day, driving into a rainy San Francisco on a chilly evening.

I was staying overnight at a friend's house so found out something that I didn't encounter on my previous trips there where I either didn't have a car or parked in a hotel's designated lot. Parking? Parking in San Francisco makes city parking in Philadelphia, Miami and DC seem like having an entire stadium parking lot to yourself. There is no parking. Period. All the houses have been split into apartments and every house has a tiny, hidden garage with no marks on the street to tell you what is open and what is not. At $6,000 per month for a nice three-bedroom apartment, I can see why.

I parked in metered parking down the block. Then, in the early morning, I had to find other metered parking. The 9 am spots fill up quickly at night and leave you the 7 am spots. Parking tickets, attached to renewing your car registration, start at $100.

Morning, with the sun coming out, and I know I will have a small reward for my day: the red marker will come back out. Across the Bay Bridge into Oakland and then north until I eventually hit old route 5 that I had ignored my last time on the west coast, favoring the scenic drive up the coast instead of the mile reducing interstate that was now my goal up to Portland.

But it's not all about the driving grind. It's amazing how beautiful 101 is when the state isn't on fire. The same with Route 5, especially through far northern California. There are epic views as you wind your way through mountains.

With the journey coming to a close, now 32,622 miles, everything is pulling me and the writing in other directions. A longer than expected winter started this entire journey, a late spring that finally came with Covid Hibernation on its heels. Everything is pointing towards another harsh winter, with more shutdowns, Covid spikes and people coming to their breaking point with the restrictions. I need to find a job and a home.

I just received an interesting "invitation" by my health care provider. They want me to participate in research. The research is in two sobering parts: Testing and research on Covid, whether I have had it or not and, the biggie, testing and research on the Covid illness.

Covid is not the flu. Agencies want to find out more, must find out more, about why some that catch the virus are now facing a multitude of health problems. Heart, liver, lung and kidney disease. I knew back in February to expect this because I trust my friends and family members who have decades of experience as doctors, researchers and educators. The initial studies will be starting to hit soon. The long-term studies are still two years out.

Parked in Seattle; November 23, 2020

I do love Seattle. I just wish I could, well, get rid of a mountain range?

The Cascade Mountain range is what keeps the Pacific Northwest lush and beautiful. It is also why there is such a gloomy winter. Despite popular belief, Seattle, and Portland, are not even in the top 10 rainiest cities in the US. It just seems that way. The average amount of rainfall is well below that of New York and even the number of rainy days is not that far beyond it. Me being the geek that I am, I investigated it.

Watching it on radar is pretty cool. The Gulf Stream pushes bands of wet weather towards the PNW. The Cascade Mountains, in the middle of the states, stops the flow and pushes it up. So, instead of clearing out, it creates cloud cover, light rain, and snow in the higher elevations. "None" is what my weather app told me under the heading, "next sunny day." Instead, you get bits and pieces of partial sunshine here and there and mark full sunny days on your calendar.

With my love of bridges and interesting highways, along with just a fascinating skyline, Seattle is ideal. Coming into Seattle, you see this beautiful skyline of high-rises as you wind your way through curvy highways and across bridges. Some of the overpasses are simply gardens.

I found a place to park, the Hilton by the airport. It's the end of the driving journey. 30,681 highway miles. Now, all that is left are some errands, a scheduled Covid test on Tuesday, and then a flight to Hawai'i. It's all coming to a close. I have my car rented and my Airbnb booked. I fly out on Thursday evening.

Me being me, I need answers: what about the mileage on Hawai'i? How about the drive back east, north and south? What of the job and home search? You'll be going along highways you haven't before, see cities you haven't been in and...

Oh, shut up. Stop it. It's over.

You must put a "The End" somewhere or else the books will never get written. Hawai'i is a good place to wrap things up. A nice enough ending. All the rest will be considered part of "next."

I had a fun day with some friends of mine. Tracie is a lab owner I met through my association, and we've become friends. Her and her wife are such incredible people. I've stopped by their house and Tracie's lab a few times, each time I came to Seattle. Today, Tracie had a special treat for me: a bike ride along the lake. There was a break in the rain so we took out her electric bikes. They are pretty cool—and she explained that everybody asks about them. When we stopped at one place, someone did a quick U-turn and stopped, asking about the bikes. The two are made to look like motorcycles. They get up to a little over 40mph. Tracie will take hers to work sometimes so they also have a pretty good range.

The ride taught me something. I think we are too used to nicer weather on the east coast. It really is just about being prepared and dressing right, not hiding in our homes when it turns cold and rainy.

I wasn't prepared. The bike ride was a surprise. I was fine for the most part but the cold got to me quickly. It could have easily been avoided. A pair of long johns underneath the jeans, wool socks and a better pair of gloves and the ride would have been ideal. I have all of that. In Alaska, I also picked up rain gear. There is a pair of pants that goes over the jeans, a waterproof hat, and water-resistant boots–though the wool socks keep your feet warm, wet or dry. It is just about getting used to something different because everything is different now.

It was nice being in a house as well. Tracie got after the dogs and I had to explain that I really didn't mind, that it is a pleasure, that I miss having dogs begging for my attention and kisses. The big one was my instant best friend, a black lab. The little one, a Chihuahua mix, was a bit wary of me at first but ended up in my lap.

Now, it is time to wrap things up, pack and then pack again. I brought everything into my hotel room, all three suitcases and two bags. My cold weather stuff needs to come out and the warm weather stuff needs to be packed right. After I get back from Hawai'i, I'll have to repack again.

I'll be heading into the snow. But I'll worry about that when I get back on the 3rd.

This is almost a wrap.

Epicenter of Dissonance; November 28 to December 2, 2020

"Oh," I thought to myself as I stepped off the plane and onto the tarmac, "this is why I didn't want to come back to my favorite place on earth."

Kona International Airport is the largest outdoor airport in the world. You step off the plane and walk across the tarmac to the gates. As I walked to the receiving line, well after sunset, to show my negative Covid test result and the information on where I would be staying, I could have dropped to the ground. I wanted to drop to the ground and huddle into a ball but the fall would have been too far. A hundred columns and a hundred days alone hit me like a blitz on a poorly defended quarterback.

My offensive line was gone; I fired them. –is it too late to throw in references to another one of my favorite movies, "The Blind Side"?

This was my first time here alone. In the past, I had always come with my wife, Tracy. This was her childhood home.

In "Once Upon a Home," I wrote about how I left an empty shell for the next family to make into a home. Now, that's how I felt about the Big Island. I didn't belong here anymore. It's about the choices we make and the consequences of those choices. You own them and move on. I owned them and stepped backwards.

When I disconnected myself from Tracy, I hadn't realized I also disconnected myself from the Big Island. In my mind, I guess, Tracy had been a conduit that connected me to the Big Island and Aloha. I had always felt at home here from the moment I stepped off the plane that very first time a little more than ten years ago.

Aloha means so much more than "hello" and "goodbye." It is an offering to someone, and to yourself. From Wikapedia, aloha means "love, affection, peace, compassion, and mercy…it is used to define a force that holds together existence." I had gotten off the plane and felt the absence of aloha.

It was as beautiful as it always is, the warm winds wrapping around me as soon as I stepped off the plane. I wanted to turn around and get on the next flight. Maybe take everybody's advice and go to one of the other islands, one I had not been to yet. But

I was there, had already paid ahead for my car and Airbnb so I decided to go for a drive and see if I could find mercy.

I had hoped to be met at my rental car by someone or something. I had hoped that mercy would find me, like some magical ideal created into form and substance. The hope dissipated on those warm breezes as I loaded my luggage into the car.

The Big Island? State #50 on my odyssey? It's an amazing place that I know well. I once wrote an eight-part series that I shared with family, friends and on my website. I struggled to write anything more about it, aloha and loneliness causing a conflict within me. Ohana, "family." The columns and posts were a reflection of that. A+ for effort, D- for substance. To me, they all read like samplings of better works, a "Greatest Hits" album, because I couldn't find the original albums with the structure, flow and uniqueness that the artist intended so just threw something together.

Up 19 to 270 to Pololu Valley, where they filmed the opening sequence to Jurassic Park where the helicopter drops straight down. It is a favorite of mine on the northern tip of the island with a black sand beach and a valley I always wanted to explore further. If dinosaurs still exist anywhere in the world, it would be here.

Route 250, my favorite drive on the island, along the saddle between Kohala and Mauna Kea. It is a beautiful drive with an unassuming beginning/ending in Hawi.

Waimai, home of the Parker Ranch, once the largest cattle ranch in the United States. I just love the story of how it began. Its origin is the old story of someone giving you a gift you don't quite know what to do with, so you just put it somewhere and forget about it. Someone gave the Hawaiian King cows. Not knowing what to do with them, he let them loose on the Big Island. Ten years went by. Boy cows and girl cows will do what boys and girls do and the island was overrun with the pests. The king brought in Spanish Cowboys and the tradition of the paniolos was born.

The drive along 2000, the Saddle Road, between Mauna Kea and Mauna Loa. It was finally finished. When I first started coming here, it was a treacherous old army road, out of bounds for rental cars. Now it is a sweeping four-lane highway with easy access to the peak of Mauna Kea, the tallest mountain in the world.

Hilo, the rainiest city in the United States, for much the same reason that the PNW is always overcast. Instead of the Gulf Stream, you have trade winds. Instead of the Cascade Mountains, you have the volcanoes. There is a constant wall of clouds between the dry side of the island and the wet side, or windward and leeward.

Right outside of Hilo are Akaka Falls and Rainbow Falls.

Southpoint. The southernmost point in the United States. It is where I want my ashes scattered. I find it fascinating that there is nothing but over half a world of ocean between it and the polar cap.

Kona, where my favorite coffee is grown—I never did find better though Alaska came close.

The touristy Kailua-Kona, that was mostly empty due to Covid. Like all of America, it was like a ghost town with many shops closed. One woman said a slow exodus began when a new management company took over the open-air mall and raised rents right before the pandemic hit. Covid turned the slow exodus into raging torrent.

Hapuna Beach, ranked as one of the best beaches in the world. I did drive and hike to a couple beaches I had never been to before. I parked my car and hiked through a blackened landscape to arrive at Mahai'ula Beach by the airport. Then Ho'okena Beach, a local favorite by Captain Cook.

Everything was beautiful but nothing was as vibrant as I remembered it. I was uneasy the entire time I was there. I don't know if it was my memories, my past, Covid or just knowing I had to return and that this was the end.

I don't know why but the most comfortable time I had on the Big Island was weeding. I've always hated weeding. On my first trip to the Big Island, my wife was in tears at a cemetery in Hawi. We couldn't find her father's grave. The cemetery had mismarked it on the map. The last time we were there, she made sure it would never happen again.

We bought tools, plants, shrubs, and flowers along with edging and a small fence. It is the tradition in Hawai'i to erect massive headstones, monuments. Tracy's idea was different.

I texted her and sent her pictures: "You will never have to worry again about finding the grave."

The shrubs, plants and flowers had grown into small trees, easily seen from anywhere. I cleaned off the small headstone, cut back the shrubs, removed dead leaves and flowers, and weeded and pruned as best as I could. With the Hawaiian tradition being what it was, I don't know how the aunties felt, but I thought the tropical garden was a far better tribute to Virginio "Ben" Tayan, a man I had never met but seemed to feel a connection with.

Hiking to Papakolea; December 3, 2020

Papakolea Beach is my favorite place. Ever. Not only is it beautiful, but it is unique. There are only four green sand beaches in the world and one is just a few miles away from Southpoint on the Big Island. (The others are in Norway, Guam and the Galapagos Islands.) The sand is formed by a certain kind of volcano, crushing up a vein of the semi-precious stone, olivine. This beach was formed when the side of the volcano fell outward, allowing the sea to pour in.

I hadn't planned on hiking, but hiking is what I had to do. The perils of traveling solo. The perils of traveling during Covid? Normally, there are a bunch of locals there making the 5 1/2-mile round trip out to Papakolea with their pick-ups filled with tourists. It's a rough drive, which is still off limits for rentals. There are some "ruts" as deep as I am tall.

There was only one guy there. He said he wasn't making the trip for one person. He said to wait but that it was slow and he hadn't seen too many people. So, I started walking. I trudged.

I felt good when I arrived. It is a fairly level hike, but twisty and rocky at times. And, you don't really know where you are going. As paths became too difficult, the trucks would make new ones, so now it is like a maze. I was glad I hiked though. It felt good, with a nice breeze coming in and I saw a lot more of the coast that you cannot fully appreciate when driving.

The way down to the beach is a lot of rock shelves that you climb down. I decided to take a cue from my friend's son in Alaska, Billy, and slid/surfed down on my feet/butt. I was feeling proud of myself. Until I realized my phone was halfway up and the only way to get it was to climb up and slide down again.

Then, I went swimming. What an awesome beach with great views and beautiful water.

A feeling welled up inside of me as I sported in the ocean, the uneasiness and uncomfortableness of being in Hawai'i alone was washed away by the waves for a few moments.

I did it!

The adventure of a lifetime, something I never thought I'd be able to do, with the sun beating down on me after a hike I wasn't expecting to take, knowing the hike back would be a pleasure and surrounded by the azure waters of Papakolea. And it was all really done by accident.

Plan A for my midlife crisis (or whatever it was), Poland, Italy and Greece, had been burned away by the raging pandemic. Plan B didn't turn out too badly.

Are my tangents epic or what?

I would stop one last time at Hapuna Beach and walk through the surf, carrying my shoes. I took some more pictures and even sat down with a cup of coffee, finally breaking out the tiny little umbrellas my cousin had given me. I recorded a video. I had another night left in Hawai'i. A flight to Seattle. And then a long drive to find a home.

But Papakolea was "The End."

Afterword

From Seattle, I drove back through Washington and up into northern Idaho to Glacier National Park and then down once again to Salt Lake City. With frozen roads and black ice a possibility, I drove south to brush up against Las Vegas and then turned east.

I took the quick way, 15 to Las Vegas and then 40 through Arizona and New Mexico, the mile eating highways. Near the border of New Mexico, I turned southeast and drove as straight as I could through Texas to a small town just north of Austin. I rented a nice little house ten minutes from some old friends of mine. Then, the trips to Target began, again, to replace the things I needed and had given away a few times.

10 months. 152 days on the road. 40,000 miles. 110 columns. Thousands of pictures.

A net formed across the United States with my travels the strands and the stops the places where the strands connect. It makes me feel like I want to bounce on it, jump higher, and see where else I can go and what else I missed. I also want to connect more dots.

A net is one of the most important tools I learned in dealing with depression and loneliness. Making it through an evening can be like a tight wire act, crossing a vast chasm with only darkness below you.

A woman I met in Seattle, Sara, is a life coach, and photographer. She explained to me that she struggled with loneliness for years. Until she learned about the net.

The paths between us and the people in our lives are the strands of the net. The more people in our lives that we allow become the connection points and make the net stronger. It's a tool I need to practice, but the fall from the high wire becomes more manageable, less frightening.

The Net. Vulnerability. Communication. Intimacy. Feeling my way along with my gut. Balance. And a few other things became tools to take with me into my new home. But I'm 49. Are they not tools that I have always known but just ignored? Chose the path of least resistance instead?

I need to think about it some more.

As I knew, no real answers were waiting for me. That was a lesson I learned a long time ago. No matter how far you run, no matter how much the motion keeps things at bay, they all catch up to you once you are at rest.

The roulette wheel had come to a stop and the ball was not on my number. Just the thought of going back into an orthodontic lab made the exhaustion rebound into me. But could I do it right this time? Finally put the pieces together.

It was time to start thinking again instead of just reacting. I really didn't know what to do with myself but, here in Texas, I could at least enjoy one winter free from snow and ice.

Murphy's Law struck again: Texas would experience their worst winter, with the most snow and ice, in 35 years. The entire state would shut down for a little over two weeks.

Aloha.